MAROON AND GOLD

The story of Inverness Harriers

by

Charles Bannerman

This book is dedicated to two late Life Members of Inverness Harriers – George Bannerman, Past President and Treasurer, and Walter Banks MBE, cross country representative and Past President of the Scottish Cross Country Union.

MAROON AND GOLD

First published in 2014 by
For The Right Reasons
(Charity no. SC037781)
Printers & Publishers
60 Grant Street, Inverness
Email: fortherightreasons@rocketmail.com

British Library Cataloguing in Publication Data.
A catalogue record of this book is available
from the British Library.

ISBN: 978-1-910205-30-3

PREFACE

Derek McGinn, the club's Vice President for a time during the 1980s, must get the ultimate credit for the appearance of this book. However that appearance is somewhat belated since it is now 30 years since Derek, following my Annual Report, told a club AGM he was chairing that I should go on to write the history of Inverness Harriers.

Many other commitments have intervened but the long delay has been a blessing in disguise. In particular club has now acquired enough history to make a book viable, which might not quite have been the case when the suggestion was first made. Four athletes at the 2014 commonwealth Games have also provided the ideal conclusion. Finding the time to research and write it before now was also an issue.

Inverness Harriers was founded in 1947 and after spending much of the 60s in effective abeyance was reconstituted in 1969. As the club member with the longest continuous association with it, going back to 1969, I didn't think that my research would produce too many major surprises. However two things have become clear. Firstly, it emerged that the level of athletic activity between 1947 and the 1969 reconstitution was much lower than I had realised. Secondly I discovered that the inward looking attitudes in North athletics which had to be overcome in order to make progress during the late 70s were a lot more deeply entrenched than I had first appreciated.

It was therefore into its fourth decade before Inverness Harriers emerged as a major force in athletics in Scotland, with membership and a strength and depth of performance of which its founding fathers could only dream.

Given the large variation in performance levels during various phases of the club's existence, there was something of a dilemma about what should and should not be included. But this is not a book of statistics with standards for inclusion such as in Athletics Weekly. It is a club history and as such the performances referred to must reflect what was going on at the time. Some periods were more productive than others and the narrative must take account this so while a particular performance would be worthy of note at one point, this may not be the case in a different era.

One further dilemma has been how, as both the author and as a participant in the story, I should treat a personal involvement which spans two thirds of the club's existence. Inevitably there have been spells where, along with others, I have had considerable input. So when referring to myself, I have decided to use the first person, "I", rather than the rather contrived and pedantic employment of the third person, "the author".

I often wonder what some of those pioneers of 1947 at the Northern Meeting Park and the Bught would think if they could visit Queens Park today and find a club of over 400 members training on an all-weather facility with fully automatic timing and electronic distance measurement equipment set beside a major sports centre. This book attempts to chart the story behind that journey.

Charles Bannerman.
Inverness – September 2014.

THE AUTHOR

Charles Bannerman is the club's longest serving member, having first joined as a teenager in 1969, and is an Honorary Life Member. His first of four spells on the Committee began in 1970 and, having held a number of offices within the club, he is currently Membership Secretary.

Following a modest early career as a 400 and 800 runner he retired for a decade to concentrate on coaching before returning as a veteran endurance runner and he continues to compete intermittently. His daughter Jenny is one of the club's leading road runners.

He turned to coaching in the late 1970s and has coached a number of Scottish and Great Britain international athletes in a variety of events. A six year spell as Chairman of the North District Committee of the SAAA concluded in 1986.

He is now a retired Chemistry teacher and continues to work as a part time freelance sports journalist. In addition to his role as athletics correspondent for The Inverness Courier, has also been the BBC's freelance sports reporter in the Highlands since 1984, which has included the reporting of football and shinty for national television and radio.

This is his sixth book. In 1997 he published "Against All Odds", the official history of the merger which created Inverness Caledonian Thistle FC and he has also produced four books about Inverness Royal Academy.

ACKNOWLEDGEMENTS

I must begin with the three club members who have made enormous contributions to filling the considerable gap between writing the words and sending the final version to the printers.

I am indebted to John Wilson for undertaking the important task of proof reading the text and to Wendy Macintosh for scanning several illustrations. The final document was then created by Mary Payne. This was a major desktop publishing undertaking which Mary overcame illness to complete and I am especially grateful.

Then publishers For The Right Reasons, and especially Kevin Swanson, were instrumental in creating this final product, including the cover design after an idea of my own.

At the time of publication I had just completed my 38th year as athletics correspondent for The Inverness Courier. The paper has been by far the major source for this book and I would like to thank editor Robert Taylor for extensive access to old files as well as permission to reproduce a 1971 report. I also have to acknowledge the scrapbooks of Courier cuttings started in 1980 by my late father which have made a lot of the information so much more easily extractable.

I was also greatly aided by interviews with club members past and present and Ian Tasker in particular filled in many gaps. The recollections of Peter Mackintosh, Charlie Forbes, Marshall Grant, Tom McCook, Audrey Munro and Ted Roodhouse have also been very helpful.

Many people have contributed photographs and illustrations and I need to thank Harry Lakeland, Brian Ross, John Wilson, Ian Tasker, Audrey Munro, Alister Cameron, George and Lee MacLennan and Charlie Forbes for their help here, along with Andy Shepherd who took the group photo in the final chapter.

I also have to record my thanks to my fellow Committee members who so readily agreed to the production of this book.

Finally it is one thing to produce a book but quite another to sell it. Exactly who will be involved here tends not to be known until after publication so, as I write, there are some still unidentified people who also need to be thanked.

A NOTE ON TERMS AND UNITS

Some readers will be more familiar with the language of athletics than others and the Imperial measurement units of earlier years may also need some explanation to the younger generation.

In 1969 athletics in Great Britain converted from Imperial units - feet, inches etc. - to the metric system, although even today some of the Highland Games still use feet and inches for the weight over the bar. As far as possible I have tried to avoid units since, in a publication like this, they could become tediously repetitive.

As a result, distances for metric events are simply quoted as "the 800", "the 5000", "the 110 hurdles" (or simply "the 110s"). Similarly, earlier Imperial distances are referred to as "the 220, 440, 880" etc with the "yards" omitted. However 440 yards and 880 yards also equate to a quarter mile and a half mile respectively. A mile is 1609m.

Although this depends on the standard of the athlete, rough conversion factors were used in the early years of metrication to compare Imperial and metric performances. The normal (approximate) differences were − 100m = 100yd + 0.9 sec, 200m = 220 yd − 0.1 or 0.2 sec, 400m = 440yd − 0.3 sec, 800m = 880yd − 0.7 sec and 1500m = 1 mile − 17-20 sec. 120yd and 110m hurdles are so close that no conversion is necessary.

Where field events are measured in Imperial units, notation such as 19' 5" (19 feet 5 inches) is used. Metric distances are simply represented by the number so 5.95 is 5 metres 95 centimetres. (1 foot = 30.48 cm).

Times will also be given simply as numbers only so 23.46 is 23.46 sec (two figures after the point indicate automatic timing) while 53.8 is 53.8 sec (one figure after the point indicates hand timing). For longer distances 16:43.65 means 16 minutes 43.65 sec while 3:05:53 is 3 hours 5 minutes 53 seconds (as opposed to 3:05.53 which is 3 minutes 5.53 seconds). There are rare instances early on when watches with accuracy poorer than 0.1 sec (ie fifth or quarter second) were used.

For record purposes, in track events up to and including 200m and in horizontal jumps, there is a following wind limit of 2 metres per second or 4.47 miles per hour. This, by the way, was never applied to club records since early on so few wind readings were available.

Age groups in male athletics in Scotland have undergone two changes during the club's history. Under 13, 15, 17 and 19 were initially as at 1st April. Then it became 1st January before moving to 1st September in line with the women, who never changed. From

2012, some competitions ran under "even" age groups of U12, 14, 16, 18, all as at 1st January, but this was then abandoned as of 1st April 2014.

Age group designation has also changed. Initially under 13s were Girls and Junior Boys, under 15s were Junior Women and Senior Boys and under 17s were Youths and Intermediate Women. Under 19 men were Junior Men while women went straight from Intermediates to full seniors at 17. Later the under 20 or Euro Junior age group was substituted for both genders and later still some under 23 competitions were also introduced, both as at 1st January in the year of competition.

Queens Park

CHAPTER 1 – THE CLUBLESS YEARS – PRE 1947

This is the story of a late arrival in the oldest sport in the world and an even later coming of age. Although organised athletics does not really begin until the 1880s, competitive running, jumping and throwing go back to Ancient Greece or possibly even to prehistoric Ireland. They have been at the heart of physical competitive activity among humans ever since.

So Inverness Harriers Amateur Athletic Club, founded in September 1947, is a rather late arrival on the scene, although this has not prevented it from making a considerable mark on local, national and international stages. This book records almost 70 years of the history of the Highlands' leading athletics club. Before that story can begin, we must first get an insight into the events leading to its formation after World War II, and the sporting environment into which it was born.

The ancient Olympic Games in Greece began in 776BC and opened out from just one event, the "stadion", a foot race of around 200 metres. Longer races and field events such as the javelin, discus and long jump were steadily added. These events remain at the heart of what can justifiably be called the most global sport in history, with 212 members of the IAAF compared with, for instance, FIFA's 208.

The ancient Olympics died out at the end of the 4th century AD but competitive running, jumping and throwing lived on in various shapes and forms. It is claimed that Malcolm Canmore, King of Scots, held the first ever hill race in the mid-11th century in order to choose a messenger. Then there was Captain Barclay Allardice of Stonehaven who in 1809 walked 1000 miles in 1000 hours for a wager of 1000 guineas. This marked the start of pedestrianism which led to race walking and professional running.

Into the second half of the 19th century, athletics became properly organised with Great Britain leading the way. But it was much later before the sport became properly established in the North of Scotland, with the creation of clubs considerably delayed. So despite its relatively late arrival, Inverness Harriers is still among the pioneers of club athletics in the North.

The late 19th century saw a massive growth in competitive sport in Britain and the reasons were varied. More liberalised working practices provided men with more free time. There was also an increasing awareness of the benefits of health and fitness while improved means of transport came with the growth of the railways.

This was accompanied by the foundation of governing bodies, both amateur and professional, in a number of sports. The Scottish Football Association and Scottish Rugby Union both began in 1873. Shinty's Camanachd Association was born in Kingussie 20 years later and the Scottish Cricket Union in 1908. The Scottish Amateur Athletic Association appeared in 1883, three years after the foundation of the AAA in England. The ongoing development of athletics meant that the Scottish Cross Country Union, and then the Scottish Women's AAA and Scottish Women's CCU, followed in the footsteps of the SAAA. Here, and in some other sports, the principles of Amateurism would be adhered to rigorously for over a century.

The creation of the AAA and the SAAA was partly a reaction to corruption, much of it motivated by betting and race fixing which had become prevalent in pedestrianism, or so called "professional" athletics. Consequently *"Betting must be rigorously suppressed"* became a prominent statement in the SAAA rule book from an early stage.

The AAA in England has its origins in the social elite of Oxford and Cambridge and the list of the 13 founder members of the Scottish AAA runs in parallel. These include privileged institutions such as the Fettesian-Lorettonian Club, Edinburgh University, Glasgow Academicals, Loretto School, Royal High School and Watsonians. The influence of social class in the early years is inescapable but this would change as the appeal of amateur athletics began to broaden from its upper class origins. Harrier clubs such as Clydesdale soon followed opening the sport, especially cross country running (the SCCU was founded in 1890), to the lower social orders. But the strong amateur ethic was paramount.

Any judgement of this strict amateur code in athletics must necessarily be mixed. On the one hand it allowed the sport to be removed from the corruption of financially motivated pedestrianism. Here the *raison d'etre* was making money which took precedence over the development of performance standards. With the new corruption of illegal drugs, some would argue that this is exactly where athletics returned once amateur principles were abandoned in the late 20th century.

From the 1880s, amateurism removed athletics to an environment where competitive standards could be developed through coaching and *bona fide* competition. An international dimension was opened up and most importantly of all, athletics adopted a club based framework. This meant that representatives of these clubs could run their own sport - apart from in the North of Scotland where there were no clubs for several decades.

However the strict amateur code was taken too far. The level of persecution of those who breached it was, in retrospect, scandalous. Apart from the rules on prizes and lost time at work, amateurs were even banned from competing in meetings without a permit issued by an amateur governing body. It was also the competitor's responsibility to establish that a permit had been granted. Among those receiving life bans for transgressing these draconian edicts was George MacNeill who might have directly challenged Allan Wells for the title of Scotland's greatest sprinter had he not signed professional football forms as a youngster in the 1960s.

The pursuit of offenders arguably sits alongside medieval witch hunters and US Senator Joe McCarthy's over-zealous persecution of communists, real and imaginary, in the 1950s. I have a clear recollection of an outburst at a mid-70s SAAA AGM from one of these moustached, ruddy faced retired Colonel types with an accent redolent of one of the posher rugby clubs. This individual took the floor and robustly asserted that children accepting threepence for competing at the Sunday School picnic should be banned for life! The implication was that the remotest connection with cash was a contagious disease which had to be eradicated, and all means were justifiable.

Among those pursued by UK amateur bodies was renowned Edinburgh coach and a very good friend of Inverness Harriers, Bill Walker. In 1978 it emerged that he was involved in so called "illegal" payments to athletes at the Edinburgh Highland Games. In practice these "brown envelope" transactions for "expenses" were commonplace and the term "Shamateurism" began to emerge. For a time Bill was ostracised but fortunately he was soon fully rehabilitated into the sport. Meanwhile excessive adherence to amateur rules, for whose demise he must receive some of the credit, is long gone.

Amateur athletics operated, and rigorously enforced, a closed shop with just a single transgression enough for permanent exclusion. It was also all or nothing. You were either in the amateur camp or permanently beyond the pale as a professional, with reinstatements a rarity. Some amateurs did, however, risk contesting professional events, often under assumed names, and some got away with it. Throughout much of Scotland the two codes glowered at each other across the divide, and the "pros" were never backward in their attempts to seduce amateurs with the promise of cash rewards.

Athletics in the North of Scotland was much more limited in the early years and very much a late developer. Professional athletics in the North has never extended past Highland Games, and by no means all of them since there is a well-established amateur circuit. Despite little competition from the professional code, it still took until after World War II for amateur athletics, especially within clubs, to begin to flourish.

The initial distinction between amateurs and professionals was whether or not money changed hands. However in terms of values and practices the two designations are arguably reversed with "amateur" athletics actually operating very professionally, while the opposite can often be said of the "professional" code. In 1996, amateurs were allowed to win cash prizes, so the financial distinction disappeared. Top athletes competing in IAAF events can now become very rich people. However two distinct sets of values and practices still persisted for half a century after Inverness Harriers was born, so the word "Amateur" was an indispensable part of the club's name and remains in place.

So how did Inverness respond to the sporting expansion of the late 19th century? Despite its remoteness, the message spread remarkably fast in most disciplines - but not in athletics. Northern Counties cricket club was founded in 1865 while of the seven founder clubs in the Highland Football League (1893), six were from Inverness. The four best known - Clach, Caley, Thistle and Citadel – all originate from the mid-1880s. Inverness had a shinty club from 1887 although Highland Rugby Club came rather later in 1922.

However the Highland metropolis didn't always lead the way in the North. Inverness Shinty Club was pipped by at least two of its rural cousins. Glenurquhart, on whose pitch at Blairbeg Park the Glenurquhart Highland Games take place, was founded in 1885. Their great rivals Strathglass, from the village of Cannich, go back even further to 1879.

In 1887 these two teams, Glen travelling by steamer up Loch Ness and Strathglass by road to Beauly and rail thereafter, met in shinty's famous and historically significant Great Game. This was played on a huge pitch, 300 yards by 200, which included the ground on which the Queens Park athletics track now stands.

In their early days there were quite strong links between shinty and athletics. For example, Bute Shinty and Athletics Club was for a long time affiliated to the Scottish AAA. In the early years of the 20th century Kyles Athletic captain Tom Nicholson was one of Scotland's leading exponents of both shot and wire hammer. A prominent

Olympic athlete, he won the national hammer title a phenomenal 21 times.

With a governing body in Scotland from 1883, athletics was developing nationally on a similar timescale to other sports, but unlike many of them club activity in the Highlands was much more belated. Locally based military were quite active but there was no public club in the Highlands until Inverness Harriers in 1947. This, however, was not quite the first club in the North since across the border in Moray, Forres Harriers trace their origins back to the late 1920s.

The development of club athletics was even further delayed elsewhere in the area. Lochaber AC came in the late 1950s from the legacy of the revived Ben Nevis Race. Even later appearances included Caithness and Elgin AACs in the 1970s and Nairn, Moray Roadrunners and Black Isle (now Ross County) in the 1980s.

All this was despite the foundation as early as 1890 of the North of Scotland Amateur Athletic Association (NSAAA). There is little on record about its first several decades when its impact seems to have been quite limited. There is also some evidence that an Inverness AAA flourished briefly after the foundation of the SAAA but the body does not appear to have survived for long.

The NSAAA seems to have been especially backward in encouraging the formation of clubs and rather more concerned with the promotion of sports meetings. Indeed it seems astonishing that the NSAAA should apparently make no effort at all to create a club even in the Highland capital. In mitigation, it should also be noted that the SAAA was, almost for the first century of its existence, a predominantly central belt institution with East and West Districts. The NSAAA and the Borders AAA were affiliated to the SAAA but largely independent of it.

The domination of the NSAAA by meeting promoters was a significant factor in the slow development of club athletics in the North which continued throughout the Association's existence. This would ultimately come to a head during the 1970s as described in later chapters.

So how did athletics fare in these early, clubless years in the North of Scotland?

It is now time to look at the Scottish championship-winning exploits of three Invernessians. They all happen to be former pupils of the town's Royal Academy and their titles are almost equally spread over exactly 100 years. Two of them competed too early to benefit from a club in the town and the third, who will figure prominently later as a key figure in the 1980s, is also included here in the interests of completeness.

With Inverness Harriers still over half a century away, the 120 yards hurdles gold medallist at the inaugural SAAA championships at Powderhall in Edinburgh in 1883 was a young army officer called Robert Carruthers. A member of the family which owned the Inverness Courier, Carruthers went on to perform distinguished military service, coming out of retirement to end his career as a Brigadier General in the First World War. His time that day in Edinburgh was 16.75 on the rather primitive clockwork stop watches of the time which read quarter seconds.

Fast forward now 100 years almost to the day and just along the road at Meadowbank. Here, at the SAAA Centenary Championships in 1983, the high hurdles champion is again from Inverness but this time is wearing the maroon and gold of the Harriers. Neil Fraser's time was 14.45 sec, which was initially excluded as a Scottish native record due to a wind reading of +2.8 but then ratified when it emerged that it was really +0.28.

Robert Carruthers

Then, almost exactly half way between Carruthers and Fraser, another Invernessian suffered acutely from the lack of an athletics club in the town while the consequences of the absence of technology are debatable. Ian Young was a member of the family which owned the drapery firm of Young and Chapman, an Inverness institution in Church Street and later in Union Street. By the mid-1930s he was one of Britain's leading sprinters, but with no club in Inverness he ran for Edinburgh Harriers which he had joined during his drapery apprenticeship in the city.

Ian remains the only Invernessian to have won Commonwealth (at the time Empire) Games medals in athletics, having struck bronze in both the 100 yards and the 4 x 110 yards relay in 1934. By 1936 he was good enough to gain selection for the 100 and 200 at the Berlin Olympics. However, he was denied a chance to run against the legendary Jesse Owens when his father took ill and Ian had to turn the opportunity down to manage the family business. He competed very little after that.

In 1952, other members of the family decided to sell the business to Aberdeen company Benzie and Miller. Probably accentuated by his sacrifice 16 years previously, this led to a major family rift whereupon he left Inverness for good and eventually settled in Devon where he became Honorary President of Dartmouth AC.

Ian Young was Inverness Royal Academy sports champion in 1926. It was also on the school's field at Diriebught that, after closing up the shop, he would do much of his training. This, he told me, included a tremendous number of sprint starts. Acting as starter would often be Duncan Fraser who founded the butcher's shop of that name on Queensgate and was a major player in north athletics for many years in the early and mid-20th century.

It seems that Ian never forgot his school or his close encounter with "Team GB" of 1936. Indeed, the very next year, on 12th May 1937, Inverness Royal Academy's log book records that, on the Coronation of King George VI, Ian Young presented every pupil in the primary department with a flag.

The occasion when the lack of technology may or may not have let him down was the 1935 Scottish championships where he twice ran inside the Scottish native record for the 100 yards. However verification of records seems to have been rather haphazard in those days, as he explained in an interview for the Inverness Courier in 1990.

"In these days wind gauges were never heard of and it was a bit breezy that day. In my heat I recorded 9.9 seconds and won the final in 9.8 seconds, both performances being better than the old (Scottish native) *record. The only way officials could estimate the wind was by looking at the flags and guessing. In the end the SAAA decided to accept my 9.9 seconds as a record but not the 9.8. I still have mixed feelings about that because a gauge might have shown my faster time to be acceptable – but on the other hand it might have ruled out what I did get."*

The name of Ian Young, the first Scotsman "legally" to break 10 seconds for 100 yards within Scotland, figures prominently in the limited programme of amateur athletics which existed in the north in the 1930s. However this sparse diet may still have been an improvement on earlier decades, and although he competed for

Edinburgh Harriers in many national events he does, in the absence of a club in Inverness, appear informally to have created one for himself

Ian Young wins the 1935 Scottish 100 yards title.

for local purposes. The Inverness Courier, reporting on the North of Scotland Amateur Sports Meeting at the Cameron Barracks in Inverness on the evening of Wednesday 27th July 1935, tells us that *"(Young) was stationed in Edinburgh for a time and was a member of Edinburgh Harriers. On his return to Inverness he founded the Inverness YMCA Harriers Club of which Eric Liddell is the Honorary President."*

That night Young won the 100 yards in 9 4/5 seconds and the 220 yards in 22 1/5 seconds. The time for the 100 is actually 0.1 sec inside the native record he was credited with at the Scottish championships the previous month and equals the time he was denied. This also seems to have been achieved in reportedly very poor weather. However we cannot account for uncertainties of wind assistance, track accuracy and the competence of timekeepers. The first two variables at least would create doubts over many track performances in the North for years to come.

As a footnote to this meeting, the programme also included the "Half Mile Telegraph Messengers' Walking Race" which is not only a sign of the times but also a rare example of race walking in the local area. This is also an example of the kind of novelty event which might turn up at a local sports from time to time.

Even though its Honorary President may have been 1924 400 Olympic champion and world record breaker Eric Liddell, I have so far seen no further evidence of any other athlete competing for Inverness

YMCA Harriers. It appears simply to have been one of these *ad hoc* bodies set up for a particular purpose - to allow Inverness's star athlete Ian Young to compete locally in the name of his home town. Inverness YMCA was possibly a product of Muscular Christianity and Scotland had one or two such athletics clubs. These included Larkhall and Bellshill YMCAs and in the 1970s Roy Baillie of Bellshill was one of the country's leading 800 runners.

Such an *ad hoc* arrangement was by no means unprecedented in the Highlands. One other body occasionally referred to is "Inverness Thistle Harriers". This is the designation of T. Urquhart who won the mile at the 1932 Forres Amateur Sports where a team representing that club also won the relay. Since Inverness Thistle was a professional football club, any link with it could only have been through some of its amateur players. At that same meeting G. G. Forbes of "Inverness AC" won the 220 and was third in the 100.

However even transient, *ad hoc* clubs seem to have been quite rare. The Courier reported that the 1926 NSAAA Sports at the Northern Meeting Park *"were excellently conducted by Messrs Angus MacDonald, Duncan Fraser, H. Chinn, W. Michie and John Bowden. The prizes were presented by Mr A Sandison, Hon. Pres. of the North of Scotland Amateur Athletic Association. The proceeds of the meeting will be donated to the Jubilee Nurses' Fund".*

This was a joint athletics and cycling meeting with a very small athletics programme of 100 and 220, the quarter mile, half mile and the mile. There is no reference to any clubs at all apart from W. MacKenzie of Greenock Glenpark Harriers who was runner up in the mile. It is also interesting that the tone of the report suggests that the officials were almost regarded as more important than the competing athletes.

Results from the 1920s and 1930s give the overwhelming impression of North athletes competing under their place of residence, as still happens in the professional code, or sometimes inventing "clubs". This has been reinforced by further evidence from Charlie Forbes, George G. Forbes' son and a major figure at Inverness Harriers from the mid-1980s, based on a discussion with his father.

Charlie said: *"My father, who was born in 1910, was great friends with, among others, Ian Young and he confirmed that there was no formal club arrangement in Inverness when they were competing in the 1930s. They did set up a group called Inverness Athletic Club but it had no formal status at all. In fact my father used to say that he used to wonder how much better they might all have become if there had been a proper club available like the Harriers."*

There is, however, a different pattern for competitors travelling from the South who are clearly listed under established clubs like West of Scotland Harriers, Greenock Glenpark Harriers and Shettleston Harriers as well as some universities. This merely confirms the impression that, before World War II and unlike the rest of the country, club activity in amateur athletics in the north was, at best, extremely limited.

George G. Forbes

Although the professional scene does not fall within the scope of this history reference must be made to one pro meeting, and another which quite soon became amateur. The jewel in the crown of local professional fixtures was the Northern Meeting Games held in and around Inverness from the 1830s. It was for these games that the Northern Meeting Park was built in the mid-1860s after the managers of Inverness Royal Academy began to charge too much for use of their school yard off Academy Street, roughly where TK Maxx now is.

Run by the local lairds, this was very much a professional event and hence barred to amateur athletes. By the 1930s it was struggling for viability and briefly tried to bail itself out by going amateur. However things got even worse and the Northern Meeting's history concludes that the death knell was the lairds, who had also been the judges, losing even more interest when judging was taken over by properly qualified SAAA officials. The Northern Meeting Games disappeared forever after 1938.

A year later organised sport as a whole largely went into limbo for the duration of World War II. Among the combatants, which included most of the leading sporting nations, activity made a quite rapid return after hostilities ceased in 1945, albeit in a difficult environment. Wartime food rationing continued into the 1950s and did nothing to assist sporting performance. Also, for many demobilized servicemen, holding down a job in hard economic times took priority over participation in amateur sport with its severely limited fringe benefits.

Straight into action to restore sporting activities were the good people of Glen Urquhart. In 1995 I was invited to write an article for the Glenurquhart Highland Games Golden Jubilee programme. These are the introductory paragraphs.

"After almost six years of World War II, Britain was desperate for community life to return to normal as soon as possible. For some sporting events this was to take years, but the people of Glenurquhart were well ahead of the game. Indeed the war in the Far East still had a month to run when, on July 8th 1945, the Minute Book records, a Public Meeting was held in Drumnadrochit's Blairbeg Hall for the purpose of constituting the Glen Urquhart Highland Gathering.

"An 18-strong committee was formed under the chairmanship of village headmaster and local legend Alistair C. McKell. Officials - including famous Inverness strong man, 'Gym' teacher and entertainer Donald Dallas - were appointed, and arrangements made for a six-a-side Shinty contest which was such an important feature of the early years. The last Saturday in August was chosen as the date, creating an instant tradition. 1773 spectators paid £73 12s 0d for the privilege of sharing that piece of history and in addition large numbers of juveniles attended for whom no charge was made."

This was initially a professional meeting but in 1954 the "Drum Games" became one of several North events to turn amateur around that time. From then on there was a very strong link between Inverness Harriers and these games in the community of Glen Urquhart, an area which has provided the club with a number of top performers, including several international athletes.

Now the scene was set for history to repeat itself. We have already seen that Glen Urquhart had its shinty club two years before one was formed in Inverness. Remarkably, exactly six decades on, the same happened in terms of Highland Games. However there is an extra twist here since the foundation of the Inverness Highland Games in 1947 very quickly led to the creation of the town's athletics club, Inverness Harriers.

The foundation of the Inverness Highland Games meant a return of Games activity to Inverness after the Northern Meeting event went defunct in 1938. However the two events are quite distinct from each other. The Northern Meeting was a pan-Highland professional event organised by the local lairds at the Northern Meeting Park as part of an annual gathering of these lairds and their associates. The Inverness Highland Games was, and still is, Inverness's meeting run under amateur rules for completely different athletes and overseen by officials of the SAAA and its successor governing bodies. There was also nine years of clear blue daylight between the demise of one and the creation of the other.

This distinction is important since the inaugural 1947 Inverness Highland Games incredibly quickly catalysed a further and much more profound development for the community - the formation of the first real athletics club in the Highlands.

The first, all-amateur Inverness Highland Games - or Inverness Gathering as it tended to be called in its earlier years - took place at the Bught on Saturday, 9th August 1947. The following Tuesday a lengthy Courier report claimed a crowd of 5000, which for the time seems not excessive. A year later 7000 would gather at Grant Street Park to watch Clachnacuddin play St Johnstone in the Scottish Cup. In this largely pre-television era, live local sport was at the peak of its popularity among a population desperate for entertainment and leisure after six years of war.

The NSAAA pulled out all the stops and used contacts elsewhere in Scotland to attract athletes from "the South". A total of 17 club athletes travelled to Inverness for the games along with some officials, and they played a major part. So did several athletes representing what was still a very substantial British military. With RNAS and RAF bases at Lossiemouth and Kinloss and Army depots at Fort George, the Cameron Barracks and elsewhere, athletes from the military would never be far away for a further half century. Competitors from the forces played a major part in post-war athletics in the Highlands at a time when clubs were still few and far between.

In contrast, local civilian athletes made a minimal impact on the prize list. Third places for J. R. MacKenzie, Inverness, in the 100 yards handicap and for M. Shaw of the Inverness District Asylum Staff in the Caber and Scots Hammer were just about it. The result for the 440 yards handicap is typical. *1 - F/Sergt Johnstone, RAF 2 - R. Russell, RAF 3 - R.S.G. Sharp, Garscube Harriers. Time - 48 4/5 sec.* The handicaps are not specified so it is difficult to assess the quality of performances on the 440 yard grass track.

However Mr. Shaw and his colleagues from the District Asylum, which would soon become Craig Dunain Hospital, found themselves on the edge of something of a controversy. The tug of war team from Auldearn duly appeared, but provoked a wrangle about their amateur status. The upshot was that they did not compete. Instead they took part in, and just won, a closely contested exhibition pull against the Asylum team who then went on to defeat Inshes and win the competition proper. Disputes over amateur status were not uncommon, with tug of war teams tending to sail closer to the wind than most. This again emphasises the sharp contrast between those within the amateur fold and those outside it.

It is perhaps slightly surprising that Auldearn were allowed on the field at all, such was the prevailing atmosphere of sporting apartheid. So it is interesting that one of the officials at the meeting was Mr. George B. Rodgers of Inverness. George Rodgers was chairman of Inverness's most successful semi-professional football team of the day, Clachnacuddin, whose paid players would have been instantly ostracised from the meeting, although their chairman seems not to have been.

In 1947 Ian Young, now into his 30s, was President of the NSAAA and after the meeting he *"thanked the South athletes and said he was sure their performances would greatly help the revival of amateur sport in Inverness and the North."* This merely reinforces the prevailing impression that the entire North athletics establishment regarded itself as inferior to and somewhat removed from the rest of the country. This view would continue to hold for another 30 years, but not a great deal longer than that.

The NSAAA can probably rightly be criticised, over a long period, for focusing too extensively on the promotion of meetings to the detriment of athlete development, especially through clubs. However their action in creating the Inverness Games as an amateur meeting was a major coup which some very quickly found inspirational.

Just six days after the Games, on Friday August 15th, the Courier reported in its *"Sports and Sportsmen - Northern Notes and Views"* column that: *"A Harriers club is to be formed in Inverness. It will have the support of the Inverness Sports and Entertainments Committee who organised the Inverness Gathering last Saturday and the North of Scotland Amateur Athletic Association. Since the War, Amateur Athletics in the North have been 'in the doldrums' but the recess (sic - success?) of the Inverness Gathering and the creditable performance of local athletes has given amateur sport a much needed fillip."*

What is frustrating about this snippet is the lack of names and details. It is also unfortunate that no follow up report can be traced during the ensuing weeks. Details of the act of formation of Inverness Harriers are regrettably sparse. They amount to one, albeit absolutely first hand, written source and some information by word of mouth. Early club records have unfortunately disappeared but there is enough available to piece together an outline.

It is now that the name of Tom MacKenzie OBE enters the scene as the best known of three founding fathers of the club and the main source of very early details. Over a long number of years, Tom played a considerable role in local affairs in the Inverness area and achieved a huge amount, despite humble beginnings.

Of farming stock, Tom was orphaned at an early age and was brought up in the Highland Orphanage in Inverness's Culduthel Road from the latter days of World War I. His autobiography "Lest We Forget", which is that single definitive source about the foundation, tells us that by 1936 he was in the Army Signals Corps and in its cross country team. For much of World War II he was a Signals Sergeant at the HQ of 152 Brigade, 51st Highland Division. As he made his way through North Africa, Sicily and North West Europe, one of his fellow sergeants in that HQ was George Bannerman who, in the 1970s and 80s, would become President and Treasurer of the as yet unthought of Inverness Harriers AAC.

On demob, Tom returned to Inverness and found a job for which he was well qualified with British Railways' Signals and Telegraphic Department. He went on to give long service to Inverness Town, Inverness District and Highland Regional Councils. The pinnacle of his career as a Labour Councillor was as Chairman of Highland Region's Social Work Committee and he was honoured by having the MacKenzie Centre in Culduthel Road named after him.

A strong advocate of public service, he was a tireless hospital

LEST WE FORGET

Memoirs of
Tom Mackenzie OBE, MM, JP

B.
M/KEN

visitor and the Town Missionary. He was a major figure in Inverness Shinty club and also the Camanachd Association which honoured him with a special centenary award in 1993. *"Lest We Forget"* tells the whole story of his life, but it is the section on athletics, and in particular on the foundation of Inverness Harriers, which is of special interest. Tom also became part of the NSAAA establishment and was its Secretary for many years.

Although he does not say so in his book, Tom frequently said that the source of his inspiration to form the club was the 1947 Inverness Games. The effect must also have been instantaneous given how soon after the Games this happened.

This is how Tom describes the formation: *"Some little time after settling into the work routine I felt there must be other fields to explore and as I was interested in and had participated in most forms of sport including athletics, football, tennis and shinty I decided to form an athletic club. Accordingly at a meeting arranged by Donald MacLeary, chemist, Alex Cameron, British Rail inspector, and myself, 15 young athletes came along to express their interest in this new club. Thus it was that on 3rd September 1947, Inverness Harriers came into being."*

And that is more or less all that is known about the act of formation of the club, although Tom does go on to list some of the early members, some of whose exploits will be examined in the next chapter. These included the Sanderson brothers, John and Sandy who were both sprinters while others from the early years included Roy Hazle, Ian Peterkin, Leslie Hodge, Donnie Davidson and Freddy Anderson who was for a time club secretary.

Two more of these pioneers died at an early age, although later generations of their families would also distinguish themselves in club colours. Ron Grant's daughter Audrey will feature later as a teenage athlete and again as a leading world-level veteran. So will the veteran sprinting successes of Kathryn Nicholson (nee Urquhart) who is the niece of the late Charles Hunter and the Charles Hunter Memorial Trophy, one of the club's most prestigious awards, was donated in his memory. Both families are among a growing number which have club members across three consecutive generations.

Jimmy Brown is also on Tom MacKenzie's list of early members, as is Willie Sutherland who later would become Sir William Sutherland, Chief Constable of Lothian and Borders Police. Tom records that he was quickly asked to become a member of the NSAAA *"which organised the Highland Games at Inverness and various other venues - some being changed from professional to amateur later - and I take some credit for visiting Nethy Bridge and several other areas to explain the benefit of handicapping in order to assist young athletes to gain the opportunity of competing more favourably with keener competition."*

So despite the slowness of the NSAAA, club athletics at last reached the Highlands during the immediate post-war period. This was thanks to the enthusiasm and vision of men like Tom MacKenzie, Donald MacLeary and Alex Cameron who founded Inverness Harriers. However, it would be a long time before this new club would become securely established and play a major part on the wider scene.

CHAPTER 2 – MODEST BEGINNINGS – 1947-69

Since the club was formed just after the end of the 1947 summer season, little if anything else appears to have happened until training began the following spring. Formal, organised whole-club, 12 months a year sessions were not introduced until the late 70s although outwith the summer, various smaller groups, especially of endurance runners, do appear to have become active on their own initiative.

Virtually no first hand accounts of the very earliest years survive, but it looks likely that training for a short and sparse three month summer season, exclusively at local sports and Highland Games, would have begun in April 1948 – apparently at the Northern Meeting Park before a fairly early move to the Bught.

Before any club embarks on competition, it must have a club vest. In its first 67 years, Inverness Harriers has had four different designs although the current one of a gold vest with maroon diagonal has been used for over half that time. The original strip was maroon with a broad horizontal gold band broken by a large club badge comprising the well-known stag's head which appears to have been the club's emblem from the start. One senses the influence of one of the founders here since the stag's head is the emblem of the Clan MacKenzie.

During the 50s a white vest with a broad gold band and narrow maroon ones on either side was adopted or the men while the women initially had a similar diagonal arrangement but there was no sign of this variation by the time of the reconstitution in 1969. Maroon and gold bands survived into the early 70s when an all gold vest briefly preceded the current design which was adopted at the 1976 AGM.

The first traceable reference to "Inverness Harriers" in published results is in the Inverness Courier of Friday 25th June 1948. The meeting was the Amateur Athletic Sports in the Northern Meeting Park where the Harriers' winners included F.R. (Fred) MacKenzie in the 100 and 220 scratch. These are relatively rare examples of scratch events at a time when handicaps reigned supreme at local meetings. But frustratingly, and unfortunately typically of the age, no times are returned so we only have limited evidence of performance levels in the early years.

The 100 Youths went to John Sanderson and other Harriers prize winners on this inaugural occasion were J. MacKay, third in the Youths' half mile, and Ron Grant who was runner up in the men's mile. There was also a large enough club presence for a winning team in the medley relay. Meanwhile a very young Marshall Notman won the message boys' cycle race. This was a tradition at sports meetings which survives to the present day at the Forres Highland Games.

There are very few survivors of the club's earliest days but one of them is Marshall Notman, now Marshall Grant, who joined up in the very first weeks of summer training in 1948. He had been a swimmer and, aged 15, needed a new challenge so turned to distance running. Marshall was no mean performer in a career which extended to the early 60s and won the NSAAA cross country championship three years in a row in the 50s. He was also North track champion across the range of endurance events from the half mile, where he broke 2 minutes, through to the 3 miles. He used to run 4:15 – 4:20 for the mile which is worth a sub 4 minute 1500.

He remembers: *"I left the High School at an early age and went to work as a message boy for MacKintosh and MacLeod the wine merchants in Bridge Street so that's maybe where I got the cycling from. I was 15 when I first went to the Harriers in the early weeks of them starting and we began at the Meeting Park but soon moved to the Bught, where we did have a marked track.*

"We used to have the dressing room on the right while the shinty players had the other one and our one would sometimes be quite full with maybe more than 20 Harriers. It was Tom MacKenzie and Paul the Pole (Machejewski) *who took training and it was really just running round the track. But in the winter I was sometimes the only one to turn up for runs on Saturdays."*

Marshall also contested the Ben Nevis Race in the 50s, and under somewhat eventful circumstances: *"I decided to take a look at the Ben the week before the race so I hitch hiked to Fort William and when I went up the mountain I got four seasons in one day. By the time I got back down, the last bus had gone so I just started walking and I had got to the Clansman Hotel* (that's 55 miles! CB) *before I got a lift into Tomnahurich Street.*

"When I got back for the race the following Saturday, I found the local Lochaber runners wearing tartan vests. At one stage I asked one of them the way but he misdirected me and sent me the wrong way and I ended up fifth. I was extremely annoyed because I am sure I could have won that race as easily as walking down the High Street."

Marshall also did the full range of Games including, he admits, on the quiet, the odd professional meeting such as Strathpeffer and Nairn in its previous incarnation *"for a few bob."* This versatile sportsman ended his career with another shift, this time to rugby, where he was a well-known hooker for Highland. However Marshall did not entirely give up running since in the 60s he delivered rolls from a mini-van –

which he was not averse to leave rolling along quiet suburban streets in neutral while he ran to and fro into various gardens with bags of rolls!

On July 24th 1948 there was further action at the Forres Sports where Ian Walker won the 100. First place in both the half mile and the mile is attributed to "D. Grant" of the Harriers but one wonders if this is really Ron Grant again. Then on August 21st, the Inverness Games made its only appearance at the Northern Meeting Park before moving back there from the Bught in 2010. According to the Courier, on a pouring wet day "only" 2000 spectators turned out.

Once again there was a party from the SAAA's East and West Districts and this would be a feature of meetings in the North for the next quarter century or so. The picture emerged in the previous chapter of a NSAAA which was decidedly not athlete centred. The local governing body could have encouraged its athletes to head south to compete in championships and other national competitions and to organize themselves in clubs. But the NSAAA instead seemed to prefer to import relatively small groups from elsewhere in Scotland to its own meetings. This might well have enhanced spectator appeal at Highland Games but it did little to integrate the sport in the North with the rest of the country and improve standards.

The early history of Inverness Harriers reveals a very similar pattern of a club which saw its function as entering athletes for the limited range of sports meetings around the local area. The sport, it seems, barely existed beyond the Highland line in the eyes of these early pioneers. Poor transport links, especially the A9, were doubtless a major factor here, as well as expense in an era of austerity. But that was the same A9 as visiting teams from the South had to travel and these inward looking attitudes would take a long time to change. There was very little concept of the wider athletics world - or of the potential of Inverness athletes to compete successfully in it.

The programme for the Elgin Gala Association Amateur Athletic Sports Meeting at Cooper Park on 1st August 1953 gives us a good insight into the sport in the North at the dawn of the New Elizabethan Age. By now Inverness Harriers as a club was making a significant impact on these local meetings.

This Elgin programme is typical of its time, with a good range of track events although the field was more restricted but included four throws - the NSAAA shot championship and the open hammer, weight over the bar and the caber. It is not clear whether this is the wire or the Scots hammer, but even outwith Highland Games, Highland heavy event throws did very much receive preference. It would take a long time for the discus and javelin to acquire anything more than a token presence at all in the North, outwith school competition.

The field for the Lossie - Elgin road race (about 6 miles), included Hugh Calder of Inverness Harriers who, almost three decades later, would become the sponsor of the Craig Dunain Hill Race. The

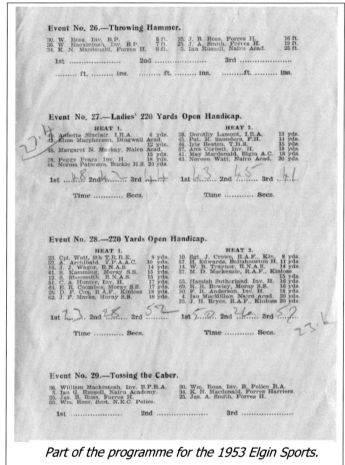

Part of the programme for the 1953 Elgin Sports.

influence of the armed forces and competitors from the South is evident again. For instance the 100 yards handicap was won in 10.4 sec by S. Shoesmith of RNAS Lossiemouth from H. Edwards of Bellahouston Harriers, and, in the best vowel-free armyspeak, "Cpl Watt, 8th Trg Regt, Pinefield".

100 yards in 10.4 sec off a 5.5 yard handicap isn't really spectacular sprinting and these runners were relative back markers.

Similarly, John Hendry of Walton AC's 4:28.4 off 70 in the mile is decidedly middle of the road although his 1:59.8 off 25 in the half mile is perhaps a little better. Runner up off 100 in the mile was Marshall Notman.

Discrimination against women would remain throughout the sport for some time and the Elgin programme only offers them a limited range of events, with 220 the strict maximum distance on the track. However there is continuing evidence of a female presence in the Harriers with Anne Corbett, Peggy Pears and Janet MacMillan all listed.

Female competitors included the reigning Scottish Schoolgirls 220 champion Annette Sinclair who is understandably back marker both times. Off just 2.5 and 4 yards, she was giving hefty 3.5 and 8 yard starts to the next on the list. Some results are pencilled into the copy of the programme which I was able to source and the harshly handicapped back marker certainly isn't among the prize winners in the 100 and doesn't even make the final of the longer sprint.

In common with several of its pupils at that time, Annette is listed under Inverness Royal Academy and was not a member of the Harriers. But running off 16 yards in the men's 220, and also missing the final, is Inverness Harrier Hamish Sutherland. In the coming years, he would become a local councillor and Annette Sinclair became Mrs. Hamish Sutherland.

As at many other meetings, the only two clubs from the North listed on the programme are Forres Harriers and Inverness Harriers with other local input from RAF Kinloss, RNAS Lossiemouth and some Army units. The referee was the well known figure of Duncan Fraser of Inverness whose son Bill was a timekeeper. Donald Duncan was Clerk of the Course and the microphone was held by that voice of North athletics Bobo MacKay.

Absent was an athlete whose name was synonymous with Inverness Harriers for two decades. In 1953 Ian Tasker was 19 and half way through his National Service with 45 Commando, Royal Marines, where his postings included Malta. Here he competed in the island's athletics championships where he discovered that the triple jump was actually an athletic event because he had only known it as the hop, step and leap at the Highland Games!

Before his National Service, whilst still working for the NAAFI in Inverness in 1950, Ian joined Inverness Harriers. He was inspired to do so by the appearance at the Inverness Games of Great Britain sprinter Emmanuel McDonald Bailey who set a Scottish all comers' 100 yards record of 9.7. On his return from the Marines, Ian resumed his athletics career in Inverness and joined the advertising department of the Inverness Courier from which for many years he also supplied the paper with regular reports on athletics. Very much a jumps specialist but something of a sprinter too, he won over 30 NSAAA titles in a career which lasted until 1972.

Ian was also no mean basketball player and this was his winter sport which kept him fit and in practice for jumping in the summer. However his abiding memory from his early athletics career in the 1950s is of a club with limited ambition, limited coaching resources, limited facilities and limited competition.

"There really weren't very many opportunities for competition available to us in the 50s and 60s," he said. *"We started training about*

Track and field athletes from the mid 50s
Rear - Hector ??, Freddie Anderson, ??, Ian Tasker, ??Matheson.
Front - ??. ??, Sheila MacDonald, Iris Beaton, Janet Macmillan.
The women are wearing the diagonal version of the early strip.

April and the competitive season started in June at the earliest and it was all over by the end of August. There were the amateur sports meetings and Highland Games, and not all that many of them, and nothing else. For us 'competing in the South' meant going to the Strathallan or Dunblane Highland Games and that was it. Very few of us had any experience at all of competitions like Scottish championships and in fact it never occurred to any of us to compete in the championships. As far as we were concerned in the Harriers we were Highland Games athletes who also did local sports meetings like the one that RAF Kinloss used to put on and that was it.

"There was one time I did go to the Strathallan Highland Games and I got a lift from Jack Frame the accountant, whose son John played rugby for Scotland. Jack was a director of Caledonian Associated Cinemas so we were taken into the cinema in Perth for lunch. Unfortunately that meant that we arrived a bit late for the Games and the long jump was the first event so I didn't get a real warm up. As a result I managed to pull a muscle which put me out for the rest of the season so that wasn't a particularly successful trip South."

Ian's personal bests for the jumping events are interesting. Although only 5 feet 8 inches tall, he cleared 5' 11" (1.80) in the high jump three times. As a member of a guest team at a Highland Games in Stromness in 1955, he stopped the pipe band dead in its tracks (a rare feat at a Highland Games!) for the crowd to watch him attempt 6 feet (1.83). His official best for the triple jump was 44' 2" (13.46) although he did also clear 13.67 with the downhill run up at the 1967 Glenurquhart Games, a club record until 1989. He says he is not sure of the validity of the 22' 3" (6.78) long jump he was once credited with, since the sobriety of the judge on duty that day was frequently in question, although another effort of 21' 7" (6.58) is definitely bona fide.

Ian can also lay claim to a 100 yard best of 10.1 although - in common with many jumps specialists - he admits to finding the 220 quite a long way! These long and triple jump marks in particular still stand up to scrutiny half a century later and provide a relatively rare insight into the kind of performance levels in an era when handicapped events deprive us of much information about standards, especially in track events.

It also has to be remembered that these performances were done off grass which was frequently rough and wet on a Games day, when athletes would contest multiple events in pursuit of prizes. What Ian might have done in a Scottish championship on a cinder run up can only be guessed at. His long and triple jump PBs are not light years away even from the winning efforts at national championships in the late 50s and into the 60s. So Ian Tasker might at least have been a strong contender for silver or bronze in the national senior championships. But it was not to be - in that era at any rate.

"There was no tradition at all of competing at national championships," Ian reiterated. "It simply never entered our heads. I just thought 'I'm not that good'."

If attitudes to competition were fairly basic, the same could be said of training. The move to the Bught after a short spell at the Meeting Park was not without some controversy. Inevitably - and understandably - local shinty interests were quite defensive about what they regarded as "their" territory so no permanent track could be marked. The nearest to a track for training was the one which was laid in whitewash for the Inter School Sports at the beginning of June and remained visible for a few weeks thereafter, depending on how wet a summer it was.

Tuesday and Thursday club sessions (a tradition which has never altered) started in April and concluded at the end of August (a tradition which most definitely has altered!) What was on offer also appears to have been rudimentary in the extreme.

Ian Tasker remembers: *"There was no coaching as such because there really were no coaches. There was a 'trainer' who just did a warm up with everybody and then we were all left to our own devices practising our own events with no coaching input at all. Ian Peterkin made a kind of starter's pistol at AI Welders and we used that instead of a cap gun. Because of lack of facilities, the only chance I ever got to practise the jumping events was at competitions because we had no pits or landing areas or anything like that to use during training. It really was quite basic."*

Ian also gives an interesting insight into the relationship in the third quarter of the 20th century between Inverness Harriers and the town's oldest school. Bill Murray became Principal Teacher of PE at Inverness Royal Academy in 1951 and retired as an Assistant Rector in 1977. His athletics CV was formidable and ranged from running the most efficient sports meetings in the North such as the Inter School and Royal Academy Sports to coaching a conveyor belt of very good athletes.

These included Jimmy Grant who as a schoolboy in the early 60s ran sub-50 for the 440 and sub-2 minutes for the half mile. And, unlike Inverness Harriers, Bill also took at least some of his athletes to SAAA national championships. For instance in 1953 Sandy Sanderson, running for Inverness Royal Academy, set a SAAA Youths 440 championship record of 50.6.

Bill also seems to have had at least some involvement with the NSAAA because one tale he told me (which Tom MacKenzie also relates in his book) is of how he and Tom went to Bonar Bridge to scythe a farmer's field to create a Highland Games venue.

However there was always a perception, including among Bill's pupils of which I was one, that he had something against the Harriers.

Certainly there was the feeling that he at least did nothing to encourage pupils to go along to the club and maybe even emitted an aura which even suggested that he discouraged this. Ian Tasker, on the other hand, has an interesting take on this apparently uneasy relationship between school and club, which continued until Bill's retiral.

"I don't think that was a surprising attitude on Bill Murray's part at all. After all here was someone who knew exactly how it should be done and fitted his school athletes out with training schedules and gave them opportunities to compete. And here was a club where to be quite honest they didn't have much of a clue about what they were doing. At that time, why should Bill Murray want to encourage his athletes to go along there?"

In the early 1950s, rivalry between the Royal Academy and the then Technical High School was as intense as ever during a golden era for Inverness sprinting. At the top of Stephen's Brae, Sandy Sanderson and his older brother John, who was club secretary for a short time in the early 70s, were among Scotland's fastest teenagers. But over the shorter sprints they still had to play second fiddle to a fellow Harrier from the "Teckie" called Donnie MacKintosh, who also seems to have been a rare example of an Inverness athlete who did sometimes go south for competition.

In 1951 Donnie beat John Sanderson over 100 yards but was too

young to be given the NSAAA title. Then the following year, and now fully eligible, he won both the 100 and 220. His personal best times - on grass - of 10.1 and 23.1 are extremely good for a 16 year old in any era. But he

Donnie Mackintosh in action at the Inverness High School Sports.

was never in a position to follow them up since he was also an outstanding footballer and at 17 signed professional forms for

Rangers. Consequently he was lost - for the time being at any rate - to athletics, as he explained in a Courier interview in 2002, the 50th anniversary of his double NSAAA triumph.

"Running was probably my first love and I might have preferred to stay there. But every time I had to go south to compete it would cost my father a week's wages. On the other hand at 17 I could get an average wage myself from Rangers and that made a big difference in my decision."

After three years at Ibrox, Donnie returned North to play in the Highland League before giving up football because he had to work on Saturdays. He applied for and, apparently unusually, received reinstatement to amateur athletics where he competed for another couple of seasons for Inverness Harriers.

Donnie's story perhaps introduces a further reason for so few athletes from the North competing in mainstream athletics elsewhere and restricting themselves to local Highland Games type events. Apart from a locally based mindset which ran through the sport in the north and the physical difficulty of getting out of the Highlands, costs were clearly also a significant factor.

The club's minute and cash books from the mid-1950s give an interesting insight into its affairs at the time. In 1953-54 there were 26 members. Then the breakdown for 1956-57 shows 21, comprising 12 men paying a 6/- (30p) subscription, one woman and four juniors at 2/6d each and four juveniles at 1/6d. Total expenditure for 1954-55 was £38 1s 4d, of which £4 10s was for hire of the Bught for training for the six summer months.

Index linked to 2014 values, where a typical bill for the Queens Park for a single month is now £1000, these figures correspond to £875 total running costs for the year, including £103.50 for facility hire. The biggest single item of expenditure of the period was £13 14s 0d on January 15th 1954 to Munros cycle agents in Baron Taylor's street for a bike for the coach.

The attendance of 16 at the AGM in the YWCA clubrooms on Raining's Stairs on 6th October 1954 was fairly typical of that period. Provost J. M. Grigor, apparently in line with the custom of the time, was elected Honorary President while founder members Donald MacLeary and Tom MacKenzie became Honorary Vice Presidents. The committee was – President J.M. Brown, Vice President – P. Machajewski, Secretary and Treasurer and assistant – J. R. MacLennan and H. Morrison, Club captain – Ian Tasker, Vice Captain – J. MacKenzie, Ladies' captain – Miss J. MacMillan, Trainer and assistant – P. Machajewski and T. MacKenzie.

The other committee members were Dave Fotheringham, J. R. MacKenzie (who also won the MacKenzie Cup), G. J. Crichton and J. Taylor. Apart from the still unrequited desire for a permanent track at the Bught, very little of an athletic nature seems to have been discussed but "the evening was concluded by a very cordial and plentiful tea."

The Queens Park track, which has its origins in the 1950s, has an interesting but initially sorry history. Constructed on land set aside "for the youth of the town" it was built to the specification of the 1952 Olympic track in Helsinki. The original facility may only have had a very short useful lifetime but one of its features would reap very positive benefits quarter of a century later.

Through the father of two of his rugby boys, a senior figure in Wm Tawse Construction, Bill Murray made the arrangements for the bottoming for the new facility. So sound was that bottoming that when construction of the current track began on the same site in 1983, the base was simply kept in place and the polymer laid on top of it, saving a lot of money on the contract.

The track, to be administered by a Queens Park Committee, was opened with great pomp and ceremony in the mid-50s, However the committee very quickly went defunct and after a very few years the place was disused and abandoned to the elements. So until it made an all-weather track possible in the 80s it was regarded as a monstrous white elephant and a waste of public money. Ian Tasker gives it short shrift. *"In the 50s it had one meeting on it and that was it. It never came into question to use it for Harriers training and we always used the Bught."*

It now seems incredible that such a facility should have so easily have been allowed to lapse into disrepair and that the town's athletics club should have shown no interest in it during its short heyday. Given its potential for performance development, this once again asks serious questions about where Inverness Harriers' ambitions and aspirations – and those of the NSAAA - lay. The post war history of athletics in the North is littered with missed opportunities.

By the mid-50s, references to the club in Highland Games reports become relatively thin again but in the summer of 1955 there is an account of Tasker following up his 5'11" in Stromness with 5'10" (1.78) at the Forres Sports where he also long jumped 21'5" (6.52). By now the Nairn Games, held on the first Saturday after the Glorious 12th of August, had become an amateur meeting at a time when the NSAAA also persuaded Glenurquhart, Abernethy and Newtonmore to make the same Damascene conversion.

26

Nairn also appears to have had some features of a conventional athletics meeting which were highly unusual for a Highland Games. For instance there was a low hurdles race, won by J. Taylor of Inverness Harriers which, from the winning time of 13.5 sec, we can take probably to have been 100 yards.

EVENT 25

Thowing the Javelin

5	G. Bell, Heriot's A.C.	3 ft.
47	Dr K. Maksimczyk, Atalanta	15 ft.
45	A. B. Macdonald, Inverness Royal Academy	35 ft.
56	Paul Mackajewski, Inverness Harriers	25 ft.
49	M. Shaw	30 ft.
51	D. Mackintosh	30 ft.
82	Cpl. Weller, Army A.A., Pinefield	20 ft.
64	D. A. Beaton, unattached	25 ft.
78	Cpl. Douglas, R.A.F., Kinloss	20 ft.
71	F/O. Keenan, R.A.F., Kinloss	25 ft.
79	P/O. Pash, R.A.F., Kinloss	30 ft.

1st..............................., 2nd............................., 3rd...................................

ft.......... in.......... ft.......... in.......... ft.......... in..........

EVENT 26

220 Yards Open—Handicap.

Heat 1

1	E. Macdonald Bailey, Polytechnic Harriers	scr.
5	G. Bell, Heriot's A.C.	13 yds.
67	A/C. Thackerey, R.A.F., Kinloss	17 yds.
30	D. Macdonald, Inverness Harriers	20 yds.
31	D. R. Grant, Inverness Harriers	21 yds.

1st................................. Time........................secs.

Heat 2

2	A. T. Bruce, Edinburgh University	7 yds.
6	W. Curtis, V.P.A.A.C.	17 yds.
68	A/C. Mackenzie, R.A.F., Kinloss	19 yds.
22	R. J. Kirby, R.N.A.S., Lossiemouth	21 yds.
17	C. A. Hunter, Inverness Harriers	23 yds.

1st................................. Time........................secs.

Heat 3

3	W. Jack, V.P.A.A.C.	6 yds.
21	J. Sanderson, Inverness Harriers	13 yds.
69	F/Lt. Spackman, R.A.F., Kinloss	19 yds.
24	J. Barclay, R.N.A.S., Lossiemouth	21 yds.
11	L. D. Cameron, Inverness Harriers	26 yds.

1st................................. Time........................secs.

12

Entrants for the 220, with MacDonald Bailey off scratch, and a rare javelin event in the North. Inverness Highland Games 1950.

Incredibly for an arena easily too small to accommodate a full sized track (the current one is 300m) there was also a men's javelin.

More incredibly still, D. W. R. MacKenzie of Edinburgh University threw a Scottish record distance of 200' 5¼" (61.08) – apparently without impaling any spectators!

A week later he was also above 200 feet in the full sized Bught Park at the Inverness Games where Inverness Harriers took second

Celebrations at the Bught after winning the 1954 NSAAA Cross Country Championship. Tom Mackenzie is in the front row on the right, Marshall Notman is next to him, Paul Machejewski is front left with a bespectacled Donald MacLeary next to him.

place to the Royal Academy in the 4 x half lap relay. It is then with some relief that we learn from the Courier that the following week at Glenurquhart, which only has a 250m track, Blairbeg Park was deemed *"too small to accommodate the javelin event"!* On the same afternoon there were runner-up spots in the ladies 100 for Janet MacMillan and for Dave Fotheringham in the 440.

There was a purple patch in 1954 with success at two major North events three weeks apart. On March 20th, the club won the Petty Rosebowl for the 4 x 4 mile Inverness to Nairn road relay by a margin of 300 yards from RNAS Lossiemouth. Ron Grant put the Harriers into the lead on the first leg and they never looked back with further contributions from Dave Fotheringham, Freddy Anderson and Marshall Notman. The time was 95:40 which represents an average of just under 6 minutes a mile, and there is a significant chance that they had to run into a prevailing westerly wind during the season of equinoctial gales.

Then at Gordonstoun Notman won the NSAAA cross country title in 30:38 over a five mile course, leading an otherwise unnamed Harriers team to victory, again over RNAS Lossiemouth. Clearly the purchase of the coach's bike was paying dividends!

However by March 1956 there is no mention of an Inverness team in the road relay which, incredibly, took place on the main A96 right through to 1973. Then early in 1957 there is further evidence of activity in cross country. On February 23rd the club promoted its first cross country meeting of the season. No results were published by the Courier but it does say, by way of preview, that over 30 athletes were expected from the Harriers, RAF Kinloss, Gordonstoun Cameron Barracks, Fort George and Lochaber AC for a senior five mile and junior three mile races.

The preview continues: *"Both races will start from Bught Stadium, following a strenuous course over the top of Torvean and returning to the Bught by way of the canal banks."* This was at a time when Torvean Quarry was still fully operational and the geography of the area was rather different from the present.

Many of these teams were back in action the following month at the NSAAA championships at Gordonstoun, with the addition of Altyre School, Forres Harriers and Fochabers. Club involvement in athletic competition in the North therefore remained quite limited.

The Gordonstoun meeting was a further personal triumph for Marshall Notman who won another senior title in 27:15, reportedly *"quite a remarkable feat in view of the fact that the ground was very heavy because of a steady fall of rain the previous day."* The runner up was *"McFadzean of the RNAS who finished strongly"* while in the junior race, *"Taylor of Lochaber"* (19:44.6) just pipped *"Hall of Gordonstoun"* (19:45) but there is no reference to any other competitor from Inverness Harriers.

April 1957 provides a hint that all was not that well within Inverness Harriers when the Courier of Friday 19th records: *"There was a very disappointing turnout at the Bught Park Inverness on Tuesday evening when Inverness Harriers commenced their training programme for the coming season. Last year the Harriers had quite a successful season and the majority of their 20 club members took part in all of the sports meetings in the North. The first meeting of the coming season is on Saturday 29th June at the Bught Park Inverness when athletes from all over Scotland will take part."*

This suggests that early season training attendances in the spring of 1957 were well down even on the modest 20 club athletes in 1956. Competition for 1957 didn't begin until the end of June, which may explain why it was thought possible to delay the start of club training until an even later than usual 16th April.

That first meeting of the season was the Inverness Games which attracted a disappointing attendance of only 500 spectators, compared with an estimated 12,000 at Nairn less than two months later. Harriers results were about as sparse as the crowd although Marshall Notman was second in the NSAAA half mile championship while Ian Tasker was third in the 220 championship, won by Forres Mechanics player Jim Preston of RAF Kinloss in 23.5. There were third places in handicaps for Iris Beaton in the women's 100 yards and for newcomer Peter Mackintosh in the junior half mile.

Peter Mackintosh, from Nairn, was a club member from 1955, when he left school, until 1959 when he was about to leave the Highlands to work. He ran the 440, finishing third in the 1958 NSAAA championship, one of the few races to take place on the Queens Park, and also contested the half mile and cross country.

By the time he returned North in 1963, the club had effectively gone defunct. Peter rose to become Highland Regional Council's Director of Economic Development and after he retired became chairman of Nairn County Football Club.

"Tom MacKenzie had a mission in that he wanted harrier clubs in all the communities in the area and was instrumental in starting Nairn Harriers which unfortunately had a lifespan of only about 18 months," Peter recollects. *"I was also a member of Nairn Harriers and Tom encouraged me to compete for them in events in the town and for Inverness Harriers in events furth of Nairn.*

"On Tuesdays and Thursdays I would quite often drop into the Locarno Cafe where Renzo Serafini would give me a cheese sandwich and a cup of tea for sixpence, or you could get bread and soup in Burnett's restaurant across the road for a shilling. After that I would run over to the Bught to train. I really don't think I ate well enough to be a runner but I got by although I never really weighed more than nine and a half stone. Training was usually at the Bught but sometimes at the Meeting Park although effectively there was no actual coaching done. Then I would have to get back over to the town to catch the 9:30 bus home to Nairn.

"The distance runners also did limited winter training in that between five and eight of us would meet on a Saturday morning to go for a run sometimes in behind Torvean or on other occasions along

the riverside and through the Ness Islands. On some Saturdays there would be cross country races and I even remember a few girls there although I'm not entirely sure if they were running in these days or whether they were just friends of some of the boys who were competing."

One clubmate whom Peter Mackintosh remembers well is Ken MacLeod who was another endurance runner and a great team man. He went on to play a prominent part in the community in roles as diverse as a local solicitor, councillor and a leading light in the judo club. In his professional role he had a high profile in the early 1990s for his part in saving Clachnacuddin Football Club and representing one of the Thistle fans opposed to the merger which created Caley Thistle.

The early 1960s saw one or two interesting developments in the North. In May 1960 H.A.L. Chapman, the National Coach, made by no means his only visit to the area for a clinic. This was a tradition which one of his successors Frank Dick would carry on with massive effect in the 70s. However at Inverness Harriers there is still little evidence of any coherent coaching strategy.

One sports venue at the time was McKessack Park Rothes, but in 1960 there seems to have been a very poor turnout, although R. J. Aitken of the Harriers won the high jump. Then what was very probably the first – and, before Sportshall, almost the only – indoor athletics meeting in the North took place in Golspie Drill Hall on 19th February 1961. This was the brainchild of Norrie Brown, Principal Teacher of PE at Golspie High School and a former Scottish pole vault champion. This was a time when athletics in Golspie was booming with stars in athletics like thrower Sandy Sutherland. Indeed in the early 60s the Courier had probably more to say about the achievements of athletes from Golspie, and their contemporaries from Inverness Royal Academy, than it did about the local club Inverness Harriers.

This indoor meeting was Sportshall Athletics years before its time. It must have been an amazing event with 400 spectators also crammed into the hall to witness competition among athletes from locations including Dumfries, Golspie, Inverness and Glasgow. It even managed to attract the legendary 1960 Olympic high jumper and Scottish record holder Crawford Fairbrother. During the mid-50s Fairbrother had been in the RAF Meterorological Office at Dalcross airfield near Inverness so knew the Highlands well. Perhaps it was his experience of the Highland weather which drew him to an indoor meeting!

On his return to compete at Golspie, he amazingly cleared a Scottish indoor record 6' 2" (1.88) off the drill hall floor, with Tasker second on 5'9 (1.75). Not to be outdone, Tasker got the better of Fairbrother in the 100 yards which was three lengths of the drill hall. Typical of a horizontal jumper, Tasker was famous for his acceleration, as many Highland Games rivals knew from sprint handicaps on tracks with tight bends. This was a strength which the Harrier presumably exploited at Golspie on all three occasions offered by this unusual sprint.

By the early 60s, Inverness Harriers had clearly got into poor shape as a club. Existence effectively in name only from 1961-69 was now imminent. Over this period the club appears to have existed as a shell and mainly as a medium for Tasker to continue his prodigious local track and field prizewinning career, with a limited and intermittent supporting cast.

However these hard times also briefly saw probably the most accomplished athlete of the early days, whose achievements as a senior competitor went unmatched until the early 1980s. The son of the Free Church minister in Alness, Calum Laing, a distance specialist, spent much of his competitive years as a student in Glasgow but, for a while at least, competed for Inverness Harriers. He had a particularly good 1961 which he began by winning the inter university cross country match in Aberdeen with 35:28 for the 6.5 mile course. The following month he returned there, this time to lift the Scottish Universities' title.

Four weeks later he was in Inverness for a NSAAA victory by 72 seconds in 34:43 over D. Gifford of Lochaber on the six mile course which began at the Queens Park and went over the canal to Craig Dunain Hospital, up what was known as "Nurses' Brae". Lochaber AC had been formed in 1959 and provided a valuable increase in the tiny number of clubs in the North, albeit principally in hill running and cross country.

The only other Inverness successes among 176 competitors in three male age groups that day were Dave MacFarquhar of the Royal Academy who won the three mile under 17 race in 19:57 and H. MacKenzie of Inverness High School, runner up in the two mile under 15 boys' contest in 15:38. Apart from Laing there are no other Inverness Harriers on the prize list – and quite possibly even on the start list.

Among his other 1961 achievements, Laing could also list the Scottish Universities' three mile track title, with a record of 14:37.8 (equivalent to around 15:09 for 5000m) and the NSAAA two miles.

Across the piece he was awarded the MacKenzie Cup as the outstanding male competitor within his struggling club.

In the chapter on the North District for Colin Shields' "Whatever The Weather", the centenary history of the Scottish Cross Country Union, Walter Banks lists some of Laing's achievements, ending with the observation: *"In 1962 he finished third in the national cross country championships at Hamilton racecourse and was selected to represent Scotland in international events in 1962 and 1963."*

This revelation appears to help resolve the question of who the Harriers' first senior internationalist was to the extent that it seems not to have been Calum Laing. Because by 1962, Inverness Harriers appears even to have lost its most successful athlete, and the only one thus far to have been a major national player. For Calum Laing, who won the Scottish 6 mile title that year and the Scottish Universities' mile and 3 mile championships with record performances, is now reported as running for Ross shire Sports Club. Laing was an Alness boy so this hardly seems contentious. Club activity in Ross shire would stutter in and out of existence until Black Isle AAC became a permanent fixture in the 1980s.

Even though Inverness Harriers was seriously struggling by the early 60s, it battled on gamely and on March 31st 1961 The Courier's "Sports and Sportsmen − Northern Notes and Views" column records that training would begin the following Tuesday, April 4th, at Bught Park.

However attendance at the AGM in November 1961 was so low that the meeting had to be postponed for a month and even then just nine people gathered in the Tower Hotel. The minute refers to poor attendances both at track and field and cross country events and a committee was assembled under the chairmanship of Tom MacKenzie. Thereafter there were no further general meetings until May 1966.

By now the name of Tom McCook was beginning to appear as a regular prize winner, principally in the half mile and the mile. But sometimes he is listed under the Harriers and others as Inverness Royal Academy. This reflects the distance between school and club and even the few who broke ranks and joined the Harriers felt obliged at least on some occasions to compete in their white, blue and gold vests.

Notwithstanding this, another of the few to compete under that dual identity was Bill Macdonald, the son of the school's Rector W. S. Macdonald and a keen distance runner. There was also some representation in the heavy events through Ronnie Ross and John Morrison who were later joined by Tony Cohen.

Tom McCook's interest in athletics was inspired by the 1960 Olympics in Rome, and 1500m champion Herb Elliott. Tom joined the Harriers that year and in 1967, two years after leaving school, went to work for the Post Office in Birmingham. There he met and married Carol Stewart, a member of the Stewart dynasty of distance athletes. Her brother Ian became World cross country champion and Commonwealth 5000m champion while siblings Peter and Mary were also major internationalists.

Their name was synonymous with Birchfield Harriers and Tom got involved as well – so much so that over the years he became both Chairman and President of Britain's biggest club. So it was rather ironic that Tom had come to Birchfield from what must have been Britain's smallest club!

"I was the Harriers club Secretary for a while in the mid-60s when there really wasn't a lot going on," he said. *"Apart from Ian Tasker, we did have several club members who used to compete on the Highland Games circuit on grass tracks.*

"At other times of the year, there were cross country and occasional hill races and the Nairn to Inverness four man Road Relay which finished outside the Town Hall. After I became an Inverness Harrier, I was joined by three of my friends, Tommy Malcolm, Brian MacKenzie and Bill MacDonald.

"Although they did not train with us we would meet up at the various Highland Games with two Highlanders who were studying at Glasgow University. One was the endurance runner Calum Laing from Alness and thrower Sandy Sutherland from Golspie whom I first met at The Highlanders' Institute in Glasgow on the eve of the 1962 Scottish Schools Track and Field Championship. At that time there were very few female club members. One was Rosie Johnson whose father was a Technical Official.

"Looking back, I realise how fortunate we were to have such dedicated and enthusiastic officials as Tom MacKenzie, Walter Banks, Donald Duncan, David Thom, Gerald Pollitt, John Johnson and the legendary "Bobo" MacKay doing the commentary and announcements on the microphone.

"One of the topical issues of the time was the plaques which were awarded for first places at every N of Scotland AAA championships. Ian Tasker, for instance, had a suitcase full of them so at the one and only NSAAA AGM that I attended as Club Secretary, I suggested that there should be a change of policy. However one gentleman told me quite bluntly that this had been a tradition since 1946 and it wasn't going to change. I later learned that the individual in question was Mr.

Jeans, who owned the shop in the market which had supplied these plaques for twenty years! On another occasion, I remember winning a Half Mile race at Nethy Bridge where my prize was somewhat incongruously a silver cigarette case which I hasten to add I never utilised for its intended purpose."

The 1963 Inverness Games produced an interesting anecdote. The Courier states that Frenchman Jean Bazile of Inverness Harriers won the mile in a remarkably respectable time of 4:13.4, the equivalent of about 3:55 for the 1500. Locally, this was the kind of performance which only Laing might have approached. At the Bught there can be no doubt about the accuracy of the distance and the paper goes on to explain that *"M(onsieur) Bazile, who is a former French junior 1500m champion, is a hairdresser who lives in Inverness."*

1965 saw the inaugural match between the NSAAA and Aberdeen at RNAS Lossiemouth where the discus and javelin made rare appearances. The North team won by 78-57 and a triple winner was international decathlete Peter Gabbett of the RNAS. Tasker won the high jump.

An attempt was made to revive the club at a meeting in May 1966 which, like its predecessor in 1961, had an attendance of nine compared with a roll of 11 competing members and some officials. A committee, again under Tom MacKenzie, was formed and it was resolved to investigate changing the club's name since "the word 'Harrier' gave a false picture of a club interested merely in cross country". This was referred to the next general meeting which in the end never took place before the club was reformed in 1969, by which time the suggestion had been forgotten about. There is also a single set of accounts for 1962-67 which show just four members including, intriguingly, Bill Murray and almost the only item of expenditure the one guinea (£1.05) annual NSAAA subscription.

By the late 60s the club's profile had dropped almost to zero although further athletes who featured after the 1969 reconstitution began to appear. Future Secretary and Treasurer Sandy MacKenzie's name appears in results, as does that of sprinter Brian Milne who also ran for Aberdeen AAC. And by 1968 Audrey Grant and Josephine Gunn were on the fringes but competing for Inverness High School.

But when it gets to the stage where you can more or less list the entire competitive force of the surviving shell of a club in a couple of paragraphs, it is clear that it has effectively died.

Then, Phoenix like, there was a resurrection from the very ashes of the former club.

CHAPTER 3 – BRIEF RENAISSANCE – 1969-76

After much of the 60s had been spent in the doldrums, 1969 was a good time to attempt a revival and that was just what a few pioneering individuals went out and did. Already there was some anticipation of the 1970 Edinburgh Commonwealth Games and the re-formed club had been up and running for a year when these Games arrived. What is now called their "legacy", fuelled by gold medal successes from legends such as Iain Stewart, Lachie Stewart and Rosemary Payne, certainly led to an increased interest in athletics. 1969 was also the year when athletics in the UK - or at least most of it - went metric.

The meeting to reconstitute Inverness Harriers was held in the Tower Hotel on January 22nd 1969. The 15 people taking up the baton again were a blend of the old guard and a new regime. Inevitably Ian Tasker, whose name had been synonymous with Inverness Harriers for so long, was right in there. He had been ready "to pack it up" due to the lack of a proper club, but the reconstitution changed his mind for him. Appropriately he became President, and co-founder Tom MacKenzie was also initially involved. However Tom and local solicitor Donald Duncan who was a major figure on the national scene preferred to watch and encourage developments from a distance as office bearers of the NSAAA, where Tom latterly sat as a representative of the Newtonmore Highland Games.

Tasker's longstanding team mate Dave Fotheringham also eventually returned and the new blood at that meeting importantly included PE teachers from two of the town's three secondary schools. This would be hugely influential in the development of a junior section.

Elizabeth Horne of the High School was elected Vice Chair but, although he was content simply to be an ordinary committee member, the vital coaching role fell to Millburn's Colin Baillie who had been involved in the 1966 attempt to revive the club. The town's other secondary school, the Royal Academy, had no teacher presence and, compared with Millburn and the High School, tended to be under represented by athletes in the initial years.

Originally from Dundee, Baillie had by now been in Inverness for six years. It would be some time yet before his massive reputation for getting things done in sport would develop fully, but his legendary fierceness matured much more rapidly. His many other commitments, especially to Highland Rugby Club, limited his regular input to the Harriers over the years but he was never far away during these earliest days of this second era.

Colin Baillie stamped his personality on club coaching right from the start and in particular established the need for a work ethic in training. Anyone who knows Colin also knows when he is blowing a whistle, even if they can't see him! The purposeful intonation is unique. It was probably Colin who gave the club its first real, proactive, focused coaching, the absence of which in the 1950s Ian Tasker had regretted so much.

The Courier's report on January 24th reads: *"A working committee to revitalise and develop the Inverness Harriers Amateur Athletic Club was formed at a reorganisation meeting held in the Tower Hotel, Inverness on Wednesday evening. Mr Tom MacKenzie, who has been an office bearer of the club since its inception in 1946/47 (sic) expressed his pleasure at such a good attendance which was most encouraging, particularly as the club had existed practically in name only for the past number of years. The first duty of the committee will be to establish as soon as possible training facilities for both men and women. The office bearers appointed are as follows:- President – Ian Tasker, Vice President – Elizabeth Horne, Secretary/ Treasurer – Sandy MacKenzie, Assistant Secretary/ Treasurer – Miss Audrey Grant, Committee – Donald Reid, John Morrison, Colin Baillie, John Gunn, Miss Josephine Gunn and William Junor.*

"It is interesting to note that a second generation of "Harriers" has evolved for Miss Audrey Grant's father Mr Ron Grant was a popular member of the club around 1950."

Then on Tuesday March 25th, Inverness Harriers swung back into action for real for the first time in eight years: *"The recently reformed Inverness Harriers Amateur Athletic Club starts its training sessions at Fraser Park, Kingsmills tonight. Changing facilities are now available for both men's and women's sections and coaching in various events will be given by Colin Baillie, Ian Tasker and Elizabeth Horne. New members will be made welcome and training will continue throughout the season on Tuesday and Thursday evenings."*

Use of Fraser Park and its changing rooms had been negotiated with the Town Council, although not with the blessing of the park's other users, Highland Cricket club. Indeed the next Secretary John Sanderson's original 1970 AGM report has a rather derogatory reference to both these parties where he referred to *"the uncooperative attitude of the Town Council (combined of course with the ignorance of the members of the Highland Cricket Club)".* This, and a similar but milder reference in Colin Baillie's Chief Coach's report, did not survive the following year's AGM and both had to be struck out in red pen. Initially it was proposed to revert to a maroon vest but nothing more came of this and the white with maroon and gold horizontals carried on.

It certainly didn't take Colin Baillie long to make inroads into coaching and it was hard interval training from day one for everyone. The Fraser Park track was 300 metres, so 400 was a lap and a bit. There was also something of a hill in it just at the pavilion, so Baillie arranged his 400 intervals so you always had to climb the hill twice!

Unfortunately that very basic 300 track was just about it. There were no jumping facilities at all. Nor, with no local competition in the Olympic throws, were there any throwers apart from one or two heavies including Tony Cohen and Ronnie Ross. In any case, any attempt to throw implements on the Fraser Park surface would have turned the cricketers apoplectic! Training facilities were hence extremely limited and it was only possible to prepare in a rudimentary fashion for running events.

I first joined Inverness Harriers as a fourth year Inverness Royal Academy pupil at the end of June 1969 – three months after training began at Fraser Park. But for the next year or so, it was for the school and not the Harriers that I competed at the games. This was in line with the practice of Royal Academy pupils during the club's earlier history, but was not unique to that school.

For many years the Harriers did not provide many facilities for junior athletes who had to depend on their schools to enter them for the likes of NSAAA cross country championships. So when the club did start a junior section from 1969, it took a long time for this to die out in local competition. It wasn't as if the schools vigorously enforced their first claim rights; it was merely accepted that this was how things were done in Inverness. It was only when school sport returned after the teachers' industrial action of the mid 1980s that previous practice was not reverted to and schools restricted their activities to school competitions only.

The event at Fraser Park on that June night was described by the Highland News as the *"first ever club championships"* of an organisation which had already reportedly expanded to 70 junior members from the age of six upwards. It is worth recounting these championships in some detail since they were the first competitive event of the new era for members of Inverness Harriers.

Pat MacKay became the first ladies club champion, winning the 400 in 65.9 and the 800 in 2:54.4 and, in the absence of pits, took the standing long jump with 2.00. Pat was a pioneer of women's endurance running in the north and the athlete she pipped for the title was Josephine Gunn who won the 100 in 13.5 and the 200 in 27.1.

On the men's side Brian Milne, formerly of Aberdeen AAC but at that time a gynaecologist at Raigmore Hospital, won the 100 in 12.0 and the 200 in a very respectable (if the distance was accurate) 23.3 in the wet conditions. The men's championship went to rugby and later rowing stalwart Roy Sinclair. His only victory was in the 400 (61.7) where he edged the evergreen Dave Fotheringham. But if Milne's 200 wasn't the star turn of the night, it was Tasker's 2.59 in the standing long jump.

Gordon Melville, who took the 100, 200 and long jump, beat me to the Youths' title although my 60.9 400 bettered the men's time. However this compared very poorly with my 55.7 elsewhere the previous week. The girls' champion was Diane Roodhouse and her apparently modest 14.5 for the 100 asks questions of the accuracy of the Fraser Park straight as well as the outer ring. Alastair Sinclair and Nicola Pledger were the junior champions.

The start of that season's open competition at the Forres Games was not far away and here more Harriers were well in evidence. Josie Gunn and Diane Roodhouse dominated the women's sprints and jumps with Roy Sinclair (400), Ian Tasker (HJ) and Ronnie Ross (Scots Hammer) on the men's prize list.

Then on Wednesday 30th July 1969 there took place what I like to call "Inverness Harriers' first overseas trip" since a party went across the Kessock Ferry to the Avoch Gala Sports. It was here that Tasker's sometimes erratic punctuality emerged. We were all on the "Rosehaugh" which was just pulling away on its short trip to North Kessock when Tasker's black MG screeched down Kessock Avenue and ground to a halt at the bottom of the jetty. Our club president would have to wait for the next ferry!

The meeting itself saw a great scrap in the ladies' (as they were still called) 80 yards. Josie Gunn just edged Audrey Grant but Audrey then relegated Josie to third in the 220, with Diane Roodhouse splitting them. Athletics may have gone metric in the UK that year, but someone forgot to tell the Black Isle!

The "gents'" half mile provided the most memorable moment of the night. Calum MacDonald and I, both on our last legs, were battling neck and neck down the finishing straight when Bobo MacKay emerged from a group of judges to intone: *"We're not quite ready lads, you'll have to run another lap."* Calum must have accommodated the trauma better than I did and eventually took first place!

Local opportunities expanded quite rapidly. The 1970 Inverness Games acted as a warm up competition for 11 athletes from a several countries in advance of the Commonwealth Games. This was another instance of the NSAAA's ability to attract good athletes to their games meetings.

Two Jamaican competitors were sufficiently unimpressed by the high jump facilities to decline to take part but Yvonne Saunders instead won the 200 in 25.8 ahead of Audrey Grant (27.0). At the same meeting Keith Clubb, from Inverness but educated at Gordonstoun, made one of his intermittent appearances for the Harriers and cleared 6' 2" (1.88) in the high jump.

1970 also saw a growing junior section compete in an inter club match at Morriston Park, Elgin and the club championships, organised by Dave Marwick at Inverness High School, had 60 athletes competing in 40 events. Among the prize winners was a nine year old called Kevin MacDonald who went on to be one of the most successful professional footballers Inverness ever produced, winning the English League and Cup double with Liverpool in 1986.

At two inter club competitions at RAF Lossiemouth in the spring of 1971 we see the appearance of Brian Ledingham. During the early and mid-70s, Brian was prominent in local sprint competition along with Willie Junor who had been an original 1969 committee member at the age of 13. During the early 70s, both also did a lot of supportive work, Willie serving as Secretary and Brian as Treasurer for a while. The underlying trend for most of that decade of flares and male perms was that the women made the progress at national level while the men tended to make little if any impression outwith the local area.

After two years at Fraser Park the club had not only outgrown the venue but was also no longer prepared to tolerate Highland Cricket Club's persistently obstructive attitude. The Highland News in 1970 headlined **"Harriers' record 140 members need a track"**. The following year that wish was granted with a return to the Bught where Inverness Shinty Club were also reluctant to have their surface altered by a running track.

Initially markings were restricted to temporary whitewash for the Inter School Sports and Inverness Games. That was soon extended to the rest of the summer and ultimately creosote markings were permitted. The availability of a 400m track with long jump pits on one of the best grass surfaces in the North represented huge progress compared with Fraser Park. The Bught Park was Inverness Harriers' home for the next 23 years.

The extra space also helped accommodate rapidly growing numbers of juniors from right across the town and beyond. There had been some concern that a move across Inverness might deter some of the original clientele but this seemed to have quite the opposite effect and numbers of youngsters actually grew. Affectionately dubbed "the sprachlers" by Ian Tasker, they created a completely new dimension.

One of the early influx of junior members was Dianne Brand who joined as a Dalneigh Primary School pupil in 1970. Apart from myself, Dianne is now the only member to have been continuously involved since the Fraser Park days. She will figure prominently in later chapters as an athlete, an office bearer and the coach of a Commonwealth Games athlete.

Another major figure who joined shortly after the reconstitution was Ted Roodhouse who quickly rose to become Secretary and then, from 1972, Chairman for five years. Originally from London and a sprinter during his youth, Ted had come to Inverness in 1957. When the Harriers sprang back into life, his daughters Diane and Jackie were getting to an age for competing in athletics. Ted took them along to the club, then got involved in coaching and before long had his own group of mainly female sprinters.

The vital and still novel concept which Ted introduced was the importance of athletes seeking competition outwith the Highland Games and indeed outwith the Highlands in order to progress. This demanded an entirely new way of thinking for Inverness Harriers and also for athletics in the north. Ted Roodhouse must get the credit for introducing this vital concept – for flying that initial kite – although its main implementation would not begin until later in the 70s after he was no longer involved.

In promoting this largely untried notion in the North, Ted was certainly out of step with the thinking of at least some of his fellow NSAAA committee members. But he was sowing the first seeds of the progress begun later in the 70s, away from the long established, inward looking NSAAA attitudes and towards integration into the mainstream.

"When I first came along to the Harriers with Diane and Jackie I decided to get involved in coaching at that point and did my qualifications in sprints in Edinburgh," he said. *"But I did think that it was important to go South for competition, to meetings like the Scottish Championships, the East District Championships and others and in fact I got Diane and Jackie to join Dundee Hawkhill Harriers to get some of these other competitions. We did go round the local circuit first before we decided to try our hand down South but that was an important move."*

Four Harriers athletes emerged as significant players in Scottish women's sprinting. Right from the start Josephine Gunn and Audrey Grant made notable marks and they were followed by Diane

Roodhouse and Ann Leith. Among them they managed to cover the entire 100 – 400 range.

A big breakthrough began on 16th May, 1971 at the women's East v West match at Meadowbank where Audrey in the senior age group and Diane and Ann as Intermediates, were all in the East team. These trips to championships like this were the first fruits of Ted's policy of getting the athletes more competitive exposure outwith the area.

The real headline grabber was Audrey's 12.0 for fourth in the 100 during a period of strength for Scottish women's sprinting. This also placed her fourth in the Great Britain junior rankings. Alongside Calum Laing's distance exploits and the now expanding throwing achievements of Hamish Davidson, this was arguably the best performance by an Inverness Harrier thus far. But Audrey's run also had an extra dimension since, unlike the others, she created a sprinting legacy which led straight to growth in future years

Audrey said: "I started round about 1967 before the club was re-formed and I was just training with Ian Tasker. At that time there were just a couple of us girls and all the rest were men. I remember getting a lift to training in Marshall Grant's mini-van but he used to keep his Alsatian dogs in the back which was very scary. Then Dave Marwick became involved as well but eventually Diane and Ann and myself were all working with Ted Roodhouse. The three of us used to go off together to East District and Scottish championships and the East versus West match but it's only now that I'm realising that we were the first club athletes ever to do that."

Inverness Girls at Edinburgh

Inverness Harriers have every reason to be pleased with the performances of their three members who competed at Meadowbank, Edinburgh, on Sunday for the East of Scotland in the Scottish Women's Amateur Athletic Association's annual match against the West of Scotland. The latter won a close contest by 212 points to 206.

Audrey Grant, competing in the senior section, recorded a personal best time of 12 seconds for the 100 metres, in which she finished a close 4th, and in the long jump event she was placed 6th.

Diane Roodhouse ran a remarkable 400 metres race in the intermediate section to win second place, also in a personal best time of 61.1 seconds. She also finished 4th in the 100 metres, recording 12.7 secs.

In the same section, Ann Leith finished 6th in the 200 metres and 7th in the 400 metres.

Inverness Courier May 1971

Audrey Grant, pictured around 1990 as Audrey Munro, leading veteran sprinter

Diane also excelled that day, taking second place in the Intermediate 400 in 61.7 and fourth in the 100 in 12.7. Ann took minor places in the 200 and 400 but her finest hour came a few weeks later at the Scottish Schoolgirls' championships where she won both the 100 (12.5) and 200 (25.7). Diane's 400 gold here in 61.4 meant that both gained the first of two Schools international selections. Audrey, meanwhile, was third in the over 17 100, 200 and long jump. Ann and Diane also broke new ground for the club when they were selected for the Scottish Intermediate team at the 1971 WAAA Championships in Wolverhampton.

Hamish Davidson was also beginning to make his emphatic but short lived mark on the fortunes of Inverness Harriers. Of sheep farming stock from Cawdor near Nairn, this athlete of enormous physique spent a couple of seasons with the club but his talents demanded a rapid move to Edinburgh Southern. However his sojourn there was limited too, because quite soon he moved to the professional Highland Games heavyweight circuit.

At the 1971 Scottish Schoolboys' Championships Hamish won the 15-17 shot with 15.91 and the discus with 50.41 which certainly put the North on the map. He had posted his intent at the North Schools at Grantown-on-Spey the previous Saturday. Distant spectators had laughed when they were advised to vacate the suggested landing place for his discus throw, only to scatter in disarray seconds later.

By this time Ann Leith's uncle Eddie Sharp, a notable school athlete of the early 60s, had set up a dental practice in Hilton and embarked on around three years of coaching sprinters at the club, including Willie Junor, Brian Ledingham and myself. One of Eddie's favourite sessions was 6 x 300 with 3 minute recoveries which could have anyone retching at the best of times, but all the more so in an era when pre-season preparations was rather less comprehensive.

He also held weight training sessions in his garage on Midmills Road on Monday nights. Hamish rapidly became a legend for the enormous poundages he shifted - and for the breakneck speeds at which he drove his car down the narrow streets of the Crown on his way home.

So now here were performances at national level by members of Inverness Harriers in unprecedented numbers. Two years into its second lifetime, the club was at last featuring notably beyond the Highlands and on the national scene. Brief consideration was also given in 1972 to joining a league but came to nothing.

Activity continued on the Highland Games circuit as well. At the inaugural Elgin Games in 1971 Ann Leith, (12.6) won an 80m hurdles race which was almost unique in the North outwith schools competition. Then the following month at Nairn, Tony Cohen retained his Scottish Heavyweight title whilst at Glenurqhart Iain Johnstone won the NSAAA 1500 title.

The 1968 Olympics had seen a breakthrough in the high jump when Dick Fosbury won gold using his revolutionary flop technique. A lack of foam landing areas slowed down the Fosbury Flop's spread to more remote areas but by the early 70s, Inverness Harriers had its own pioneer "flopper" in Iain MacDonald. At the 1972 Forres Games Iain, who soon after moved to Perth Strathtay, cleared 1.73 to defeat back marker and Scottish record holder Crawford Fairbrother on handicap.

The 1972 AGM in Hilton's Jolly Drover was an historic occasion since the man who had been synonymous with Inverness Harriers for the previous 22 years was departing the ranks. Ian Tasker retired from competition at the end of the 1972 summer season – a move marked in the Highland News by the excellent headline **"Ian the original Harriers jump jet calls it a day."** He also agreed to take on the major responsibility of NSAAA Handicapper, setting a huge number of marks for the series of seven Highland Games.

This was a job which had to be done and be seen to be done fairly, so Ian decided he had to become completely independent and sever his association with the Harriers. This meant the loss of the club's overwhelming personality, and also of its President - a role inherited by Ted Roodhouse. After a few years of divorce from the club he loved so much, Ian came back into the fold as an Honorary Life Member as over and 40 years of setting handicaps progressed.

There was still only very limited activity in road racing and cross country. It seems incredible now that road racing could have taken place on the main A96 and the Nairn – Inverness relay was switched to a safer course in the Dores area after Mike Scott of Forres Harriers was knocked off the road in 1972. The Alves to Forres "6" actually survived further out the A96 until 1988. The only reference to Inverness Harriers in the 1971 NSAAA cross country championship results is that the junior men's team finished third equal. The first finisher here for Inverness was Calum MacDonald, another veteran of 1969 and the club's leading distance runner. Further attempts were made to develop cross country through matches against Inverness High School.

The 1973 cross country championships well and truly put Inverness Harriers on the map for the strangest of reasons. With a couple of inches of snow on the ground, the leaders set off at a tremendous pace from the Queens Park and off up "Nurses' Brae" towards Craig Dunain Hospital, with Ian Johnstone of Inverness strongly challenging defending champion Ian MacKenzie of Forres.

This is how Walter Banks, in his chapter on the North District for Colin Shields' "Whatever The Weather", described what happened next: *"Having battled through five miles of sleet, snow and hazards, and with the finishing line virtually in sight, the runners suddenly came across a final obstacle which was insurmountable. Before their eyes, on the run in, the bridge over the Caledonian Canal was being opened to let a boat pass through. Officials at the finishing line some 200 yards away, having been assured that there would be no traffic for the duration of the race, could only watch in dismay – helpless to avert the crisis. One of the leading athletes, in sheer frustration, took the plunge into the chilly waters of the canal but quickly turned back."*

The athlete in question was Johnstone who had by then built up a winning lead. By the time I arrived at the bridge to join a steadily accumulating crowd of frustrated runners my team mate, teeth chattering, was disconsolately climbing back out of the water. They re-ran the race in Forres a few weeks later, but Iain's moment of glory had passed and he eventually dropped out, leaving the title to MacKenzie.

By 1973 things were on the wane again after the early flush following the reconstitution. The junior section, which had expanded so rapidly, contracted with equal suddenness. This was partly because the committee decided to increase the minimum age for membership to 11, to which Colin Baillie objected vigorously but this was a decision which stood for over 30 years. Senior track and field activity also shrank back to little more than half a dozen men and three or four women doing the Highland Games. The club's name is also absent from results for the likes of the Cairngorm and Knockfarrel Hill Races and the 4 x 4 mile road relay over the new Scaniport course, but this lack of endurance activity was by no means unprecedented.

1973 saw an attempt to revive the blaes track at the Queens Park after a decade and a half of dereliction. Ambitious plans were made to bring in sand to try to fill in the holes which were beginning to appear in the Queens Park surface. However this was a scheme doomed to failure on two counts.

Firstly, sand was no substitute for compacted blaes and however much of it Willie Junor, Brian Ledingham and I laid, the holes soon reappeared. And secondly it emerged that there was no enthusiasm within the Town Council for our plan to revive a facility over which they said they had no influence, since the ground had been donated to the defunct Queens Park Committee "for the youth of the town". However it emerged that this Council viewpoint also carried an element of ambiguity.

It soon became apparent that the track was being used by horses towing buggies, which very quickly made the surface a whole lot worse, and Council minutes quickly revealed what had happened. Although the Council apparently felt it had insufficient ownership of the track to help the Harriers in their efforts, it emerged that it did feel entitled to give permission for the horse owners to achieve terminal ruination of a once fine running surface. So after one summer only, because organised club training still only ran from April to early September, there was a return to the Bught in 1974. But not before one final titanic competition on a Queens Park surface which could still muster a narrow, unblemished 100 metre straight.

Club members were amazed and delighted to have a visit during that summer of 1973 from Garscube Harrier, GB sprinter and Munich Olympian Les Piggott. He wanted to use Queens Park, whose best sections were faster than grass, for training and the Inverness athletes were astounded to witness his sheer acceleration at close quarters. Clearly no Inverness Harrier was going to volunteer to race him, but race that night he did - against Colin Baillie's dog Rusty. The clash ended in a canine victory over his distinguished two legged opponent!

Back at the Bught, 1974 saw a brief revival. Inverness Harriers' prize winners at the Games became rather more prevalent again, with a number of new names, especially among the junior ranks. It was around this time that new recruits included Mike Wallace, Sandra MacLaren, Donald MacMillan, Graham Whyte, Dougie Phimister and Eileen Turnbull. Following very soon after would be Wilma Brownlee, Catriona MacCallum, Melanie Robertson and Jock and Mirren Ramsay. This was important because, although things would get worse again before they got better, this cohort included some of the athletes who would play a part in the earliest stages of the major revival which was now not far away. Very tentatively, the seeds of that revival were being sown here.

Mike Wallace was from Perth and the leader at the Cameron Youth Club. He was a fine sprinter and long jumper while his wife Maureen had sprinted for Scotland in the 1970 Commonwealth Games. Although both retained their affiliation to Perth Strathtay, they both also played a significant part for Inverness Harriers, and Mike was Vice President for a time.

One of an amateur club's biggest sources of coaches and officials is the parents of its young athletes. So while Donald, Eileen and Sandra were valuable athletes, so also were their fathers on the sidelines. Walter Turnbull and Alastair MacMillan both became club Treasurers while Allan MacLaren served on the committee. It was also at this time that Dianne Brand's mother Eileen began a lengthy period as Secretary, bearing much of the brunt of controversial letters to the NSAAA and the interminable correspondence which was apparently necessary simply to hire the Bught Park.

Although now a PE student in Edinburgh and doing much of her serious competition for Dundee, Diane Roodhouse produced the performance of 1974 when her time of 25.9 in the women's NSAAA 200 at the Elgin Games broke Audrey's championship record. The Morriston Park black cinder track would soon deteriorate hugely, but even in its prime it was never a wonderful surface. So a time like this, especially for a 400m specialist, was right up with the best that Audrey and Ann Leith had done over the shorter distances. Meanwhile on the men's side Willie Junor, Brian Ledingham and I generally played second fiddle in most North championships to Forres brothers Iain and Alan MacKenzie and their clubmate Donnie MacLean.

There was a modest morale booster when Mike McAusland, Ross MacDonald, Bill MacDonald and I managed to take a recently unprecedented fourth place in the 4 x 4 mile road relay. This led Tasker, now well into his second decade as the Courier's athletics correspondent, to express the ultimately unfulfilled hope that: "*(this performance) marked a start at least for the Harriers to return to winter competition.*"

Bill MacDonald and Mike McAusland, one of two Australian brothers resident in the area, contested the Knockfarrel Hill Race that September, but attempts to become involved in the embryonic north cross country league, which was still for senior men only, were very limited.

That 1974 recovery was a brief one before the club almost ended up back where it had been in the 1960s. Membership for 1975 shrank to just 24, although much of that did comprise the nucleus mentioned above, from which re-growth would be achieved. That two dozen also included new recruits Marie Inglis, Debbie Heath and Lucy Vaughan, Fortrose Academy pupils from the Black Isle, who got some financial assistance from the club to come over on the ferry to train and compete.

Numbers were so small that no viable age group club championship could be held, so an age graded performance graph was developed to allow one all-in competition. In the end it was one of the youngest members, 10 year old Peter Hardie, who emerged as club champion. But overall, competition had largely retreated once again to a tour round the games and in numbers sometimes struggling to reach half a dozen.

The 1975 AGM took place on September 10th at the now regular Harriers meeting venue of the Cummings Hotel which succeeded the Tower Hotel. Despite, or perhaps rather because of the low numbers, there emerged a revived will to do something about the situation. And although competitive strength had reached a low point, the 1975-76 committee included a number of people who were right behind that aim. There was great regret that fortunes had fallen so low again and, aided by a new intake of club officials in the coming months, this committee took the initial steps towards an unprecedented resurgence.

The 1975-76 committee comprised: President – Ted Roodhouse, Vice President – Ronnie Ross, Secretary - Eileen Brand, Treasurer – George Bannerman, Club Captains – Charles Bannerman and Dianne Brand, Committee - Allan MacLaren, Mike Wallace and Alastair and Sheila MacMillan.

Within the next couple of years, Ted Roodhouse and Ronnie Ross would move on to be replaced respectively by George Bannerman and Mike Wallace while Alastair MacMillan took over the vacant Treasurer's office. 1975 was a year which Inverness Harriers was glad to see the back of. But it also marked the end of an era which would give way to much more successful times which were not only unprecedented but, until now, totally inconceivable.

The upward bounce began almost immediately. A lot of new initiatives began immediately and 1976 was a watershed year with a lot of groundbreaking developments. It was also the year that the NSAAA passed out of existence to be replaced by the North District of the men's governing body the SAAA. This left some loose ends on the women's side but open women's events were simply run alongside the official men's ones. After a bit of a struggle, this would also mean that the governing body was far more in tune with what the club wanted to do.

Informal weekend training sessions began that winter in the outer Bught Park. Some experimental winter club races were held and the age graded graph was again used to work out final awards. These were derived from results of the first club cross country championships for many years in January 1976, and of the club races. Wilma Brownlee had the fastest championship time in a mainly female field, but the overall award went by a tiny margin to the slightly younger Melanie Robertson.

The open cross country races which the club organised on January 31st in conjunction with the North League broke new ground in more ways than one. This was the first time Inverness Harriers had promoted an open cross country meeting and Wilma became what is believed to be the first Harrier ever to win a women's cross country race. With Melanie runner up, the hosts also had the top women's team the first time it ever fielded one. Women's distance running was still in its infancy in the North and these athletes were at the very cutting edge.

Other new ventures during that pioneering winter included a return to indoor athletics following pioneering efforts by the Roodhouse group. Long before Glasgow's Kelvin Hall became one of Britain's major indoor venues, there was a track at the Bells Sports Centre in Perth. The outer ring was just 153 metres in circumference, which meant that a 1500 was almost 10 laps. The longest straight sprint or hurdles that could be run was 50 metres - and that only after officials opened the double doors to allow athletes to decelerate into the car park.

The star turn of that indoor season was Simon Fraser who took what was still a very rare national silver medal at 300 in the Scottish Senior Boys' championship. A group of female athletes also attended their championships, but still with limited success.

The relative accessibility of Perth from Inverness, which made indoor competition quite user friendly, gives the opportunity to examine the role of the A9 in the developments which were about to take place. Although still heavily criticised on safety grounds, the A9 is nowadays massively faster than before the upgrade which began later on in the 70s. Whereas four hours from Inverness to Edinburgh used to be considered very good going, below three hours has now been achievable for some time.

The timing of these original A9 improvements happened to coincide with Inverness Harriers' increased need for them. As time went by, travel south became so much easier as nightmare features like the Moy bends, Glenfarg and the Daviot hairpin disappeared. But initially the journey was so slow that travelling the day before was a regular feature of competition beyond the Highlands.

This meant that somewhere inexpensive to stay was needed and the club very soon joined the Scottish Youth Hostels Association. The plus side here was that the accommodation cost little more than a pound a night but there were several negatives. Taking your breakfast with you was no inconvenience, nor was fulfilling the "duty" of cleaning and tidying the hostel. But sleeping in a large communal dormitory was rather less attractive, especially if any clubmate was prone to flatulence. And then there was the Scottish Schools cross country trip when the bus driver was a thunderous snorer!

For competitions at Meadowbank or Grangemouth, Edinburgh's Bruntsfield Youth Hostel was used regularly. For Coatbridge it was Perth and an early departure for the final hop on single carriageway. Bob and Jean, the wardens at Bruntsfield, had hearts of gold and always made us very welcome. On one occasion when my car broke down, Bob even piled us all into his Reliant Robin and drove us to Riccarton for the Scottish Schools cross country.

But let us say that hygiene was not perhaps a high priority at that particular hostel - even when their Alsatian wasn't lying about the food sales area. So the consumption of breakfast at Bruntsfield tended to be one of life's less comfortable and appetising experiences.

Eventually, improvements to the A9 made central belt tracks much more easily accessible - and hence Inverness Harriers' principal competitive strategy much more achievable. The shorter and less arduous journeys also meant far more morning departures and a reduction in overnight stays. It is also questionable whether the rigours of SYHA accommodation would nowadays be acceptable to modern youth.

It should be acknowledged here that it was coaches and athletes from Caithness AAC who led the way in driving North athletics southwards and they had some desperate 600 mile round trips on these dreadful roads. Their pioneering achievements, led by Sandy Gunn, played at least some part in showing those in Inverness what could become possible.

The 1976 track and field season got off to a flying start at the women's East District championships at Pitreavie early in May when Dianne Brand produced a sensational performance to win the senior

200 at the age of 18. Scottish women's sprinting was still very strong and this was the first of a number of performances of this period which literally took the club up to another level. It was from that day that an almost uninterrupted string of groundbreaking efforts would ultimately see Inverness Harriers athletes compete in Scottish and GB teams at all age levels, in the Commonwealth Games and at European and World Championships. If there was ever a seminal moment for the modern club, this was it.

"It was a terrible day at Pitreavie with an awful headwind," Dianne remembers. *"It was so windy that I only ran 26.7 but I was a pretty strong runner and I was also used to it with training in Inverness while a lot of the others just got blown away by the wind."*

Dianne, who also won the 100 the following year, had another good day, especially in the relay, at the East v West match. Here the club's investment in its Black Isle athletes also paid dividends when Debbie Heath added 3 metres to her personal best to win the Intermediate javelin with 28.75. She also broke completely new ground when she won the Scottish under 17 title and was selected for the Celtic International, but no credit for this can really go to Inverness Harriers which could still offer no technical coaching in the throws.

Clubs depend on people to create change and drive them on. And it so happened that in 1976 four individuals who had experienced athletics in the wider world, albeit in somewhat different environments, all arrived on the scene almost simultaneously.

Brian Turnbull was just 21 when he moved North from his native Hawick to work at McDermotts oil construction yard. Apart from being a fine endurance athlete, he already had considerable experience of how a mainstream club operated from his time at Teviotdale Harriers. In particular he was steeped in the traditions of cross country cross country which had almost been a closed book at Inverness Harriers thus far.

Peter Thompson came from the West Midlands and arrived in Inverness as Highland Regional Council's Director of Personnel. He had previously been a prominent distance runner for Birchfield Harriers, Britain's largest club. Apart from his particular interest in endurance, he vigorously spread the message of getting people along to run and his experience of the sport was vast.

Harry Lakeland had been a competitive athlete in the North East of England and now worked for the HRC Roads Department. His daughters Susan and Jane had become junior members and he came along initially to help with a growing junior section. A decade later

Harry, who like Peter ultimately served as President, would provide the Scottish Commonwealth Games team with a discus thrower and send a hammer thrower in the same direction.

Then after five years' partial absence as a student, I returned home permanently to a teaching job. I also had a huge desire to try to develop the club and came back with an insight into how the sport really worked in the wider world. My time as a member of one of Scotland's foremost training groups run by Bill Walker in Edinburgh was a big asset here. Although a 400/800 runner myself, my coaching interest developed into sprints, hurdles and high jump.

There were, of course, many others who contributed hugely to the transformation of Inverness Harriers. But among the four of us who were at the more technical end, we covered the range quite well from endurance to youth development and from a spread of track and field events to administration.

However there were one or two obstacles which had to be overcome. Expanding membership, improving coaching and the development of competition were all major requirements which started to be addressed on a vastly increased scale in 1976. But there was also the issue of the local athletics environment in which the hoped-for transformation had to begin.

One fundamental problem was that much of the rest of the North wasn't ready for the athletics revolution on which Inverness Harriers embarked in the latter half of the 1970s. In the earliest days of its renaissance, the club was still dependent on local competition which largely meant Highland Games. These in turn were controlled by the SAAA North District committee which at that stage still effectively comprised the same NSAAA cabal of Highland Games promoters who looked after their own interests.

In 1975 the SAAA and the North of Scotland AAA agreed that the latter would give up its independent financial control and become the North District of the SAAA and Scottish Cross Country Union. The women's side passed to the East Districts of the SWAAA and SWCCU who had no North District, so local control still largely rested with the former NSAAA committee men but under a different name.

Ultimately the creation of the North District would help drag the sport locally into the second half of the 20th century - and under the guidance of representatives of clubs. But for decades the NSAAA had been principally a promoters' organisation which is partly why there were only three real clubs in the North before 1970.

Inverness Harriers wanted changes in order to improve and modernise competition at the Games but these were just too much for the District Committee to take on board. They were content enough to introduce a young athletes' North championship and the first one was at Dingwall Academy in May 1976. With most athletes still competing here for their schools there was only a minimal Inverness Harriers presence. But, significantly for the future, the Junior Boys' 100 was won that day, in 13.8 seconds, by a first year Millburn pupil called Neil Fraser.

However the District Committee flatly refused to take the senior championship events away from Highland Games and hold them along with the young athletes' ones, as in the East and West. This was a knot which would remain uncut for another four years so the senior athletes continued to be denied a good quality championships venue. To a large extent this was protectionism on the part of the games promoters who were reluctant to dispense with this major incentive to attend their meetings.

There was also a regular stream of correspondence between the club and North District secretary Bill Sutherland on issues as varied as improving the range of women's events at the games to the continuing absence of an Inverness Harriers representative on the District Committee. There was the minor concession of Mike Wallace being co-opted on to that committee. But mutual backscratching at the SAAA AGM meant that Highland Games representatives would continue to exclude the North's fastest developing club until 1980.

By the mid-1970s some tension had built up between Inverness Harriers and some, but by no means all, of the games. The biggest problem was with Nethy Bridge but in complete contrast Glenurquhart was invariably popular. A major factor was the feeling among the track and jumps athletes that preferential treatment was being given to the heavies and other tartan toting tourist magnets.

This boiled over during that roasting hot summer of 1976 which saw the Bught dry out so badly that its surface began to undulate. At the time I was cutting my journalistic teeth on a series of articles for the Highland News on the North amateur games. A stingingly critical article in the HN with the headline **"Nethy Bridge Games No Fun"** reflected our frustration at the worst prize values in the North in the face of hundreds of medals for dancers.

This prompted a complaint from the games committee to the District Committee who then wrote to club secretary Eileen Hardie, objecting and asking whether I had obtained the necessary permission from the SAAA to write about athletics – which I hadn't! However I penned Eileen's robust response myself and no more was heard of the matter. But despite a local political environment not altogether conducive to the development of a mainstream athletics club with ambitions to sample the sport beyond Highland Games, huge progress was still made. At this early stage the games remained the main avenue of competition and at Glenurquhart in 1976, Gillian Cattell became the club's first female 5 foot high jumper with 1.52m.

September 4th 1976 saw the first Inverness Harriers Open Meeting at the Bught. This included visiting athletes from Elgin, Aberdeen and Caithness with a programme of 55 events. The meeting had originally been planned for a Sunday, but Inverness District Council still operated a "no Sunday sport" policy. There was such enthusiasm to include high jump that I transported to the Bught a single section of Millburn's landing area on the roof of my car, tied to the bumpers at each of its four corners.

This would be a precarious journey, repeated once in each direction for the next several years from the Merkinch Community Centre who were prepared to lend us theirs for the entire summer. That year the club did get one important piece of equipment of its own, a Wharton Electronics digital stopwatch which was the size of a small brick and got hot as its red LED display chewed batteries. The cost of £39.95 for a single watch was equivalent to almost £250 in 2014.

That year's AGM took place in Eden Court and, with an attendance of over 40, was probably the biggest to date. It took place in a vibrant atmosphere of motivation and optimism about the future. This meeting was a very significant turning point in a watershed year and people left it with a true sense of purpose. In an era of rampant inflation, subscriptions increased by a third to £1 for juniors and £2 for seniors. In terms of the club's governance, this meeting was a real watershed since it opened up a completely new era in terms of the committee and from that point of view Inverness Harriers seldom looked back during the years which were about to unfold.

One lasting legacy was the adoption of the gold strip with the maroon diagonal which has been used ever since. It was almost as if the club sensed a new beginning and wanted a new look to go with it. Two 16 year old athletes, Simon Fraser and Dougie Phimister, were commissioned to bring proposals to the meeting and it took no fewer than four ballots to achieve agreement.

Also, crucially, it was resolved to investigate entering a track and field league but that breakthrough was still another two years away. This was a bold quantum leap in thinking since just a year previously the club had struggled to exist at all, even though a large percentage of a small membership were actually active either as competitors or as committee members or indeed both.

Ted Roodhouse was re-elected President with Mike Wallace Vice President. Eileen Brand (later Hardie) continued as Secretary and George Bannerman as Treasurer although he would become President the following year and be replaced in the financial role by Alastair MacMillan.

This has been a very detailed account of the year 1976 but that is unavoidable, given its absolutely central role in the development of Inverness Harriers. In terms of performance, 22 club records had been broken as opposed to five in 1975. As a measure of where performance levels stood on the threshold of this renaissance, these are the best performances for the 1976 season, from which throws and hurdles are still conspicuous by their absence:-

MEN
100 - Mike Wallace 11.3.
200 - Simon Fraser 24.0.
400/ 800/ 1500 - Charles Bannerman 52.4/ 1:59.1/ 4:15.6.
Long jump - Wallace 6.41.
High jump - Jock Ramsay 1.73.
Triple jump - George Coghill 12.72.
4 x 100 - Wallace, Bannerman, Willie Junor, Dougie Phimister 47.8.

WOMEN
100 - Dianne Brand 12.7.
200 - Brand and Catriona MacCallum 26.7.
400 - Brand 58.9.
800 - Melanie Robertson 2:27.4.
1500 - Wilma Brownlee 5:21.3.
Long jump - Lucy Vaughan 5.20.
High jump - Gillian Cattell 1.52.
Javelin - Debbie Heath 28.72.
4 x 100 - Vaughan, Brand, MacCallum, Sandra MacLaren 51.7.

CHAPTER 4 – LIFT OFF – TRACK AND FIELD 1976-81

After a limited and often uncertain existence during its first three decades, Inverness Harriers' growth and development from the latter half of the 1970s was quite astonishing. Membership statistics are just one of several performance indicators which all began to move rapidly upwards after the low point of 1975. These also included performance standards, the range of events contested, with the field undergoing an especially dramatic transition, level of competition aspired to and the number of coaches and officials available to ensure that a rapidly growing club operated smoothly.

Just a year after the disappointing revelation at the 1975 AGM that membership had fallen to just 24, it had more than doubled to 50. By 1979 it had more than doubled again to 105, with the 200 mark surpassed in 1982 and 300 in 1987. Into the early 1990s this would rise a little more before a steady decline to around 120 early in the new millennium before another major upturn. But the dozen years from that low point of 1975 saw Inverness Harriers experience a dramatic 13 fold increase in membership.

In terms of performance, 1976 yielded just five medals in the men's North District Championships. By the early 80s this was sitting consistently in the 20s, also boosted by an increase in the number of events after the eventual creation of a single senior District Championship. Predictably, national success took a little longer and, apart from Debbie Heath's sole win in 1976, it was two more years before the medals started flowing properly. 1978 produced four, including two gold, from the Scottish age group championships (Scottish schools excluded) and by 1980 the corresponding figures were 15, including 8 gold. A year later Scottish Senior championship medals began to come up the steadily improving A9 to Inverness. And so the upswing would continue through the 80s across all aspects of the sport.

Dianne continued her fine form into 1977 and victory in the East District 100 saw her in the relay pool from which the under 21 international team would be selected. She got no further but did take a remarkable 0.3 sec off Audrey Grant's record of 12.5 for the North 100 championship on an accurate but sometimes difficult surface at Glenurquhart. Hugh Footit began a brief Harriers career and broke the North District 400 record with 52.3 at Inverness. Meanwhile Turnbull did the 800/1500 championship double at Nethy Bridge and Lochaber before sharing domination of North men's track endurance with the emerging Donald MacMillan.

The biggest step forward of 1977 came in Aberdeen that September. The North East League comprised six clubs from Grampian down to Fife. An Inverness membership application had been turned down since most of the meetings were on six lane tracks with no room for a seventh club. But this was tempered by an invitation to compete as guests in the final meeting on the seven lane all weather Balgownie facility.

A huge effort fielded the strongest available team, comprising most of the club, which took fourth place in the men's contest and fifth in the women's. League records broken included Dianne (59.5) and Rosalind MacLennan (61.4) in the women's 400 A and B. The other clubs, which the Harriers regarded as huge, were so impressed that they extended membership to seven, irrespective of the consequences of having to run some events as 4+3.

Very soon the "big three" in this league became Aberdeen, Fife Southern and Inverness Harriers. In 1979, at just the second attempt, the women's title went to the Highlands and in both 1982 and 1983, by now in straight fights with Aberdeen, Inverness Harriers did the double. In the ten seasons from 1979-88 this regional league yielded seven women's title successes, three men's and an increasing number of league records.

The first North East League match "in anger", on blaes at Kirkcaldy, began the 1978 season. While there were many fine individual performances, lack of numbers still caused difficulties with relays. That season's first major coup was at the women's East championships when Maureen MacLeod took age group sprinting to new levels with times of 12.6 and 26.1 in the Junior Women's 100 and 200. That she only struck silver did nothing to dampen the euphoria since the winner was Pitreavie's prodigious Linsey MacDonald, British 400 record holder and an Olympic 4 x 400 bronze medallist just two years later, aged just 16.

The Scottish Schools championships produced gold for Yvonne Sutherland (under 14) and George Coghill (over 17) in the sprint hurdles, which was another growth area. Then came the Scottish age group championships on June 24th.

One of the great qualities which made Neil Fraser the winner he ultimately became was a level of competitiveness and self belief which is unusual in an adult, never mind in a 15 year old boy. Despite his still relatively modest best of 1.65, Neil clearly believed that he could win the Scottish Senior Boys' high jump at Coatbridge. And that was just what he did – with a massive 11cm personal best of 1.76. This was the first major breakthrough in one of the most distinguished careers of any Harriers athlete.

On the same day at Grangemouth, admittedly without Linsey MacDonald, Maureen MacLeod ran the race of her life in difficult conditions to win the Junior Women's 200 in 26.4. Coghill also struck silver in the under 20 110 hurdles (15.0) and long jump (6.37) and Inverness Harriers had well and truly arrived on the national championship scene. Coghill went to the Bells Junior International at Meadowbank where, over the next few years, he would be followed by a procession of clubmates.

The 800 club record went twice that year. MacMillan ran 1:57.9 at the Scottish Schools but then Turnbull produced one of the performances of his career to record 1:56.4 at the Stretford Open Meeting.

An instance of the "them and us" relationship between the club and the North District, formerly the NSAAA, establishment emerged at the Inverness Games in 1978. The club was keen to promote throwing, or at least Olympic throwing events, and Derek MacKenzie entered the shot putt. Derek was barred from the competition, not for being too young at 14, but for not wearing a kilt! Since the Games offered almost the only opportunities to putt the shot, a rather angry club put a motion to the SAAA AGM to exclude the shot from the rule requiring heavy event competitors to wear the kilt and this was duly passed.

By 1979 the rest of Scotland was looking out for the swelling tide of high performers among juniors suddenly coming out of Inverness. The next was Angela MacRae who has the unique distinction of having pursued an international athletics career from the Isle of Raasay! Angela, at that time a Dingwall Academy pupil and living in Evanton, was recruited at the 1978 Dingwall Athletics Week. After a good winter's training she began to make a big impact the following year.

A string of first and second places in major Scottish events saw her best shoot up from 1.57 to 1.69 in her first season as an Intermediate. That summer of 1979 the only Scottish under 17 to defeat her was Shettleston's GB Junior internationalist and Scottish under 17 record holder Susan Brown. This also gave Angela selections for the schools international and − at just 15 − the under 21 international at Middlesborough.

Then her father David, who ran a shop in Evanton, acquired Suisnish House on Raasay off Skye and relocated there. Angela moved to Portree High School which didn't have a landing area so David bought one and she trained for an elite high jump career both there and on Raasay when she went home for the holidays. It was a remarkable tale of improvised training sessions and epic commutes to national championships and other big events, although her personal best never progressed past 1.69 after the move.

Meanwhile Neil had improved to 1.87 in matching Angela's Scottish schools gold so both were selected for the British Schools international on a July Monday afternoon in Grangemouth. Everyone was in awe of the giant 6'7" Ossie Cham of England, the red hot favourite for the boys' high jump. But when we walked into the stadium, in an attempt to reassure Neil, I said to him: *"Look, there he is talking to that chap over there. He's maybe not all that big after all since the other boy is looking him straight in the eye."* Neil looked at me and simply replied: *"Yes, but the other guy is standing on that seat!"*

In May 1979 a women's team, also including the pick of the Intermediates, went to the semi-finals of the Scottish Women's Cup in Coatbridge and qualified for the final. They returned in August to finish fourth behind the major powers of Edinburgh Southern, Shettleston Harriers Ladies and Glasgow AC, prompting more accolades. There was almost disbelief that they had made such an impact on a senior national team event.

That wasn't the only success at that meeting, which incorporated the SAAA relay championships. Here the club finished a close second in the Senior Boys' 4 x 100 in a remarkable 45.9. This was a full second faster than the senior men's club record and they ended the season third in the UK Senior Boys' rankings despite having to practise baton changes on grass for competition on an all-weather surface.

The team comprised the prodigious Peter Durham, long jump specialist Dougie Butler, Chris Brogan the national Senior Boys' 400m champion with an outstanding 53.4, and the massively strong Calum Johnston. With Allan Watson in for Johnston, two weeks later they took bronze in the 4 x 400 (3:45.0).

MacMillan, meanwhile, had reduced the 800 record to 1:54.5 in an invitation meeting at Grangemouth just a month after setting the Bught Park alight by front running a 1:56.4 on grass in the inter school sports. With his departure to Edinburgh University's Vet school now imminent, he did the North District 400/800/1500 treble, despite the close attention of 5000 champion Turnbull who set a 1500 club record of 3:57.8 at the Scottish Championships.

By 1979 the club was now established as a significant national force in sprints, hurdles and jumps, with endurance also making good progress. Throws would have to wait a few more years, but it is now worth looking at the coaching arrangements which had achieved these breakthroughs.

The Spectrum Centre had been a valuable asset for two winters, allowing the establishment of 12 months a year training. The former Inverness Royal Academy and St John's Church Hall on Southside Road were also used as winter training extended also to Thursday evenings. The lack of a proper track was an increasing handicap, but by the late 70s the club was still not securely enough established to make a strong case for one.

Ironically the events which provided much of the early breakthrough also suffered most from the lack of a proper track. High jumping on wet grass or soft ground is all but impossible and it was common to drag the landing area out of the Bught store, only to have to drag it back in again when the heavens opened. The same applied to hurdles with the additional difficulty that even slightly bumpy grass made the barriers effectively all at different heights. The lack of track markings also made technical work for 200 hurdles and 400 hurdles almost impossible. But despite that, Dorothy Kidd and Rosalind MacLennan respectively got East v West representation in these events.

Winter track sessions for sprints or endurance were out of the question and "quality" work had to be done on the roads. A road can actually be quite fast but problems ranged from having to dodge cars to early season lower leg injuries on the the change of surface from road to grass and all-weather in the spring. One favourite stretch which was handy for St John's Hall was the upper end of Southside Road where we just happened to run back and forward past Provost Sellar's house as a reminder that a track was urgently needed!

Different coaches had different routines. Turnbull used to take his endurance athletes for runs of increasing distance and intensity, on and off road, as standards steadily rose among the juniors. The youngest age groups were looked after, among others, by Harry Lakeland, Brian Ross, Dougie Bone and Dave Barnetson senior. They had a whole series of treks with stop off points for various strenuous routines which the kids loved. This achieved levels of early fitness which would later be abandoned on the advent of "Fun Athletics".

Many of my squad happened to be Royal Academy pupils so I supplemented club nights with after school sessions on Mondays, Wednesdays and Fridays - Friday being jumping night in the school games hall. My non-Royal Academy athletes frequently came there as well. Gillian Cattell soon joined the staff and fulfilled a very important role as the club's long jump coach.

An ongoing desire to improve along with clear signs that this was happening fuelled a massive work ethic among coaches and athletes alike. This would thrive until challenged by more recreational coaching methodologies in the 90s. However coaches also needed education which was done formally through coaching courses at Largs but also - vitally - through informal contacts with established coaches like Bill Walker, Alex Naylor and Bill McLellan.

Then there was National Coach Frank Dick, who helped revolutionise athletics development in the Highlands at this vital time. Apart from his technical and coaching expertise, Frank had enormous ability to inspire, so to have the entire Dingwall Athletics Week with him was invaluable. These achieved quantum leaps for coaching within Inverness Harriers. They also prompted an entirely new venture because, in the absence of a club in Ross-shire, a vibrant and extremely valuable section of Inverness Harriers was set up in Tain.

The initial contact was made at the 1979 Dingwall Week with Bill Stewart, manager at the aluminium smelter in Invergordon whose son David was a promising 400m runner, eventually becoming a schools internationalist. Robert MacGregor, Maureen Fraser and Sally Gunn were among the others with Neil Munro soon added. Before long there was a very active Tain section, coached by Bill with some help from Tain Royal Academy PE teacher Alastair McKinlay. This made a big contribution to the club for several years.

Given the take-off in performance levels, it was often difficult for initially quite inexperienced coaches to keep up with their athletes' needs. It was often a case of reacting as fast as possible as these needs developed. As a sprinter/middle distance runner myself, one of the last things on my mind was coaching hurdles and high jump. But suddenly I had hurdlers and high jumpers, and very good ones too, so I was drawn into coaching these events. Neil Fraser in particular was in the very first wave and was extremely influential in creating the need for me to learn.

A better organized club was only part of the reason for the breakthrough. Because this also happened to coincide with a generation of athletes, born roughly between 1961 and 1968, which produced a concentration of talent never seen in the club, nor indeed in the North, before or since.

Inevitably frustration at the lack of a track was occasionally reflected in my Courier reports. For instance in July 1980, when Scottish schools selections for David Stewart and Peter Durham rounded off a hugely successful period, I wrote: *"All of this is all the more remarkable given that these athletes run the gauntlet of traffic* on the road in winter and in summer only have a grass track to train on and even then are forced back on to the road on wet nights." Before long we would have a media ally in Campbell Gunn, the local reporter for the People's Journal who later shot to fame, or notoriety, during the Referendum campaign of 2014. Campbell did a number of pieces on the success of Inverness Harriers athletes in the face of inadequate training facilities. This kind of pressure continued until the Queens Park became a reality.

Given Dianne's 44 year involvement with the club by 2014, I now look with some amusement at my reference to her in the Courier as Inverness Harriers' "elder stateswoman". That was in 1980 when she was aged 22 but already she was spearheading the charge. What prompted that comment was her 100/200 East District double silver of that year which raised her medal haul from these championships to nine across all three sprints over five years.

Dianne was again a prime mover in the 1980 Women's Cup campaign, once more at senior level with a significant under 17 presence. The team list for the semi-final was:- 100/800 – Dianne Black, 200/400 – Maureen MacLeod, 1500 – Melissa Jeans, 3000 – Ann Dundas, 100H – Dorothy Kidd, 400H – Rosalind MacLennan, LJ – Sandra MacLaren, HJ – Angela MacRae, SP/JT/DT – Gillian Cattell, 4 x 100 – Maureen Fraser, MacLeod, Kidd, Black, 4 x 400 – MacLeod, MacLennan, Jeans, Black.

Only seven teams turned up so qualification was automatic and instead they held a non-counting "pre-final". Once more Inverness finished fourth behind Scotland's big three women's clubs. Come the real final in August, a largely similar but slightly weaker team even improved to third equal.

That the club was now not too far adrift of the big names of Scottish women's athletics had not gone unnoticed. In August 1980 the Courier reported that *"Inverness Harriers' women figure very prominently in the chasing group – so prominently in fact that those in the central belt who have recently been exerting a fair degree of pressure on the local club to join the Scottish Women's League have confidently predicted that it would progress very swiftly from Division 4 to Division 2."*

By now Inverness Harriers had acquired a lot of admirers throughout athletics in Scotland, including Bob and Dora Stephen. Both were leading lights in Shettleston Harriers Ladies and Dora was Secretary of the SWAAA. They had been so impressed by the cup performances that they urged us to apply for the Scottish Women's League.

This prompted a further complication of Catch 22 proportions. The SWAL, who also organised the Cup, were thinking about restricting it to members of the League. The Cup had been initially chosen by the Harriers as an ideally sized one per side competition, with no initial thoughts of the League. But here was a scenario where the club might become ineligible for the Cup unless it also took on the other, much larger commitment.

Brian Turnbull and myself on a club night at the Bught – early 1980s. The 'brick' in my left hand is the club's first every red LED digital stopwatch!

Apart from the logistics of raising and transporting a team across all four age groups, two per event, for three league meetings per season, there was also a huge cost implication. Expansion had been so rapid that travel and accommodation costs had risen from zero in 1975 to over £1000 five years later, a large sum in 1980. Adding buses for three more round trips of 300 – 350 miles would create severe strain on finances, even though a Support Group of parents was by now doing an excellent fundraising job.

The resulting dilemma was highlighted in the Courier and within days the paper became the club's salvation. The Editor and Proprietor, the formidable Miss Eveline Barron, who was an Inverness institution, duly contacted me to say that she would like to cover the cost. Application was then made to the League, initiating the task of raising a full team for the qualifying match on Sunday 21st September.

That took place at Grangemouth on a horrible day with a fierce headwind but it was a triumph for Inverness Harriers. The other very credible candidate for the two places was Colzium AC. But in the end a 33 strong Inverness team emerged resounding winners with 646 points from Colzium on 482 and Kilbarchan the best of the rest on 408. So now the club looked forward to its full league debut, the start of another epic upward journey, in 1981.

The SWAL narrative has now outstripped the rest of a 1980 track and field season which followed the now familiar format of groundbreaking progress. Three gold and two bronze from the 1979 Boys' Youths' and Junior championships had been highly gratifying, so the 1980 tally of six gold, two silver and one bronze absolutely overwhelmed everyone.

The star turn was Peter Durham whose spectacular Senior Boys' 100/ 200/ LJ treble of 11.37/23.15/6.06 was totally unprecedented. Neil Fraser took the Youths' high jump with 1.84 with Colin MacKinnon runner up on 1.80 and Tommy Leighton fifth with 1.73. Duncan Chisholm produced a massive improvement with a new club long jump record of 6.56 to win the Junior event. But the performance with the most profound implications was the one which completed Fraser's double.

After a lengthy jumping injury he told me he wanted to add a second string to his bow and try the hurdles. The product was a gold medal in the Youths' 100 hurdles in 14.2. The implications of this decision will become evident in later chapters.

One other major success area in 1980 was relays and in particular the Junior Women's 4 x 100. All amateur clubs experience clusters of talent and drought. 1980 saw an abundance of sprinting ability in this under 15 age group with no fewer than five athletes below 13 seconds. Heather MacLeod, from Tain, posted a remarkable 12.3 for silver in the Scottish Championships while Jane Lakeland added a 12.5 to her 200 silver in 25.7 which she later pruned to 25.6. Shirley Dick's favoured event was the long jump but she could still run 12.7, as could recent recruit Dawn Fletcher. So unfortunately, although Kathryn Urquhart had run 12.9, she was only the reserve for a record breaking quartet.

Before the Scottish championship at Coatbridge, there were thoughts of going to Meadowbank for baton practice since we had already discovered that the grass to all-weather conversion was problematic. In the end we opted for a trial involving the Junior and Senior teams on the Bught which the Juniors won 51.6 to 51.8. On grass, this was tremendously encouraging.

On Saturday August 9th at Coatbridge, with a running order of MacLeod, Fletcher, Dick, Lakeland, this squad took half a second off the Scottish Junior Women's championship record with 50.1 in the heats. They were then clear winners of the final, but in 50.2 with the sub-50 denied by changeover difficulties.

The following weekend it was Meadowbank for the Octavians Relays and another resounding win. But was it sub 50? An early suggestion that it probably was came from Shirley's father Angus, a Grade 1 timekeeper, who unofficially got 49.9 on the line from the far side. It didn't then take long for a friendly official timekeeper to confirm this with a thumbs up. This was the first sub-50 by a Scottish under 15 club team and it was right up with the very best in Britain.

A triumphant Octavians also saw the girls win the 4 x 200 in

1:46.6 and Dougie Butler, Calum Johnston, Chris Brogan and Robert MacGregor the Youths' 4 x 100 in 45.4 for an Inverness treble. Just for good measure the girls did another 49.9 in the final North East League meeting, which was matched minutes later by the seniors. Many of these 1980

1980 Junior Women's 4 x 100 – Shirley Dick, Jane Lakeland, Dawn Fletcher, Heather MacLeod.

breakthroughs were recorded in a monthly club magazine to which a number of members contributed. Peter Thompson arranged for it to be typed up and assembled by YTS youngsters but, probably due to other pressing club commitments, it only lasted for six issues.

With so much activity in the central belt, the focus had by now moved well and truly away from the Highland Games and towards more mainstream competition. However the size of the club compared with before meant that there was still probably a bigger presence than before at many of the Games, including some of the top performers on quiet weekends.

The 1980 AGM broke all records when over 100 packed Eden Court's Long Gallery. Many were there to see athletes receive Thistle Awards since the club had become very involved in what had begun as Frank Dick's brainchild. There were two very significant departures from the committee with Eileen Hardie and Alastair MacMillan standing down as Secretary and Treasurer respectively.

Sam McNaughton, who worked with Harry Lakeland in HRC's Roads and Transport department and was a distance runner, took over as Secretary. And George Bannerman, who three years previously had only regarded himself as an interim President, was more than content to revert to Treasurer. Harry took over as President with Derek McGinn as Vice. The rest of the committee was – Men's Captain Brian Turnbull, Women's Captain Gillian Cattell, Chief Coach Charles Bannerman,

Your Committee

INVERNESS HARRIES COMMITTEE

President: George Bannerman 6 Dores Ave.
Vice President: Harry Lakeland 76 Lagan Rd.
Secretary: Eileen Hardie 28 St. Valery Ave.
Treasurer: Alistair McMillan 52 Grigor Ave.
Club Captains: Brian Turnbull 38 Glenshiel Pl.
                Gillian Cattell Inverness R/Academy
                Peter Thompson 8 Trentham Crt.
                Derek McGinn 24 Delnies Rd.
                Diane Black 5 Ashe Rd
                Sandra McLaren 14 St. Fergus Dr.
Chief Coach: Charles Bannerman 6 Dores Ave.
Young Athletes
Representatives: Alan Watson 4 Grigor Dr.
                Maureen McLeod 55 Glenshiel Pl.

Committee – 1979 - 1980 as listed in the club magazine.

Committee – Peter Thompson, Dianne Black, Eddie Brogan, Angus Dick. SCCU representative and Auditor – Walter Banks, Candidates for SAAA General Committee – Charles Bannerman, Peter Thompson.

The SWAL Division 4 debut was on April 26th 1981 at Dumbarton. The team got there feeling decidedly disorientated after a lot of "spew stops" on a nightmare journey down the A82 by Loch Lomond side. But again they emerged triumphant, once more with Colzium second, albeit by the narrower margin of 572 to 550, and Vale of Leven third on 282. The tighter result was due to some particularly good Junior Women going up to the already strong Intermediates, leaving us slightly weaker in the lower reaches while Colzium had generally strengthened. The second and third match margins were wider and the team ended the season in September as Division 4 champions. The first part of Bob and Dora Stephen's prophecy was vindicated.

As team manager, I used to spend much of the outward journey permutating places to maximize points. This did tend to mean asking athletes to undertake ambitious and sometimes unusual commitments. Over 30 years on, I would not feel as comfortable making what were probably unreasonable demands on athletes, including the star performers. On the other hand, at the advent of league competition, everyone looked on this as groundbreaking progress and were happy to do their bit. Leagues were still some way short of becoming bread and butter and commonplace.

At long last the first SAAA North District championships for all age groups, including senior, at the same venue took place in 1981. Since 1975, when the NSAAA gave way to the SAAA North District, it had been club policy to pursue this objective. So far this had fallen foul of the Highland Games interests which dominated a North District committee, from which the area's fastest growing and now largest club had been excluded by the Games block vote.

Then, at the December 1980 SAAA AGM, Inverness Harriers at last got a fully elected member which happened to be myself. Possibly as a challenge to put my money where my mouth was, at the first meeting I was elected North District chairman – a post I held until the end of 1986. Things were really going the club's way by early 1981, and I was able to push through a deal whereby the men's championships were added to the young athletes' at the single venue. The *quid pro quo* was that they would be replaced by "North Of Scotland Amateur Highland Games" championships. These events never were going to have the same status as the District Championships but the Games promoters seemed happy enough.

Another part of the deal was for me to convene the championships at the Bught. Against a good entry, across the board the Harriers won more than half the titles. One conspicuous absentee was Neil Fraser who had opted instead for the following weekend's East championships at Meadowbank, for which he qualified by having been born in Perth.

That coincided with a dinner to celebrate Walter Banks' SCCU Presidential year (see Chapter 6). One of Walter's comments in his address was that he hoped that Inverness Harriers might have an athlete in the Scottish team for the 1986 Commonwealth Games in Edinburgh. Many of us had all been out all day in intense sunshine at the Primary Inter School Sports and the consensus was that Walter was perhaps suffering from mild sunstroke, given the still apparently fantastic nature of his suggestion.

He had not long sat down when news arrived that Neil had taken the East senior silver medal in the 110 hurdles. Not only that, here was a first year Junior defeating most of a top quality field in his first race over the full specification 3'6" hurdles. Over the winter the hurdles had figured more and more prominently. And here was a spectacular debut despite having to make the triple transition from 100m 3' to 110s 3'6" using soft blaes and paving stones at Inverness

Royal Academy where we rejected trying an empty corridor! Neil still had a long way to go, but this outing was the first step towards the realisation – three times over as it happened - of Walter's apparently delusional suggestion!

That summer's other spectacular breakthrough came from Tommy Leighton who only turned 16 that March. The previous year his high jump progressed hugely from 1.48 to 1.80. Then in the spring of 1981, he posted a remarkable 1.93 on grass at a schools competition in Inverness. This was just 2cm short of Fraser's pb, and it was no flash in the pan. He then followed up a Scottish Schools gold (1.91) with a phenomenal championship record of 1.98 (6'6") in the Scottish Youths' championships. So in less than two years, Tommy had improved by half a metre.

A couple of weeks later he became the club's highest ever finisher in the schools international in Dublin – second with 1.88. Then at the end of July, there was a development which, until recently, would have been unthinkable – except perhaps to Walter Banks!

Neil (18 that June) had only left the Royal Academy a few weeks previously while Tommy (16) was eagerly awaiting his "O" Grade results there. Neil had made the wise decision to pass on a final

Jane Lakeland winning a sprint at Meadowbank – early 1980s.

Scottish schools championship to contest the SAAA senior championships the same June weekend. His reward was another breakthrough with a national silver medal and a further advance to 14.89. Next he posted 14.99 for Edinburgh AC in the British League, with Olympic decathlon champion Daley Thomson trailing behind him in 15.22.

However it was still with some disbelief blended with sheer delight that it emerged that both Neil and Tommy had been selected for the Scottish senior team to meet England, Hungary and Norway at

Gateshead on July 25th and Denmark and Ireland at Meadowbank a week later. Since Calum Laing had apparently moved on from the club by the time he gained his selection, these are very probably the first senior international honours for Inverness Harriers, and certainly in track and field.

Realistically, this was possibly a massive step just too soon for athletes whose selection had appeared totally inconceivable just a couple of months previously. They both underachieved at Gateshead, taking 8th places. Then in the second match Tommy was reduced to 1.80 while Neil actually declined his place to contest the AAAs junior championships where he finished 7th.

The women were in the headlines that July as well. The Scottish junior relay record holders were now Intermediates and hence eligible as Seniors. So in 1981 the club could field a 4 x 100 team of Heather MacLeod (pb 12.3), Jane Lakeland (12.4), Sandra MacDonald (MacLaren) 12.6 and Dianne 12.1. At an early North East League match they improved the club record to 49.0. Then in July it was the unusual venue of the Carluke Highland Games, on a fast Rubkor-type surface, for the Scottish senior championship. Here they emerged triumphant over opponents which included Edinburgh Southern Harriers and Shettleston to win the title in 48.2.

Despite all this massive top level progress, the Highland Games were not entirely forgotten, especially Glenurquhart which was most people's favourite and where a large club squad included no fewer than five internationalists, both junior and senior.

By now Harry Lakeland's coaching aspirations were evolving from overseeing the junior group into specialist throws and he was also trying to build a team of qualified officials. He had come into the club as the parent of sprinters Susan and Jane and, now as President, had not been slow to recruit other parents for officiating and coaching.

Harry Lakeland on starting duty at the Queens Park

Officials were vital, with league competition and the Open Meeting creating an increased demand. Meanwhile a rapidly increasing membership continually stretched coaching resources. It was round about this time that the likes of Dougie Bone and Dave Barnetson senior had joined the coaching force while Angus Dick, and Hilary MacLean were budding officials with Brian Ross and John Wilson active in both departments. Brian had a number of strings to his bow since he not only became a javelin coach and field official specializing in that event. In the early 80s he also held the club javelin record at 40.32.

Sandra MacLaren (facing camera) and clubmates preparing for action at Pitreavie around 1980.

Since 1977 the club had published an annual records and rankings booklet. This was started by Mike and Maureen Wallace and charted annual improvement. The 1981 edition, with cover design by Jane Lakeland (P79), was especially elaborate and the leading senior performances for that year (preceded by club records at that stage in brackets) were:-

Men 100 (G. Coghill 11.0) N. Fraser (J) 11.2, P. Durham (Y) 11.3, D. Chisholm 11.3.
200 (B. Milne, Durham 23.2) Chisholm 23.3, Durham 23.6.
400 (H. Footit, D. MacMillian, D. Stewart (Y), K. MacKintosh 51.3) Stewart, MacKintosh 51.3.
800 (D. MacMillan 1:54.9) S. Catto (Y) 1:57.9, MacKintosh 1:58.7, A.Watson (Y) 1:59.0.
1500 (B. Turnbull 3:57.8) M. Mitchell (Y) 4:15.4.
5000 (I Johnstone 14:47.0) Turnbull 16:26.7.
110H (Fraser 14.9) Fraser 14.9.
400H (Turnbull 57.1) Catto 60.6.
3000SC (I. Johnstone 9:27.0) MacKintosh 10:51.0. LJ (Chisholm 6.56) Chisholm 6.56, D. Butler (Y) 6.44, Durham 6.07, Fraser 6.02.
HJ (T. Leighton (Y) 1.98) T. Leighton 1.98, Fraser 1.95, C. MacKinnon (Y) 1.80.
TJ (I. Tasker 13.67) Durham 13.35, Butler 13.24.

SP (Fraser 11.04) Fraser 11.04.
DT (P.Flockhart 29.00) Flockhart 29.00.
JT (B.Ross 40.32) Ross 40.32.
4 x 100 (Scottish Championship Youths 1981 45.4) North East League Men 48.2.
4 x 400 (Scottish Championship Youths 3:30.8) Scottish Championship Youths 3:30.8.
Women - 100 (A. Grant 12.0) D. Black 12.3, H. MacLeod (I) 12.4, J. Lakeland (I) 12.4, S. MacDonald 12.6, M.MacLeod (I) 12.7.
200 (M. Wallace 25.1) Black 25.4, Lakeland 25.5, H. MacLeod 25.8.
400 (Black 57.7) Black 58.1, M. MacLeod 59.8.
800 (M. MacLeod 2:21.9) M. MacLeod 2:21.9.
1500 (M. Jeans 4:51.5) L. Lobban (I) 5:06.2.
3000 (M. Jeans 11:03.5) Jeans 11:37.3.
100H (D.Kidd 15.4) Kidd 15.8, S. MacDonald 16.6.
LJ (S.Dick (I) 5.46) Dick 5.46, Kidd 5.12, MacDonald 5.11.
HJ (A. MacRae 1.69) MacRae 1.68.
SP (H. Carey 10.15) Carey 10.15.
DT (G. Cattell 24.10) Cattell 23.70.
JT (D. Heath 29.40) F. Coote (J) 22.56.
4 x 100 (Scottish Senior Champions 48.2) Scottish Senior Champions 48.2 + 5 sub 50 performances.
4 x 400 (1979 Cup semi final 4:06.3) SWAL2 4:07.8.

The convention at that time for club rankings and records was, for consistency with the majority of hand timed performances, to round up and return as tenths any still rare automatic timings. So Fraser's 110H record was actually 14.89 while in the men's 200, Peter Durham was the sole record holder with 23.15. There was inevitably some year on year variation and some events were clearly more developed than others. In particular the throws still lagged well behind, principally due to a lack of coaching which was being addressed.

Senior internationalists Fraser and Leighton were respectively awarded the MacKenzie Cup for the top senior performer and the Post Office Cup for the top Boy or Youth. The corresponding Charles Hunter Memorial Trophy and Mrs. D. M. Duncan Rosebowl went to Angela MacRae and Shirley Dick. When Neil gained his first senior cap, his parents donated what they wanted to name the Charles Bannerman Trophy which the committee decided to award to the most promising under 13. The inaugural award was a joint one to Margaret McGilvray for performances in the high jump and Alan Bone for the endurance events.

One other measure of progress was the club's travel and accommodation expenditure which had risen to over £2000 in 1981 when the price of an average house was just £24,000. The club tried to meet half the costs with the athletes contributing the rest and this placed pressure on fundraising. There was a very good relationship with Fraser's Coaches of Elgin whose driver Colin was particularly popular among athletes and coaches alike. He even had a special "Inverness Harriers AAC" sign for the front window of the bus. On one occasion his prompt action in swerving off the old A9 near Blair Atholl to reduce the impact from an irresponsible overtaking motorist probably saved the lives of the car's occupants.

During the winter of 1981-82 there was an increased presence of the leading athletes in the national training squad and far more in the regional squad which was set up to bring athletes from all over the North together during the non-competitive months. But while a regional squad was one thing, the recently re-formed Ross shire AAC's proposal for a regional club was entirely another. At a time when Inverness Harriers was developing at an unprecedented rate on its own, there was no appetite at all for any amalgamation and this was very quickly rejected. Inverness Harriers would continue onwards and upwards with complete independence.

CHAPTER 5 – EDINBURGH GAMES IN SIGHT – TRACK AND FIELD 1982 - 86

The achievements of 1976-81 were enormous, but it was during the next five seasons that Inverness Harriers really came of age as a major track and field club. This latter period also began with the first appearance of one of the athletes who dominated these years, and beyond.

Jayne Barnetson

Jayne Barnetson's first medal for Inverness Harriers was at the 1982 East District championships at Meadowbank. She took the Junior Women's high jump with a modest and unremarkable 1.50 while Angela MacRae took the senior event with 1.60. This was a championship where lower leg injuries, due to conversion from grass to all-weather, blighted the Inverness contingent. However there were still 25 athletes staying in the Perth Youth Hostel the night before.

Like Angela, Jayne started high jumping at Dingwall Academy. She was one of many prodigious talents spotted and initially developed by Jack Sutherland who encouraged her parents, Sheila and Dave, to contact the club during the summer of 1981. Five years later Jayne had emerged as a world class high jumper.

By 1982 another dominant figure, Neil Fraser, was an established senior internationalist and a student in Edinburgh. Neil and Tommy Leighton both needed more competition at a higher level than the club could provide and found that with Edinburgh clubs in the British League, but at this stage retained their first claim with Inverness.

The 1982 season started indifferently for the women with a narrow defeat by a strengthened Colzium in the opening SWAL match at Glenrothes. This turned out to be a minor blemish in a year of dramatic success. The second and third matches both went the Harriers' way, confirming the Division 3 title and another promotion. Then right at the end of the season the grand slam of all league titles was achieved with the men's and women's North East League crowns.

The men's District Championships saw 21 of the 36 titles come to Inverness including four each for long jumper Dougie Butler and

Fraser, who beat the highly fancied Alan MacKenzie in both 100 and 200. Alisdair Ferguson had a shot and discus double at the Scottish schools where Jayne Barnetson (1.62), Margaret McGilvray (1.56) and Lorna Ross (1.56) were first, third and fourth in the under 15 high jump.

1982 also saw the zenith of the unfortunately all too brief athletics career of "the man who beat Colin Jackson". Ronnie Sharp, from Nairn, was an outstanding sprinter and hurdler. As a Youth, he ran 10.9 for the 100 and, as Scottish Schools 100 hurdles champion, became the first Harrier to win a Schools international event with 13.3 at Colwyn Bay. It was only some years later that the significance of this emerged when Welsh rival Jackson became 110 hurdles world champion and record holder. However Ronnie's first love had always been football and he made an early departure from athletics to play for, and for a time to manage, Nairn County FC. That year another IH Nairnite, Andrew Thain, ran 11.4 to top the British Senior Boys' 80 hurdles rankings.

The 1982 AGM was told of a record membership of 207 and oversaw another change of President. Harry Lakeland, by now very much focused on the throws, stood down from the top job and succeeded me as Chief Coach. I had become so involved with so many different strands of athletics that there were some I had to relinquish. Harry passed the Presidential baton to Peter Thompson, who had the benefit of previous experience at Birchfield and also remained on the SAAA North District committee along with myself.

Donald MacMillan had not been idle in Edinburgh and in May 1983, en route to the UK final at Meadowbank, took the club 800 record to an impressive 1:50.08. This also led to Don joining Fraser and Leighton in the ranks of the senior internationalists in a year when he improved his 1500 club record to 3:48.1.

Inverness domination extended to 26 of the 37 titles at the 1983 North District Championships in Elgin. These included a 1500/5000 double from Paul Kenney, the 5000 with a club record 14:37.7 on a track which was by now beginning to deteriorate. A week later Kenney completed the district treble with the 10000 in a very creditable 30:59.8 in pouring rain on the undulating grass track at Millburn.

Other 1983 highlights included Eddie Leighton's Scottish Schools under 17 high jump title to follow his older brother into the international team. At the still separate Schoolgirls' Championships Lee Lobban, now the club Senior and Intermediate 1500 record holder at 4:45.9, was second in that event. But it was in the 3000 that she joined Leighton in the international during the brief period when the all-powerful English team withdrew from it. However the two Royal Academy pupils still excelled themselves and both won their events in this three country, six athlete competition against Wales and Ireland at Pitreavie. Lee set a club record of 10:31.5 while Eddie cleared 1.88.

At that year's Scottish Senior Championships 15 year old Eddie cleared an impressive best of 1.95, while his brother became the first Inverness 2 metre jumper with 2.00 in the British League in July. Also in the schools international were Andrew Thain, now up to 100 hurdles, along with a new club member called Russell Devine.

By now Harry Lakeland's throws group was progressing well and his first major success was Devine who came to the club from Golspie High School. Russell set the SAAA Senior Boys' championships alight when he won the discus by 11 metres with a championship record of 48.30 and the shot by almost 4 metres with 15.89. This brought Inverness Harriers' throwing into a completely new dimension in a year when George Patience joined the club. George was still principally involved in Highland Games and would not emerge into mainstream athletics until the following year.

The major individual highlight of 1983 was Neil Fraser's, and the club's, first Scottish senior title in the Centenary Scottish Championships at Meadowbank on June 18th, as related in Chapter 1. This was a multi-faceted triumph for a 20 year old athlete in his first year as a full senior. An Electrical Engineering student at Heriot Watt University, he had been training with Bill Walker at Meadowbank as the lead coach with some back up from myself, especially during vacations. Neil produced a remarkable 14.45 for the 110s to take gold from the rest of the Scottish top three, Glen MacDonald and John Wallace. This was a personal best and a club record, but the following wind denied him a Scottish native record. He also went fifth in the UK senior rankings.

The other club record at these championships was in the 10000 where Kenney improved to 29:33.4 for fourth. In April he had run 2:19:04 in the London Marathon so suddenly here was a top class 5000/ 10000/ marathon club record treble. Remarkably this means that all the current men's club records from 800 upwards were set in the early summer of 1983.

Performance levels, not only at senior level but across the age range, had progressed by light years since those dark days of 1975 and near extinction. 1983 saw many of the club's best ever athletes in place and already making a big impression on the national and international scenes, with a lot more still to come. Fraser, Tommy Leighton, Macmillan, Kenney and Patience all either were, or would soon become, Scottish senior internationalists. But this was very one sided progress since the first senior woman internationalist was still awaited.

The athlete who would achieve that distinction, in 1984, was taking great strides forward, or more specifically upwards. These strides were - literally - not uninterrupted since early in the 1983 season Jayne Barnetson fell over a hurdle in a league match in Dundee. The fall did not look particularly serious and, to my eventual embarrassment, I shouted "Get up and finish. We need the points!" It wasn't until she was X-rayed shortly afterwards that we learned that she was lying there with a broken leg!

This kept her out of all schools competition, but remarkably by mid-July she was back. Just two months after the leg break she won the Scottish under 17 title with a personal best by 4cm and championship record of 1.72. The following month she progressed even further to win the Celtic International with 1.76.

Alongside all this individual success, team competition yielded another title and promotion to Division 1 of the SWAL. Division 2 was won with three straight victories, so the team had gone straight from 4 to 1 in three consecutive seasons. The narrow reverse in the opening Division 3 fixture in 1982 was the only blemish on a totally unbeaten record in nine matches. So Bob and Dora Stephen's prophesy had in fact been exceeded.

As the dramas of 1983 unfolded on tracks across the land, there were equally dramatic developments towards one being provided in Inverness. Given the club's size and the performance levels it had achieved, the case for this was now cast iron. There was also a willingness within Inverness District Council, which was responsible for Leisure and Recreation in the two tier local government structure, to provide a track.

Two important allies were Bill McAllister, chairman of the Leisure and Recreation Committee, and Allan Jones the department's director. Club officials had already approached Councillor McAllister, a high profile figure in the National Playing Fields Association so such projects were close to his heart. The L and R Committee minute of May 9th, 1983 records: "*After full discussion, and in particular having heard the chairman on informal discussions he had had with representatives of Inverness Harriers, the committee recommended to the Policy and Resources committee that the following items constitute the Leisure and Recreation committee's bids for any outstanding sums available:*
1 Beauly Sports Field £20,000.
2 Capital grants to sports clubs £25,000.

3 Provision of an all-weather running track at the Queens Park £150,000.

Two days later, the P and R committee approved all of these bids from a total available sum of £318,000 and this was rubber stamped by the full council on May 23rd. So, after years of campaigning and of training for high profile competition on dark roads and wet grass, the prospect of a six lane all-weather running track the following summer at the Queens Park was at last a reality!

The club's preferred location was the Bught. But politically that was a non-starter since the Bught had long been the accepted home of shinty which cannot be played within a 400 metre running track. The contract would probably also have been significantly more expensive there since providing additional bottoming would have been necessary.

To get the money spent within the financial year, things had to move very fast indeed and from a short list of five companies, Sportworks were awarded the contract. This was eventually valued at £168,858 with the additional £18,858 added from the L and R budget to broaden the use of the facility to other activities.

Such a notion was not particularly appealing to the club. As a result its delegation, headed by Peter Thompson, Derek McGinn and Harry Lakeland, met with Council representatives in the Town Hall on July 18th, armed with a proposed layout which had all the field event areas inside the track itself! This of course meant that almost no other games could take place on the infield. Miraculously, the Council accepted this after a meeting which lasted almost two hours.

There was some initial doubt about how many, if any, field areas could be provided within the strict budget - and hence whether the track could ever be used for competition. The club representatives said that they would reluctantly accept whatever could be done, but in the end council officials and the contractors worked a minor miracle. Not only did they provide all field areas, they also managed to extend the finishing straight from six lanes to eight. Savings due to the integrity of the very sound bottoming from the original 1950s track may well have been a factor. But, by any standards, what was obtained for the available money was outstanding.

The weather closed in to prevent a proper start in 1983 and some financial gymnastics were necessary to overcome the problem of the delayed spend. The club used cash from the previous year's Land's End to John O'Groats run to provide two ex-Kessock Bridge portakabins for shelter, administration and storage which were available to all track users.

With the sports centre still a long way away, one important addition was a large second hand wooden hut donated by Weldex International Offshore supremo, Dougie McGilvray. His daughter, Margaret, was among a group of talented high jumpers who had come through the under 15 ranks. Turnbull's proposal to call it "The Weldex Building" was rejected as somewhat grandiose. "The club hut" would be a Harriers institution for over a decade and there was great sadness when it had to be abandoned after the Sports Centre opened. When it was finally demolished in the mid-1990s, it greatly enhanced the District Council's Guy Fawkes bonfire!

By the time the 1984 track and field season, the club's last at the Bught, got under way that April, a start had been made on the track. It was due to be finished and in use by August once the polymer surface had been laid during the necessary appropriate weather window.

The first highlight of 1984 came in April at the opening SWAL meeting at Meadowbank. Jayne Barnetson, recently back from warm weather training in Portugal, set a Scottish under 17 high jump record, going second in the national senior all-time list with 1.82. This clinched her senior international debut in Hungary on May 18th. Like Tommy Leighton she was 16 years and 4 months. The weekend before that, her East District title was part of a record for the club of 3 gold, 6 silver and 3 bronze.

The Hungary match was a triumph for Inverness Harriers with no fewer than four athletes selected for the Scottish senior team, the others being Fraser in the hurdles, Patience in the shot and Kenney in the 10000m. However Kenney, who had just left Inverness but was still a club member, declined selection due to a prior commitment to the London marathon. This was Patience's senior international debut and he raised his shot pb to 14.92. Despite Jayne's excellent form, her first senior cap had still come somewhat unexpectedly and her passport had expired. However all was resolved in the nick of time by the intervention of Charles Kennedy, Ross and Cromarty's recently elected young MP.

Late in the afternoon of Thursday June 7th, Jayne received a phone call with an invitation to the Olympic Trials at Gateshead that Sunday. "Plan A" - the Scottish schools pentathlon - was quickly abandoned. Being dropped into this level of competition was a frightening prospect for a 16 year old. Her father was an indispensable part of "Team Barnetson" who regularly transported her about the country and could again have taken her. But she insisted that she needed her coach with her this time.

Off we set that Saturday morning to Gateshead, and a television-inspired starting height of 1.75! Following Tommy's "no height" at the same venue in 1981, my heart was in my mouth. She cleared it at the third attempt but went no further. On return we were amazed at the number of people outwith the club who couldn't understand that this teenager was just there for the experience and wouldn't actually be going to Los Angeles!

Next came a championship record of 1.79 to bring the Scottish Schools best performance trophy, the Frances Barker Shield, north for the first time. Then at the following month's British Schools international in Crawley, six days after her first six foot jump of 1.83 in the British Airways Games, she cleared a phenomenal 1.85. At 16 years and six months this improved both her Scottish under 17 and under 19 records, took her within 2cm of the Scottish senior record and within 6cm of the British junior record. But with the return of the English this still left her second on countback to Debbie Marti.

Neil Fraser as depicted by Jane Lakeland in the 1981 club records and rankings booklet

Andrew Thain captained the Scottish schools team and was runner up in the 100 hurdles in 13.6 while Russell Devine missed out in the shot by just 7cm with 16.26. His best hammer throwing days were some time off yet, but he was still fifth there with 55.28. The British Airways Games saw Eddie Leighton clear 2 metres to break his brother's Youths' club record so both were now 2 metre performers.

In the senior championships, Fraser, neck and neck with John Wallace, hit the deck a couple of hurdles from home. The athletes had adjacent trail legs and Fraser was judged to have been impeded, so Wallace was initially disqualified. On review, a re-run was ordered instead and Wallace got the verdict in 14.66 from defending champion Fraser.

Harry Lakeland was now making fine progress with Devine and Patience, who rapidly homed in on 50 metres with the discus. His shot improved to 15.22 and he also retained his SAAA heavyweight title in addition to a clean sweep of all the heavy events at the Inverness Games. However he was denied an attempt at the Scottish record of 15' 2" for the 56lb weight because the stands would not go past 15'! But there were more strings to Harry's bow with throwers such as Alisdair Ferguson, John Morrison and especially David Allan.

Then attention returned to Jayne with an invitation to travel to the future 1988 Olympic venue of Seoul in South Korea with a Scottish team and her phenomenal year did not even end there. On September 15th she became the first Inverness Harrier to compete for Great Britain at an international in Karlovak, Yugoslavia although 1.78 for fourth place suggested that this was just too late in an exhausting season.

In this atmosphere of high powered individual performance, the club's SWAL Division 1 debut in 1984 almost faded into the background. This always was going to be an uphill struggle against some of the best clubs in Britain and two sixth places followed by a fifth meant an always inevitable relegation.

Alongside all this frantic activity there was a huge effort to prepare for the opening of the new track. Over the winter, plans had been hatched for a spectacular official opening meeting. This included a match between a North District select and a Scottish Junior select (a decidedly sniffy SAAA took severe exception to the team being referred to, even informally, as "Scotland"!) with a number of high profile guest athletes. An organising committee, with Turnbull and McGinn to the fore, put a huge amount of work into the meeting held on Sunday August 19th 1984.

Problems included hospitality for visiting athletes and officials. The council was in principle very happy to give a civic reception for 300, but asked for this to be on the Saturday night since it was council policy not to offer entertainment on a Sunday. Just a few years earlier the Sunday meeting could not have taken place at all because there was still a complete council ban on Sunday sport.

Councillor Dan Corbett moved an amendment to have the hospitality rule suspended but councillors, some perhaps with an eye on the religious vote, turned that down by 16 to 10. In the end the council made a £250 contribution to help the club provide the hospitality at Highland Rugby Club.

Several councillors still attended the function and one of them overheard Neil Fraser and European 200 silver medallist Cameron Sharp discussing the wearing of 9mm spikes. There had been a stipulation, albeit unrealistic, that 5mm should be the maximum on the track. So what the councillor overheard led to a huge furore and a large warning notice at the entrance. This went largely unheeded since 5mm spikes raise significant safety issues, but the incident did raise speculation about the thickness of the original polymer, given what was obtained for just £150,000!

I can claim to be the first Inverness Harrier to run a lap of that track that July, along with Bill McAllister whom I was interviewing for the BBC. Then the contractors moved out and the club was allowed in for its first experience of training luxury on our doorstep. Equipment, including the high jump landing area, still had to be carried 200 metres from the Bught before the club made its own rock hard one from a canvas envelope and foam offcuts. The club was initially charged £5 per training session while members of the public could get unlimited use for a year with a ticket costing adults £10 and juveniles £5.

INVERNESS HARRIERS AMATEUR ATHLETIC CLUB

INVERNESS DISTRICT COUNCIL HARRIERS
1984

OPENING OF NEW

ALL WEATHER TRACK

and

ATHLETICS MATCH

NORTH DISTRICT SELECT

versus

SCOTLAND

Sunday 19th August 1984

Queen's Park • Bught Drive • Inverness

A crowd of 2000 attended the opening meeting at the new track on Sunday 19th August 1984 and were not disappointed on a day of warm sunshine and ideal conditions. This was just as well because a grandstand and covered accommodation were still some time away. However the overwhelming need - the track and field facilities - was now fulfilled and this meeting was a fitting celebration of that huge milestone. The organising committee had worked wonders to assemble a star studded field to complement the team contest and this grand opening suitably Christened the new surface.

Cameron Sharp produced a sparkling double of 10.4 and 20.9, times comparable with some of that year's Olympic semi-finals. Better still, Craig Bonnington, one of a number of athletes from Grantown Grammar, set an amazing pair of club senior and junior records of 10.8 and 21.8 in second place. This instantly confirmed that we had an extremely fast surface. However that is significantly compromised because it faces the prevailing south westerly wind. This means that fast sprint and hurdles times can only be achieved on rare occasions when the wind is coming from the east - as was the case that day. This has seriously devalued the track as a competitive venue for sprints and hurdles.

Geoff Parsons delivered the first 7 foot high jump in the north with 2.15 but failed to improve his national record to 2.27. The Leighton brothers, Tommy for the North District and Eddie for the Scottish Junior select, tied for second on 1.95. Scottish record holder Moira McGuire won the women's event with 1.80 and that might have been an interesting contest had Barnetson not been on her way to Korea. There was also the first sub-1:50 800 in the north when Tom McKean ran 1:49.8.

Patience, who also took the 56lb weight and caber, won the shot with 15.32 and the meeting was brought to a resounding conclusion when Bonnington and Fraser, joined by Duncan Chisholm and Forres Harrier Alan MacKenzie, pipped the juniors in the 4 x 100 with a brisk 43.0. Among several young athletes' events, the under 15 sprints went to the emerging Linda Wilson and to Keith Geddes.

The curtain was brought down on yet another season of major progress by the final North East League match in Aberdeen where the women retained their title but the men had to settle for second.

By now the 1986 Commonwealth Games in Edinburgh were very much in sight. For Patience (top Scottish discus thrower in 1984 with 50.86), Barnetson and Fraser, 1985 was very much about consolidating their strong selection prospects. Several other athletes continued their emergence, not the least Russell Devine who had already topped 50 metres to break the SAAA Youth discus championship record in 1984.

OFFICIALS

Convener	D. McGinn
Manager of Meeting	W. Banks
Arena Manager	T. Mackenzie
Referees — *Track*	J. Wilson
Field	H. Lakeland
Timekeepers	G. Aithie, D. McSwein, J. Mitchell, A. Dick, D. Davidson
Judges/Umpires — *Track*	D. Lyall, W. Murray, J. Cassells, Mrs M. Johnston, D. Bone, D. Robertson, Miss D. Brand, D. Aitchison
— *Jumps*	I. Tasker, Mrs M. Cooke, Mrs H. Hall, J. Crossman, Mrs P. Wilson, Miss A. Tuach
— *Throws*	W. Sutherland, A. Valentine, K. MacDonald, B. Ross, J. Sutherland, Mrs G. Ramage, D. MacPherson
Starters	R. Southcott, D. Patience
Mark Stewards	C. Baillie, J. Johnston
Recorders	R. MacDonald, Mrs R. MacDonald
Announcers	C. Bannerman, A. Hamilton
Athletes Declaration and Assembly	G. Bannerman, Mrs S. Bannerman, Mrs A. Tasker, J. Mackay
Officials Reception	W. Murray
Presentation Stewards	B. Turnbull, R. MacDonald
Visiting Teams and Guests Reception	P. Thompson, D. McGinn, D. Duncan, Mrs M. Banks
Press Liaison	P. Lewis
Stewards	Members of Inverness Harriers
Organising Committee	D. McGinn, B. Turnbull, R. MacDonald, C. Baillie, W. Banks, C. Bannerman, M. MacDonald, P. Lewis

293 MIKE MURRAY Airac ✓   294 BARRY HOLT ✓ Birchfield

MORAY FIRTH ADVERTISERS

EVENT No. 5   800 METRES MEN   2.20 p.m.

Scottish All-Comers Record   1min 45.5secs
Scottish Native Record   1min 47.7sec

33 COLIN DONALD, ND ✓   38 PAUL FORBES, Edinburgh ✓
34 DONALD McMILLAN, ND ✓   39 TOM McKEAN, Clyde Valley ✓
35 ALISTAIR CURRIE, Scot   40 CRAIG MOCHRIE, Loughborough
36 TOM RITCHIE, Scot   41 ALAN SMITH, Edinburgh SH ✓
37 ROLAND WEDDEN, Essex ✓   282 CHRIS PULFORD, Darlington ✓

1st .... 2nd .... 3rd ....

Time .... m .... s   Time .... m .... s   Time .... m .... s

Opening Meeting – Men's 800 Line up

Apart from the August 84 head wetting, the open meeting on April 14th 1985 was the first regular event at the Queens Park and had the three senior office bearers of the SAAA present. A record turnout of 330 athletes from 15 clubs flocked to the track and the manual system, with all entries made on the day, coped with the influx with the start only delayed by 15 minutes. Russell took the meeting by storm with Scottish under 17 records of 16.95 in the shot and 59.72 in the hammer (both 5kg). The following Wednesday at Meadowbank he just missed the treble when his discus throw of 52.74 was just 6cm short of that record.

Safety procedures were still fairly rudimentary and on one occasion the hammer bounced off the back straight. Russell already had something of a reputation for firing off missiles at diverse angles and Harry once had to call out his council colleagues in the lighting department to rescue a hammer which had lodged in a tree at the Bught. This open meeting also gives us an early sight of the name of David Allan, winner of the Senior Boys' shot with 13.33.

The Queens Park came into its own at the North District championships where the pouring rain would have created mayhem at the Bught, and even caused problems at this new venue which still had no cover for athletes and spectators. Patience, although slightly under par in a wet circle, improved the discus record to 49.10 while Eddie Leighton showed that a 2 metre high jumper could still long jump 6.64. Andrew Thain, now a Junior, made his 110m hurdles 3'6" debut in 15.7.

Mid June saw a highly successful purple patch for the club's junior athletes, especially the boys. The Boys' Youths' and Junior championships at Meadowbank yielded 5 gold, 3 silver and 2 bronze. Four of the golds came from Lakeland's increasingly successful throws group with Devine taking the Youths' shot (15.97), discus (49.38) and hammer with a championship record of 55.44 while Allan won the Boys' shot with 12.05. The other gold went to Thain in the Junior 110 hurdles with a cracking 14.54 over the 3'3" barriers. One feature of Thain's 110 hurdling was a bigger time differential than normal between his 3'3 and 3'6 performances, possibly because he was quite small for a high hurdler so found the 3'6 barriers disproportionately difficult.

It got even better at the following weekend's Scottish Schools championships where Inverness Harriers' athletes produced the bulk of the medals on a triumphant day for the north. According to Sandy Sutherland in The Scotsman on Monday June 17th: *"The North of Scotland made an astonishing assault on the Scottish Schools' athletics championships on Saturday. Records fell and medals were plundered in a way which must have made the sophisticated south wonder whether the Pictish hordes were returning. The plunder reached a tally of 30 medals - 13 gold, 9 silver and 8 bronze, and the top two trophies at the Schoolboys' meeting in Glasgow both went to Inverness Harriers."*

By now, Thain's family had moved to the Glasgow area and, although he stuck with the Harriers, he was completing his sixth year at Douglas Academy music school. He was awarded the Eric Liddell Trophy for the top boy performer for a sparkling double of a record 14.7 in the 110 hurdles and 6.90 in the over 17 long jump. Then the A.H. Dalrymple Trophy for the top thrower very much "came home" to Golspie High School when Devine, in the same age group, set records of 52.98 in the hammer and 45.04 in the discus. Dalrymple, who died of cancer aged just 39, had been Principal Teacher of PE at Golspie High, of which Sandy Sutherland was also an FP.

At this time the schools, who had added an under 14 age group, operated, as now, September age groups while the SAAA used April. This meant that Devine (but not Thain) was a SAAA Youth but a schools over 17, using heavier implements. To these two records, Barnetson added the senior girls' high jump with an injury affected 1.75 which eliminated her as a candidate to retain the Barker Shield. One other gold at the girls' championships went to Eilidh Johnson who took the under 15 75m hurdles in 11.7, which was still 0.2 short of her impressive club record of 11.5.

Eilidh's parents Joe and Margaret were prime examples of what parent power was doing for the club at this time. Lakeland was still very active recruiting coaches and officials as the club underwent its expected expansion after the track opened. By 1985, membership had risen to 275 and continued to increase. Even after they moved to Fort William when Joe became chief of police in Lochaber, they continued to assist and other parents who arrived around this time included John Wilson, Hilary MacLean, Brian and Trish Ross and Alan Hards. Many who began as interested parents, some with an athletics background and others without, went on to occupy some very senior positions.

Commonwealth Games qualification was becoming a live issue and two Harriers reached standards with their gold medals at the 1985 Scottish Championships at Meadowbank. Patience retained his discus title with 50.06 while Barnetson made a characteristically quick recovery from injury to take the high jump with 1.83.

That, however, was still not the sum total of an outstanding year's haul of national (including schools) championship gold medals. This rose to 21 (including 8 championship records) at the SWAAA age group championships in July. The titles included Eilidh Johnson equalling her high powered 75 hurdles club record of 11.5 - but into a 2.7 wind this time! This meeting also saw significant short sprint performances from developing youngsters Linda Wilson and Alison Edmonds, who remain in the club 100m all-time top four. Johnson and Edmonds went on to Celtic Games selection later in the summer and won the 75 hurdles and 100 respectively.

By this time it could be said with confidence that every Scottish track and field team in any age group included at least one Inverness Harrier. Barnetson, as Britain's number one, was a regular fixture in the GB Junior team with one year still remaining in the age group. The 1985 European Junior championships were in Cottbus, East Germany but the BAAB qualifying standard was a phenomenally difficult 1.88. So if Jayne was going to get there, she was going to have to add a centimetre to Moira McGuire's Scottish senior record.

Serious ankle problems, partly due to an instability of the joints, and other injuries had hugely disrupted her progress early in 1985 and by the end of July she still had not matched her 1984 best of 1.85. The selection deadline was Sunday August 4th so her last opportunity to qualify was the under 21 international at Middlesborough on the 3rd. Harry Lakeland was also appointed the Scottish throws coach here.

What happened at Middlesborough was typical of an athlete who was the supreme competitor. Jumping on her own once the runner up departed after 1.81, she cleared the 1.88 standard to qualify for the European Juniors. She also became Inverness Harriers' first Scottish national record holder - a record which, at the time of writing, she still holds 29 years later.

From this last gasp qualification, it was on to Cottbus where Jayne took herself and her club into the major international championship arena for the first time on Sunday 28th August. At one point she led this European junior final with a first time clearance at 1.84. But it became a case of so near yet so far since the vertical jumps, with their countback rules, are cruel events. A single failure at 1.88 imposed on Jayne that ultimately frustrating championship experience of a fourth place. The medallists were two Soviets (including world junior record holder Olga Turchak) and a Bulgarian on a day when the Inverness Harrier was only denied a major European medal by a heel catching the bar on one of her attempts at 1.91.

Returning to London the following night, she had 30 minutes to catch the Edinburgh shuttle and was whisked up the road to Dingwall by her dad in the early hours. That evening it was back down the A9 to join a Scottish team bound for Tel Aviv, arriving at 5am on the Wednesday.

Of the other two major international stars, Fraser was having rather a barren period while Patience's discus career was going from strength to strength. He had taken to the event quite by accident in Hungary in 1984. He was there as a shot putter but asked for a guest spot in the discus. He beat both Scottish representatives and never looked back. Later that season he won, and went on to retain, the Scottish discus title. 1985 also saw him become Irish champion and gain a Great Britain "B" selection in France where he upped the club record to 53.14.

Jamie Bell Leads Kevin MacKintosh in Augsburg.

That summer saw a completely new venture when a group of club athletes and officials took part in a trip to Augsburg as part of Inverness's town twinning arrangements with the German community. The venture included a highly entertaining Highland Games.

By the autumn of 1985, club membership was approaching 300. Athletes were undertaking an ever expanding range of competitions – road, hill, cross country and, in track and field, league, open, championship and internationals. The sheer volume was becoming very difficult for the committee to handle through its current monolithic structure. On 21st August, over 50 members at a special

Lorna Ross and Dianne at the Augsburg Games with Tommy Leighton in the background.

meeting resolved overwhelmingly to recommend radical changes to committee structure. This involved creating five sub committees with each of their conveners sitting on the main committee. This was yet another reflection of the rapid, across the board progress which was being made.

With a young family on the way and, it has to be admitted, a degree of burn out, I had decided to stand down from all my administrative and coaching commitments. My coaching group was quite well placed to be wound down at the end of the 1985 season although I did commit to taking Jayne on hopefully to the 1986 World Juniors and Commonwealth Games. Sam McNaughton also stood down as Secretary.

The necessary constitutional changes were placed before the AGM on September 23rd and the new look committee was - President - Peter Thompson, Vice President - Dougie Bone, Secretary - Hilary MacLean, Treasurer - George Swanson, Newsletter editor - Jamie Willis. Sub-committee conveners - Finance and Social - George Reynolds, Coaching and Officials - Harry Lakeland, Road, hill and cross country - Brian Turnbull, Track and Field - Brian Ross. The PR convenership initially remained unfilled. Young athletes - Alan Bone, Corinne Campbell. Commitee members - Bill Arthur, Neil Martin, Alan Hards, David Ross. Firemaster Donnie Grant presented the awards, including the senior club championship trophies to Julie Wilson and Kevin MacKintosh.

The 1986 Commonwealth Games season began with a great deal of anticipation, but there was also some apprehension over the club's three team contenders. Patience had a back injury while Fraser, also not entirely injury free, had not been in the best of form and still needed to stake his claim. Meanwhile Barnetson, already named in an SWAAA "provisional" squad, had not long recovered from a cracked vertebra following an autumn 1985 landing area accident in Norway.

The Open Meeting in April saw Devine tackle adult implements for the first time. He threw the discus 41.50 while Linda Wilson and Alison Edmonds cleaned up in the senior and junior sprints. Neil Munro ran 22.7 to edge two very classy Aberdeen opponents in the men's 200 and Eddie Leighton beat his brother by 1.97 to 1.93 in the high jump. This was in advance of a 2 metre North championship countback win over Eddie for Tommy, who then joined George and Jayne in the Scottish team for Barcelona early in June.

At the Scottish Junior Championships the brotherly duel swung back towards Eddie who won gold with a new club record of 2.03, but it was too late to stake a claim for his senior international debut since Tommy was already on the plane to Barcelona where he cleared 1.95. Eddie's success was the club's 25th national high jump title since Fraser's pioneering under 15 success in 1978. This was a triumphant day for Inverness Harriers who won seven gold, two silver and three bronze. The gold medallists included another Barnetson - Jayne's younger brother David, who was now very much on the up, breaking Fraser's Senior Boys' high jump club record with an outstanding 1.84. The "Golspie hammer school" was on song too when, along with the discus (47.26), Devine took the Junior title with 58.52. John Morrison succeeded him as Youth champion with 50.64 ahead of training partner Barry Brown, silver medalist with 44.60.

Nowhere were Neil Fraser's outstanding competitiveness and self-belief more evident than at the 1986 Scottish Championships, effectively the Commonwealth trials. His previous couple of seasons had been decidedly unrewarding and some had already written him off as a Commonwealth contender. Neil Fraser, however, had not! When it really mattered, he produced one of the runs of his life to win his first title for three years in a personal best of 14.23, losing out on a native record with a wind of +2.02. Against all the odds he had put himself right back into the frame.

Although the outsider had won gold, this eluded both his more highly fancied clubmates. Jayne was taken to a four round jump-off before she lost the women's high jump title to English Commonwealth team member Jenny Little, both clearing 1.82. Meanwhile George, who gave the Highland Games, including the defence of his Scottish heavyweight title, a complete miss in 1986, was third in the discus with 50.04 but neither athlete's selection was threatened.

Neil Fraser, Harry Lakeland and George Patience at Meadowbank – 1986.

As a result, when the Scottish team was announced from Edinburgh Castle on the morning of Monday 23rd June it included the names of these three Inverness Harriers. So, far from suffering from delusional sunstroke on that May evening five years previously, Walter Banks had actually been correct three times over. But before we end this chapter with the Games themselves, it is now time to round off the rest of what happened during that historic summer for Inverness Harriers.

Jayne Barnetson found selection for the 1986 World Juniors in Athens easier than for the previous year's Europeans. Before the world event, she remained on fire with two international wins in five days late in June. In Swansea it was 1.88 against the juniors of Switzerland and Oceania. Then, on what was her own and the club's GB senior debut, she cleared 1.87 to defeat nine Eastern Europeans in Czechoslovakia.

In Athens, the high jump had to go ahead at 7:30am local time, 5:30 UK time, to avoid the excessive heat. This had meant changes to her daily routine before leaving the UK to allow biorhythms to adjust. In the end she again missed a major medal on countback. This time the height was 1.86 for another fourth place behind three Eastern Europeans. After the Berlin Wall came down, it became clear that there had been long term institutionalised drugs abuse in the Communist bloc. It can therefore reasonably be claimed that, in 1985, Jayne Barnetson was the best "clean" junior high jumper in Europe, and in 1986 the best in the world.

Scottish Schools records of 54.12 with the 6.25 hammer and 50.92 with the 1.75 discus saw Devine lift the premier award, the Liddell Trophy in succession to Thain, and retain the Dalrymple Trophy. This meant that four SSAA top awards had come to Inverness Harriers athletes in three years. While Jayne was in Athens, her brother David was making his international debut in the British schools in Swansea along with David Allan (discus) and John Morrison (hammer) while Linda Wilson had to withdraw from the relay pool due to injury.

That summer saw the start of a longstanding link with the Australian Boys' Touring Team which led the way to annual visits. Their leader, eminent Australian sprints coach Neville Sillitoe, suddenly appeared at the Queens Park one day and asked Harry Lakeland if there was any chance of a match with the club. This is a fixture which still goes ahead early each July and the first time they visited there were spontaneous celebrations all over the Queens Park the day Pat Cash won the men's singles at Wimbledon.

As time went on, speculation grew and grew that each year must surely be Neville's last on tour, but come the following July he would always be there. At the time of writing his latest appearance was in 2014 when he and his athletes did the usual double of the Forres Games on the Saturday and the Inverness Harriers open graded meeting on the Sunday.

Two years on from relegation, the club won its way back to Division 1 of the Scottish Women's League whilst taking second place in the Junior Women's section of the Cup. The North East League yielded a fourth women's title in five years and second place for the men. At the club's home match on a wet August Sunday, Peter Thompson was able to assure visiting clubs that by the following summer a grandstand would be in place at the Queens Park - and it was.

Officials John Wilson, Harry Lakeland, Brian Ross and Ian Tasker before the Edinburgh 1986 closing ceremony.

Before looking at the competitive side of the XIIIth Commonwealth Games at the end of July 1986, it is worth examining the role of the half dozen Inverness Harriers who were highly honoured as officials. On the track, the venerable Walter Banks was Assistant Chief Umpire and Harry Lakeland and John Wilson were officials. Colin Baillie was on wind gauge, Ian Tasker on jumps and Brian Ross on throws. This was high recognition for the club's efforts, driven forwards by Lakeland, to develop officiating as well as coaching. This policy also left the club well provided at its own local meetings.

The TV quiz "Question of Sport" is said to have featured a question relating to these rainsoaked Games. The action in the javelin suddenly freezes and the question is put. "What Happens Next?" The answer is that javelin official Brian Ross falls on his backside as he runs across the greasy surface to mark the throw!

The Inverness athletes' parents, friends and family gathered in Edinburgh for the Games. The night before Jayne's high jump, I stayed in Neil's flat overlooking Meadowbank itself, Neil having temporarily come out of the Village at Pollock Halls to be mine host. He immediately warned me not to look out over the stadium with binoculars. This was what his father had done a few days previously and he had been spotted from the roof of the stadium. Within minutes, a squad of police, highly wary of IRA terrorists, were at the door.

When the action began, Patience finished seventh with 52.54 in the final throw of a series all over 50 metres. Fraser ran 14.28, his second fastest ever, in the semis of the hurdles and missed the final by 0.15. And in the women's high jump, Barnetson's sparkling form was clearly continuing when she had three superb first time clearances up to and including 1.83. Looking at the other jumpers, a medal appeared at least a good possibility.

Then, running in to plant on her first attempt at 1.86 she suddenly crumpled into the ground, holding her left, jumping ankle in agony. Despite severe pain and an obviously serious injury, she incredibly made two more attempts before being carried out of the 1986 Commonwealth Games on a stretcher.

As her coach, all I could do, from the terraces behind the high jump area, was to look on in horror at this unfolding tragedy. Security was so tight that there was absolutely no chance of getting near her. So before the advent of mobile phones and, it has to be said, in the face of very poor feedback from team management, all I could do was to drive disconsolately home to Inverness and await very belated news. This also was my final act as a coach since, for the foreseeable future, I had now retired. The upshot for Jayne was serious ligament and bone damage in an already unstable ankle. It was only after extensive reconstruction that she was able to resume training very cautiously.

She was now due to begin a course at Lafayette University in Indiana, USA. The coaches there had made all manner of promises about what they could offer and how athlete friendly their competitive requirements would be. This was soon exposed as complete fantasy. In the best traditions of American Universities, they wanted their full pound of competitive flesh, irrespective of injury rehab. When she abandoned the course in despair and came home after just five weeks, it was with tales of rudimentary technical knowhow on the part of coaches who apparently had little knowledge of the compilation of training schedules.

This was a sad end to a hugely successful season which topped off a period of unprecedented progress. A decade on from those tentative track and field beginnings of the mid-70s, Inverness Harriers had become a major contributor to Scottish teams and had entered the British arena. Thanks latterly to a revolution in facility provision, there had been athletes at three international championships, a rising flood of national titles plus medals and team performances which made even the bigger clubs look to their laurels as membership burst through 300.

But track and field was only part of the club's extensive activities and the next chapter looks at off-track competition across the decade which the previous two have covered in track and field.

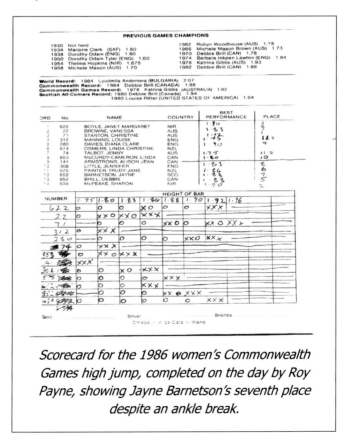

Scorecard for the 1986 women's Commonwealth Games high jump, completed on the day by Roy Payne, showing Jayne Barnetson's seventh place despite an ankle break.

CHAPTER 6 – THE OFF-TRACK REVOLUTION – 1976-86

Endurance running had generally been the poor relation within a club which, from the start, had only really functioned during the summer. There had been Marshall Notman, Ron Grant and some others before Calum Laing's influential but relatively brief involvement. Then Ian Johnstone played his part but the sparsity of organised winter training was a big handicap, especially in cross country. Also, until the 1970s, there was a complete lack of club endurance competition for women.

Along with everything else, it was all change in that pivotal year of 1976. The open cross country meeting and embryonic winter club races of early 76 were a start. Then when Brian Turnbull arrived that spring he did so with a mission, as well as a lot of experience for his 21 years.

Although much of my own competitive background was in endurance my entry into coaching was determined largely by where the need arose. Apart from some input for Donald MacMillan that happened to be in the sprints. This was initially prompted by Dianne emerging as the lead athlete in a sprints group which also included Simon Fraser, Dougie Phimister and Sandra MacLaren. Coaching hence moved forwards with Turnbull running the endurance side while I focused on sprints, hurdles and some jumps, although we each supported the other.

Brian Turnbull wasted no time. That autumn saw an increased presence at the Knockfarrell Hill Race and the Alves to Forres "6" but it was a case of boosting numbers first while the quality took a little longer. October 1976 also included second place behind Forres in the road relay for a quartet comprising Turnbull, Peter Thompson, Mike McAusland and myself.

In November the club hosted the North District cross country relays for the first time and Turnbull's expertise in setting out courses came into its own. His speciality was de-stapling fences and wrapping the barbed wire in sacking, a technique entirely new to inverness. Over the years, urban development has steadily eaten into viable cross country territory in Inverness and this course was on the land which soon became the second nine holes of Torvean Golf Course. The outcome of the men's race was a carbon copy of the road relay but the event came too soon for the developing young athletes who came seventh. This also carried through to the cross country league where for the first time Inverness Harriers had a full men's team at all six races, again finishing second to Forres by 2315 to 2158.

The 1977 summer season saw only limited progress in endurance events but into the next winter activity moved up another notch. When the NSAAA evolved into the SAAA North District in 1976, the latter no longer had financial autonomy. This meant that new promoters had to be found for two open competitions run by the NSAAA. The Amenities Association took over the Inverness Games while the club made a major commitment by taking on the 4 x 4 mile road relay.

Turnbull was very keen on projecting the sport to the public and proposed an alternative route with each leg comprising two laps, starting and finishing on the quiet second carriageway opposite St Andrew's Cathedral. The two miles took runners as far as the Ness Islands in one direction and across the Ness Bridge –hence in the public eye – in the other. It was a good fast, flat route although there were one or two problems with runners making their way through Saturday crowds on the Ness Bridge. Indeed race officials once found themselves confronted by an irate shopper demanding compensation for the eggs knocked from her grasp by a speeding athlete!

With Johnstone unavailable, Brian Turnbull (23:51), Innes Mitchell (22:54), Donnie MacPherson (25:11) and Ross MacDonald (25:12) finished third. Donald MacMillan won the Youths' open 4 miles over the same route in a promising 25:12. There then followed a still rare foray outwith the Highlands for the Kingsway relay in Dundee and the Allan Scally in Glasgow, which yielded a creditable 14th out of 84 teams.

To achieve the club's objectives, training had to be for the entire year and not just the summer. This was especially important if the organisation was going to be kept together over the winter for cross country. A winter training venue with

A North cross country race at what could well be Lochaber – 1980s

indoor facilities and access to running areas outside was therefore needed urgently. Clearly the Bught was useless in the pitch dark and salvation came at the Spectrum Centre in Farraline Park.

This had changing rooms and a hall as well as access to the still largely traffic free Longman. The Kessock Bridge approach was being built on Longman Road, and offered an unused, metalled surface illuminated by nearby street lights. Spectrum sessions were on Tuesdays and St John's Hall in Southside Road was later added on Thursdays.

The 1977 North relays were held in Fort William. The hosts, hillrunning specialists Lochaber, appeared to have their own view of what was appropriate underfoot and gradient. The men's race was hence effectively a hill race across some horrendously slippy and dangerous country. The junior events passed without incident on a different course but the men's was so unrunnable and downright dangerous that Forres Harriers and all three Inverness teams withdrew before the start on safety grounds. The race began with just Lochaber and the RAF but was abandoned by the officials after a single lap.

New ventures were coming thick and fast and the autumn of 1977 saw the formal start of the club handicaps which have been a major winter feature ever since. Runners start at different times according to ability and these races were another idea which Turnbull took from Teviotdale. The inaugural series had an ambitious seven events - five handicaps of 3 to 4.9 miles over various terrains, a club cross country championship and the Christmas Relay.

However the very first "club handicap" was actually a scratch contest on Saturday, October 29th. Mitchell won the men's race in 19:09 from Turnbull

---

Club News

OCTOBER AND NOVEMBER CLUB RACES

Included in the Craig Dunain Club races on November 15th will be a friendly Inter Club match against Ross-shire Athletic Club.

With these being handicap races Ross-shire athletes will be "Slotted into the Handicaps" and the scores determined through the net times of the declared team runners.

Handicaps for this and the Holm Mains club races on October 26th will be posted on Club nights from a week before each respective race. If your name is not included and you intend running you should see Bryan Turnbull as just turning up for the race may result in you getting an unsatisfactory handicap.

All athletes should have declared for all club races by 1.30 p.m.

Changing accommodation is at the Bught Stadium.

Club fixture lists for the cross country season can be obtained from Bryan Turnbull.

I.H. SHOULDER BAGS

Liesuropa Ltd., in a bid to become more associated with our club have aquired a stock of shoulder bags with the club badge embossed on the side. These smart bags, a must for anyone wishing to be identified with the club, cost £5.99.

A page from the club magazine which ran for six months of 1980

(19:21) and Ross MacDonald (20:09). No record of the route survives, but the times suggest that it may have been Kinmylies. The boys' race went to Kevin MacKintosh in 9:26 and Dianne moved up several distances to take the women's in 10:26. It would be some years before the senior women ran not with the girls but with the men on the longer course.

The first proper handicap followed, and the Courier records that I got the best of a tight sprint finish with Turnbull and Donnie MacPherson. Initially the men's fields were around half a dozen, eventually rising over the years to a peak of 37 before declining again.

Essentially four of the five club handicap routes – Holm Mains, Craig Dunain, Bught and Kinmylies – have remained the same although Inverness's steady development has enforced various changes in detail. After about 20 years the club championship route via Dunain and Dunain House from Torvean Golf Course became unusable and the championship was then incorporated in the Balnacraig handicap which in 2013 became the only route to undergo significant change to avoid the A82.

Although the Bught race became the traditional start of the club year, the inaugural one was held on 25th February 1978. The handicap winner, by a hefty 37 seconds from Derek McGinn, was Peter Thompson who made this fixture his own.

Ian Johnstone had been running so well that he was selected for the SCCU versus Scottish Universities, Civil Service and Northern Ireland match in Stirling that December. This was a huge honour for the club at the time.

Inverness Harriers hosted its first North District cross country championships in January 1978 at Castle Heather where a good course was only available on this one occasion. The club's first women's team championship came from Dianne 3rd, Rosalind MacLennan 4th and Melanie Robertson 7th. Another sprinter, Maureen MacLeod, took the Junior Women's title.

The North cross country league saw many of the young athletes compete for their schools. The men were again runners up to Forres, whose Iain MacKenzie won the individual title ahead of Mitchell and Turnbull. A small party at the national cross country championships in Glasgow failed to make any real impression.

The summer programme included a small contingent in the Ben Nevis Race before the 1978-79 winter season produced further progress. November 25th 1978 was a red letter day since, in Thurso, it marked the first ever win for an Inverness Harriers' men's team in the North cross country league. By now MacMillan was in his final year in school and improving fast. He was the first counter in fourth place ahead of Turnbull (6th), Mitchell (8th) and MacDonald (12th). Victory by three points was followed by another win at Fort William after agreement that courses there would be more realistic.

Turnbull won the fifth race but a narrow team success for Forres sent the two clubs into the last match at Inverness on March 17th 1979 dead level. Here the hosts rose to the occasion in fine style. Turnbull posted another victory with Mitchell 2nd, MacMillan 5th and MacDonald 8th. This gave an unbeatable 388 points to win the final match and the title by 12 points. This was spectacular progress in just three years and was matched by the women when individual champion Dianne led that team to success.

Early 1979 saw the hardest weather conditions in the Highlands for many years. It was so cold in Inverness that Thistle's Scottish Cup tie against Falkirk had to be postponed a record 29 times. On January 27th the only outdoor sporting event in the North was Inverness Harriers' club cross country championships. In deep snow and temperatures well below zero the senior winners were Donald MacMillan and Melissa Jeans.

Cross country racing outwith the North was on the increase too, with Aberdeen's Hydrasun meeting often a successful day out. National penetration continued to be difficult but at the Scottish schools MacMillan took over 17 bronze while Jeans was fifth under 17. Initially there was optimism that Melissa might be selected for the British schools under 17 international in Inverness at the end of that month. That was then dashed when it emerged that selections were across two different age groups and she would only be a reserve.

The schools' international over the club's own Kinmylies course was hugely successful with a number of Harriers' officials and members supporting the main organiser, the recently retired Bill Murray. The area above race HQ at Charleston Academy and up towards Craig Dunain Hospital served the club very well for many years although development eventually rendered it unusable.

Turnbull and MacMillan continued to dominate North distance running on the track during the summer of 1979. Then by October, MacMillan was lost for university term time at least since he began a Veterinary Medicine course in Edinburgh. However Innes Mitchell was by now alongside Turnbull over the country and, with further support from Ross MacDonald and Mike McAusland, there came the 1979 North cross country relay title.

The women spread their net to the East District championships and league and Melissa – described in the Courier as looking "unbeatable in the North" - secured a top four finish in the East under 17 championships. North female runners benefited here by having both the East championships and the unofficial women's events at the men's North championships, both in track and field and cross country.

Turnbull's form was good enough in the early winter of 1979 for selection for the SCCU representative match at Stirling while MacMillan's strong start in Edinburgh saw him in the Universities team.

Into 1980, the men's North league race in Elgin on January 12th had to be abandoned when the leading six runners were sent the wrong way. The Royal Academy – mainly fielding club runners from Turnbull's endurance squad – won three of the six young athletes' team contests. A week later the men's team was tipped for a very close contest with Forres in the North championships before Lochaber, infrequent league competitors but prone to assembling a strong squad for championships, upset that particular applecart.

The league campaign brought better news despite boiling down to a cliffhanger. Inverness went into the final match in Thurso with a slender lead of just ten points which Forres reduced to just four by the end. Central to that second successful league campaign were Turnbull and Mitchell who also took the top two individual prizes. Melissa Jeans (women) and Calum Martin (under 13 boys) had clean sweeps of six wins out of six. A week later the all-Harriers quartet of Martin, Michael Mitchell, George MacLennan and Paul Mitchell produced another national breakthrough with Scottish schools under 14 silver for the Royal Academy.

The Courier's summary of the 1979-80 cross country season, which had seen another huge leap forward, said: *"Inverness Harriers have put even more of their resources into cross country and this season has taken them in even greater numbers to the national individual and relay championships as well as their being seen for the first time at open races at Hawick and Aberdeen."* By now Turnbull's programmed endurance coaching was really having an effect on an expanding squad. However he still seemed to manage to perform well himself, whilst also undertaking a plethora of other club commitments.

One of these was a completely new enterprise with Caledonian FC at Telford Street Park. The idea was half time races and the "Leisuropa 2000m" was born. Leisuropa was a local sports shop which became official stockist of club vests and one or two other branded items, including shoulder bags, at least one of which, purchased in 1980, is still going strong!

The inaugural 2000 took place at Caley v Fraserburgh on 12th April 1980, with Leisuropa vouchers for £12, £8 and £4 for the top three. Track marking was done in two minutes flat by a squad of youngsters sticking in flags at pre-determined points. A dozen top North runners assembled and Ross Arbuckle of Keith held off a late challenge from Derek Taylor of Caithness, with Turnbull adding third place to his organisational duties. Other similar events followed and these were well received by the Howden Enders.

In the history of the Ben Nevis Race, no year has been more controversial than 1980. The weather in Fort William on September 6th was so severe that the officials, led by race referee Tom MacKenzie, had to cancel the event. Predictably some of the hard line hillrunners disagreed but this was absolutely the correct decision. The cancellation was especially unfortunate for the Harriers who had made a special effort to be well represented for the first time. However the demise of their day prompted another idea.

This is how the Courier described the next step on Friday September 12th:- *"The cancellation of last Saturday's Ben Nevis Race was a severe blow to the 400 competitors - not least to the eleven entrants from Inverness Harriers, many of whom had travelled to Fort William some time prior to the race to study the ground and had done a lot of specialist training for the event.*

BEN NEVIS RACE
6th September.

It looks as though at least some eight club members will toe the line for the start of Britains highest mountain race up and down 1,344 metres (4418ft.) of the Ben. Last year 356 runners including nine women completed the gruelling test. Our own Linda Lamb made her debut on that occasion finishing well clear of a number of the male competitors. In for their baptism this year and hopefully for the first of many races are Brian Turnbull, Bob Cooper and David Hughes. Your first Ben is always your last until the pain has gone - and then its roll-on for the next Ben.

The 1980 Ben Nevis race was much anticipated in the club magazine but never took place

"Therefore, by way of compensation, Brian Turnbull and Derek McGinn have devised an alternative race which will take place tomorrow (Saturday) from the Bught at 1.30 p.m. Although nowhere near the scale of Ben Nevis, Craig Dunain which many athletes used for training, is the highest there is in the immediate vicinity of Inverness and a course of 5.3 miles, leading ultimately to the summit, has been worked out. An invitation has been sent to the Ross-shire club to take part as well and it is hoped that a fairly large field will assemble."

So, Phoenix-like out of the ashes of the previous Saturday's Ben Race, a North athletics institution was born. Since this was put together in few days there was no time to obtain an SAAA permit which theoretically limited competition to two clubs. Eventually 21 athletes assembled to run an out and back course up the A82 as far as the forest path leading to what is universally known by local runners as "The Cottages" and hence to the summit by "The Zigzags".

Turnbull won in 32:36 from Ian Johnston of Forres (34:11), with Ross MacDonald third in 36:04. The event was so successful that the Craig Dunain Hill Race became an annual fixture with generous sponsorship from Hugh Calder, managing director of Las Plant crane hire, whom we met in Chapter 2 as a competitor in the 1953 Lossie to Elgin road race. The start was later changed, initially to one of the fairways of Torvean golf course and then to the nearby canal bank. This new route accessed the "cottages" path by the canal banks and "Dosser's Brae", avoiding the A82 apart from one rather tricky crossing. Very quickly the Craig Dunain Hill Race became a prominent North fixture usually attracting a smallish but often unusually high quality field.

That area West of the Caledonian Canal has been a favourite among local runners since the 1950s. It became even more so after the club's Joggers section appeared in 1985, with various geographical features steadily acquiring specific titles. Apart from those already mentioned, there are also "The Old Ruin", "Davy Moy's Route", "Gordy Fraser's Route" and "Barking Dogs" - a cottage above Dunain House where passing runners could be sure of attracting the wrath of some extremely bad tempered canines. Hence statements like "We'll regroup at the Old Ruin" or "Let's do an effort as far as Barking Dogs" became standard currency on both Joggers' and Harriers' training nights.

The most famous feature of all is undoubtedly "The Mast", local runner-speak for the summit of Craig Dunain which accommodates a communications hub. The Mast has become an obsession among some members of the Inverness running community. Indeed over frequent, slow paced slogs up to it – in daylight and pitch dark - may not have entirely helped competitive standards.

The 1980-81 cross country season got off to a bad start for the men's team and went downhill after that. A strong Lochaber side appeared more frequently than usual and dominated, with Inverness well off the pace. The junior contests were different and the club squad made further advances. Athletes like Michael Mitchell, Callum Martin, Allan Watson, Lesley Munro, Karen Luke and Lee Lobban were very much on a rapid improvement curve which continued for some time. The club presence at some meetings rose to over 50 runners, young and old.

Club-school cooperation was well illustrated in the boys' District Relays when the Harriers and the Royal Academy divided their resources and scooped the top two prizes. Ewan Scott with Martin and

Watson took the title for the club while, for the Academy, Mitchell linked up with high jumpers Tommy and Eddie Leighton to take silver.

History was made in 1980 when the National cross country relay championships took place at Charleston over the same course as the previous year's international. This was a triumph for Walter Banks, now in his SCCU Vice Presidential year as Inverness Harriers' representative. Not only did he persuade central belt sceptics to come North in numbers, he also organised a superb event which was universally praised by athletes and officials from Galashiels to Thurso. The local young athletes were 11th and the men 19th.

December 1980 saw the Stirling select meeting expand into a Scottish inter district match where Martin and Mitchell were 10th and 11th. However this would continue to be more of a mismatch, with the sparsely populated North almost always unable to come close to the East or the West.

There was a massive breakthrough for Lee Lobban who ran out of her skin to finish eighth in the 1981 under 15 Scottish schools and win selection for the British schools international. 1981 also saw the first ever London Marathon where Inverness Harriers were represented by Derek McGinn, who ran 2:54, Chris McDermott and Alan Young.

The club's results in that year's Alves to Forres road race offer an interesting insight into overall men's distance running standards compared with more recent years. The course, at just over 6 miles, was effectively a 10K and run East to West, into the prevailing wind. In 1981 Inverness Harriers' leading finishers were - Innes Mitchell 32:29, Brian Turnbull 32:49, Donald MacMillan 32:59, Les Hunter 33:06 and, in 15th place, Ross MacDonald 33:50. In comparison 15th in the 2013 Dyke 10K, the historical successor of the Alves to Forres, was 37:47.

The first five years of recovery from 1976 saw dramatic developments right across the event range, both on and off track. Cross country began in a state of virtual non-existence. Now the club, also with some athletes competing for Inverness High School, Inverness Royal Academy and Culloden Academy, had become North leaders in many age groups. The men found it toughest against strong opposition mainly from Moray and sometimes Lochaber. The women's fortunes were often variable before a long period of complete domination. The strongest age groups varied, depending on where the talent was as time went by. Elgin AAC, Moray Roadrunners, Black Isle and Fraserburgh did at various times present significant challenges.

National breakthrough remained a lot more difficult but on 26th February 1982 the Courier's preview of the following day's Scottish championships at Irvine said: *"No honours have come to Inverness from these championships as yet, but that may very well change as a result of tomorrow's senior boys' (13-15) race. In this section, the Harriers' team is unbeaten this season so far either locally or nationally, and as a result they must be regarded as major contenders for an award. So far, Callum Martin, George MacLennan, Jamie Bell and Stephen Pierce have made most of the running this season."*

Inverness Harriers had already benefited from clusters of talent producing success in sprint relays. Now it was the turn of cross country where more recent recruits Bell and Pierce joined established team members Martin and MacLennan. They had already posted their intent outwith the North with victories at the Teviotdale and Aberdeen open meetings before heading for the nationals. On that triumphant day at Irvine, Pierce was 7th, Bell 13th, Martin 14th and MacLennan 34th in a field of over 200 to take Inverness Harriers' first Scottish cross country team title by 19 points from Shettleston.

This was also a red letter day for Walter Banks in his SCCU Presidential year and the boys' awards were presented by Mary Banks. According to Walter: *"I could hardly have dreamed of a more fitting end to my year as President".* His year had also included trips to Poland for the World Championships and to Rome where he had an audience with the Pope at the Vatican.

To mark his Presidency, Walter donated trophies to the club for annual award to the outstanding male and female cross country performers. In 1982 the inaugural winner of the Walter Banks Rosebowl was George MacLennan who had been ever present throughout this unbeaten

Lee Lobban and George MacLennan with Mary and Walter Banks at the inaugural presentation of the Banks Cross Country Awards

season. The Mary Banks Salver went to Lee Lobban who had

succeeded Melissa Jeans as leading lady in endurance. Even by this stage George and Lee had become "an item" and went on to marry and produce a new generation of athletic talent – but not before doing the Banks double again in 1984.

Alongside the excitement of the Scottish team title, one major project dominated much of 1982. A free newspaper called the Inverness Focus was running its "Hamish Appeal" for a spina bifida charity. This prompted the Turnbull and McGinn ideas production line towards the notion of assembling a team of Harriers for a sponsored run from Land's End to John O'Groats. The start of this near 900 mile effort by a team of 14 runners took place in August and the proceeds were split between the Harriers and the Hamish Appeal.

To raise funds a number of local sponsors were lined up and, over several weeks, introduced in the paper along with one of the runners. The team ranged in age from Callum Martin at 16 to Bob Cooper who, at 42, was still regarded as quite a mature runner. There were two women, Linda Lamb and Louise MacDonald, and the athletes did late and early shifts totalling 13 hours a day.

They received a great welcome at various places on the route, and not the least at Inverness. Here a fun run coincided with their arrival and onward progress towards John O'Groats which they reached around a week after starting. In the end over £2500 went to the charity while the club retained the other half for the fund which was part of a now very active campaign to persuade Inverness District Council to provide an all-weather track. As noted in the previous chapter, the money eventually helped with ancillary facilities at the Queens Park.

In September 1982, after 29 years, the tradition of a 4 x 4 mile relay finally died. It was replaced by a 4 mile road race and a fun run organised by Inverness District Sports Council while the young athletes' races carried on. The inaugural 4 mile winner was Paul Kenney, a major force in Scottish distance running who had just joined the club after becoming assistant manager of the new Marks and Spencer store. When he left two years later it was as the holder of three club records of huge longevity.

That year's Teviotdale trip saw Lee Lobban finish second in the women's race behind an Edinburgh AC runner three years older than herself. In 1994 Yvonne Murray went on to become Commonwealth 10000 champion. Performances like this won Lee further international honours, including an under 17 selection for the Five Countries match in Dublin early in 1983. So it was no surprise when Lee became Inverness District Sports Council's inaugural female sports personality for 1982, part of a clean sweep where Neil Fraser won the male award and Inverness Harriers took the new Club of the Year title. As further markers of Inverness Harriers' developing status in the local area, Lee and the club went on to retain these titles in 1983.

By now the 1980s running boom was well under way which meant a lot of people on the streets, many of them in the dark. This became a road safety issue and Chief Constable Donald Henderson once even jumped out of his car to have a word with an inconspicuous jogger with whom he had had a near miss. One problem was that Harriers athletes - probably not totally innocent but also likely to be literally more "streetwise" than less experienced joggers - were getting a disproportionate amount of criticism over the problem.

So enter "Hot Dots". These were light reflecting adhesive discs which club runners were given, along with armbands, to stick on themselves to increase visibility, and they certainly were effective. During the debate over this road safety issue the club, never missing a trick, also let it be known that a proper running track in the town would mean less use of the streets as a training venue.

The club hosted the 1982 North District championships, but at Culloden Academy since the previous Kinmylies course had fallen victim to Inverness's inexorable expansion. The championships provided evidence that female distance running was matching the earlier development of men's when the club had a clean sweep of all three titles – Senior (with Lobban as inevitable individual champion), Junior and Girls. With the four male events producing one team win and three seconds, two of them very close, here was further evidence of the club's ability, on its day, to dominate the North.

When his job allowed him to run on Saturdays, Kenney was the clear North leader. Performances elsewhere clinched his selection for the full Scottish team for the Home Countries international in March 1983, matching the track and field achievements of Leighton and Fraser. However there was an honest realism about the club over this selection. Kenney had arrived in Inverness as an established internationalist and Inverness Harriers certainly could take no credit for his athletic development.

The early 80s obsession with marathons reached Inverness like everywhere else. Kenney ran a club record 2:19:04 in London in 1983 and one popular event was the Aberdeen Milk Marathon. That September Bobby MacDonald led a Harriers pack of seven runners with 2:42 there, ahead of Ross MacDonald, and Bob Cooper on 3:01. One athlete who joined as a marathon runner was Alex Sutherland, but he then moved down distance to become 1984 club cross country champion.

Forres regained the upper hand again in North men's cross country, but Kenney's arrival very much swung things back Inverness's way. At the 1983 District Relays at Forres, Turnbull, Bobby MacDonald and Les Hunter battled out a narrow 4 second lead going into the last lap. The final Forres runner, Mike McCulloch, would have been more than a match for almost anyone else but Kenney produced a 26 second margin of victory.

The women's mixed age group title, by 75 seconds, made it an Inverness double. The successful trio was the diminutive Vicky Allan, one of Scotland's leading under 13 girls, Catriona Bell (Junior Woman) and, with the fastest lap, Lee Lobban (Senior). The boys were second but in the following Saturday's National relays David Bell, Simon Garland and George MacLennan achieved a best ever finish of sixth.

Turnbull's junior endurance group continued to thrive and by the winter of 1983-84 Lee had established a claim to be Scotland's top under 17 cross country runner. With a total of six international appearances she was a regular Scottish team member and in the open national championships finished top Scot as runner up to an English athlete.

Walter Banks had by now negotiated a place for a North select in the SCCU's premier club team event, the eight stage Edinburgh to Glasgow road relay. In 1983 Kenney, Turnbull and Bobby MacDonald contributed to 14th place. It had not taken long for the Craig Dunain Hill Race to make its mark and by 1984 it was attracting some leading performers, with internationalist Colin Donnelly the winner. He was followed by Neil Martin, who had just changed clubs from Forres to Inverness, and Lochaber's Ronnie Campbell.

Inverness's response to the 80s running boom was diverse. The Harriers set up a Wednesday evening recreational running group, officially called Inverness Joggers but soon simply dubbed The Joggers as they became an integral part of the club. Although the general thrust was recreational, Joggers over the years have consistently appeared in a range of competitive events. The name should, as a result, have long since been changed to reflect that, but it has stuck.

Group members have also given important backup to Inverness Harriers in areas such as catering and fundraising. It is almost invidious to pick out individuals, but from the very early days Bill Arthur and Bob Cooper were among the founding fathers. Two other stalwarts and driving forces were, and still are, the "Two Lizzes" - Forbes and Gray. There has always been a strong social component within the Joggers which has ranged from a Christmas night out to a midsummer barbecue, with a post-run cuppa an indispensable Wednesday night ritual. Joggers members also played a big part in organising the club's dinner dance which for a time hosted the end of season presentation of cross country and club handicap awards.

The Inverness District Sports Council fun run which superseded the road relay quickly expanded, and had a field of 500 in 1983. Then in July 1984 Inverness saw its first commercially run road event, the Turnbull Sports 10000m fun run, which also included a competitive 10K race.

By now Brian Turnbull had opened a sports and specialist running shop, initially in the Crown but latterly in Church Street and this event was partly an early effort to boost business. One consequence of this strategy of business promotion through athletics was some tension within the club. A number of members felt quite strongly that a body run by unpaid volunteers should not be allowed to become a vehicle for commercial gain.

Prime among a range of controversies was the formation of the Turnbull Sports Race Team whose members, largely recruited from leading Inverness Harriers youngsters, wore Turnbull Sports branded tracksuits to competitions. The main bone of contention was that this was a club within a club and Inverness Harriers' identity was being sacrificed for external commercial gain.

The inaugural Turnbull Sports race was one of the earlier 10Ks in the North since longer established events were normally in miles or were specific "point to points" such as Inverness to Drumnadrochit and Spean Bridge to Fort William. The entry was over 800 and it started and finished at the Town Hall, running over a very flat and fast course in the Dalneigh and Merkinch areas. However this doesn't quite explain the inaugural event's phenomenally fast times and a somewhat amended route was later used.

Callum Murray of the RAF won in an almost incredible 29:00. Graham Laing of Aberdeen was runner up in 29:11 and Inverness Harriers' star new recruit, Welshman Simon Axon was third in 29:41. Other leading Harriers were 9 - Donald MacMillan (30:50) 17 - Bobby MacDonald (32:43) 18 - Andrew Gordon 32:43 28 - John Day 35:04. George MacLennan was the first junior man in 33:08 and Lee Lobban, at 17, recorded 38:51.

Axon had just moved North to work at the Ardersier oil yard and effectively replaced the departed Kenney. So with Neil Martin also now on board, retaining the men's District Relay title in 1984 at Culloden Academy, with the additional support of Turnbull and Bobby

MacDonald, was almost a formality with an extended victory margin of a minute.

Despite Kenney's departure to Blackpool the men's team was now enjoying another period of North cross country domination, and one which was even more emphatic than in the late 70s. Next came the main District Championships at Fort William in February 1985 when Axon was runaway winner and the other Harriers counters were 4 - Brian Turnbull, 11 - Peter Golding, 13 - Alex Sutherland, 18 - Ross MacDonald 19 - Bobby MacDonald.

This took the incredibly tight team scores to - Inverness and Lochaber 66, Forres 67. The men's tie breaker rule of the day - compare the teams as if they were the only ones racing - still left deadlock. The secondary rule of better last finisher, which is now the only one used and is guaranteed to produce a result, then determined that Inverness Harriers had won their first North District men's cross country team title. With six to count rather than four in the league, the club had always regarded the District title as an especially tough nut to crack. This was a win so far matched only by the 1954 NSAAA success.

So with both SCCU district titles on board, a very first North clean sweep was in sight if the men could also land their first league success since 1979. That was achieved on home ground at Culloden on March 2nd. Runner up Axon was denied an individual clean sweep before Turnbull, MacLennan and Neil Martin completed a famous treble. In parallel, Catriona Bell secured the individual women's award and led a victorious team on a day which ended with five individual and four team successes across seven age groups. By now the Bells of Drumnadrochit - Jamie, Catriona and David - were prominent contributors. There were "Triple Bells" headlines when they had a clean sweep of all three individual South Highland schools titles.

March 1985 saw another new event, much more durable than the 10K which was discontinued in the early 1990s. The Inverness Half Marathon was the latest Turnbull creation and after he withdrew from event promotion before leaving Inverness, it transferred to a committee of volunteers. The leading lights for 20 years after that were Roy and Lorraine MacDonald who had strong Joggers roots but always ran the event separately from, but with the very supportive blessing of the club.

The Inverness Half has for a long time been based around the Bught but with the course mainly east of the Ness. However the earlier events started in Kenneth St and finished in the Northern Meeting Park with the initial stages and the 4 mile fun run via

Kinmylies. The inaugural winner from a field of over 600 was 1982 Commonwealth Games marathon runner Graham Laing in a very impressive 64:37 which is still a race record. Axon was runner up in 66:14 with George MacLennan, who had just reached the minimum age of 18, the next local in 72 minutes. The women's fun run was won by Catriona Bell a week before her schools international cross country debut in Wales.

These were also the earlier days of the career of George Mitchell, even though he became a 40 year old veteran in December 1985. That career still lasted almost 30 years and latterly took him to the top of the tree in the over 55 age groups. In July 1985 he completed the 28 mile Lairig Ghru race in a time of 4:17, three minutes ahead of clubmate Roy Morris.

September 1985 saw Inverness's third new road race in just over a year, this time promoted by the club. The Ness Motors "10" filled the gap between the 10K and the half marathon both in timing and distance. Over 200 runners tackled a course which included the old A9 north and a stiff hill in mile five at Delmore.

At the front was the familiar sight of Graham Laing (49:44) and Simon Axon (50:22) while Aberdeen's Lynda Bain's latest impressive appearance in Inverness gave her the women's race in 56:28. The host club won the team contest with Neil Martin, Ross MacDonald and Bob Cooper. The prizes included the Petty Rosebowl which had begun life with the Nairn to Inverness relay in 1953.

There was a strong start in the cross country league and the opening club handicap attracted a record 63 competitors, including 35 men. A month later there was another record of 112 runners in 22 teams for the Christmas relays where winning captain Jamie Bell

Jamie Bell in cross country action at Bught Park – mid 1980s.

had the fastest Whin Park lap of 8:33 for around 3K. The third league match at Elgin yielded thin pickings, not helped by a clash with the women's East District championships and a weakened men's team but number four in January 1986 made history. On a horrible day at Muir of Ord, Inverness Harriers became the first club to win all seven team events and remains the only club ever likely to pull off such a feat. Unusually, the league returned to the same venue five weeks later - and the club did the same again.

Come the final match in Inverness, but back at Charleston, Inverness Harriers became team champions in all four male age groups and in the Junior Women's, with second places in the Girls' and Women's. There were individual titles for Roma Davidson (Girls), Jenny Rankine (Junior Women), Chris Buchanan (Senior Boys), Neil Martin (Men) and Jimmy Neil (Veterans). This followed five team successes in the North District championships at Kinloss where the men failed to retain their crown.

The second Inverness Half Marathon attracted 1136 with over 400 in the fun run which, in practice, had already become a competitive short race for the club's youngsters and some seniors. Simon Axon, who had now moved to Aberdeen, won the half in 65:20 with success in the fun run for Alan Bone.

If anyone were to ask "who was the first Inverness Harrier to compete in the world championships?", most would say either Jayne Barnetson or Jamie Bowie. But the correct answer is actually Jamie Bell who, when Scotland still had separate cross country representation, was in the junior team in Neuchatel, Switzerland in March 1986. That came with a seventh place in the Scottish Championships. Coincidentally, this was almost exactly a decade on from his club's fortunes starting their battle upwards from absolute zero.

The ten years from 1976-86 had seen Inverness Harriers steadily establish itself as the North's top endurance running club. It was never complete domination, especially since the men were challenged regularly by Forres on road and country while Lochaber ruled hillrunning. A national cross country team title had been won along with a number of international honours, including this latest one on the world stage.

CHAPTER 7 – MORE HALCYON DAYS – TRACK AND FIELD
1987-91

The Commonwealth Games gave huge extra momentum which carried on into 1987 and beyond. The three athletes who competed in these Games enjoyed somewhat contrasting fortunes over the next year or two but all three became Scottish champions in 1987. That number of Scottish titles in a single day is in stark contrast with the 1950s belief that Inverness athletes just weren't good enough to contest national championships. Fraser set a native record of 14.31 to take his third 110s gold, Barnetson's ankle restricted her winning clearance to 1.83 and Patience made it three discus wins in a row with 51.44.

Come the end of the year at the SAAA AGM, Fraser was presented with the Crabbie Cup for the best performance at the senior championships. He still sees this as one of the highlights of his career. He said: *"Getting my name on that trophy meant a huge amount to me because it meant that I was able to share a place with all the megastars of athletics in Scotland over the years."*

July 1987 brought the Welsh Games in Swansea where Fraser's winning 14.11 was a Scottish national record which he held for another seven years. He also lowered the native record to 14.29 via 14.31 and clocked 14.17 for fifth in the 1987 UK championships. However a campaign to reach the 1988 Seoul Olympic qualifying standard of 13.94 failed to bear fruit.

Patience was another Welsh Games winner with 53.48 so two club records, which still stand in 2014, were set on the same day, July 11th 1987. That May, Patience competed in the Tokyo Highland Games, winning all five events, four with ground records. Then in June 1988, despite the prospect of at least one further Commonwealth selection, he decided to turn professional and concentrate on Highland Games so was completely lost to amateur athletics.

Fraser was among the first Inverness athletes to benefit from the new Kelvin Hall indoor arena where he set a Scottish indoor record of 7.90 for the 60 hurdles in February 1988 before heading back to hard winter training. Or so he thought, because it then emerged that he would be making his GB debut at the European indoor championships in Budapest where he ran 8.08.

Meanwhile Barnetson's relationship with the high jump became more and more ambiguous as it emerged that bone fragments were still lodged in her ankle and further treatment was needed. At one point in 1988 she even announced her retiral from the event and turned to the 400 hurdles, eventually clocking a very respectable 60.70 and, in a further demonstration of her versatility, receiving an international selection.

That first post-Commonwealth Games summer season of 1987 had its traditional start with the open meeting in April where £150,000 worth of new facilities, including a 600 seater grandstand, were being used at Queens Park for the first time. This source of shelter from the elements hugely increased the amenity of the track.

Just a few weeks before that season began, one of the club's high jumpers featured on the news pages. Jackie Lyall was at work in a Dingwall sports shop when she became aware that a man had left the premises wearing a £115 weatherproof jacket without paying. The Press and Journal reported that Jackie *"chased (the man) through the streets into a housing scheme and eventually on to the Kyle rail line near Dingwall Academy playing fields. At the railway the girl asked for the jacket back - and got it."*

Long Jump action at Queens Park

Fining the culprit £75, Sheriff James Fraser told him: *"You won't go back to MacLean's Sport in a hurry after that."* Jackie herself said: *"It was instinct that made me run after him and yes, I would do the same again in a similar situation. When I came face to face with him at the railway I just said 'you better let me have that back because the police are behind me' and he threw the jacket to me. I was away from the shop for 20 minutes."*

The main local attraction that year was the appearance of 1980 Olympic 100 metre champion Allan Wells at the Inverness Games. Promoters, the Inverness Amenities Association, were not quizzed too deeply about the arrangements! Despite being on painkillers for a groin injury Wells took his marks in the 100 handicap, predictably off scratch. But handicapper Ian Tasker was possibly just too much in awe of this sprinting legend and gave the rest of the field up to 17 metres start! So Wells, despite a very decent 10.5 on grass, never came close to reaching the final. This was won in 9.8 off 10.5 metres by Tain based Harrier Neil Munro, who was instantly dubbed "the man who beat Allan Wells". To his credit Wells asked for an extra 200 scratch to be organised and cruised to a 22.2 to 22.8 victory over Munro.

The next major new undertaking was entry, in 1987, to the Scottish Young Athletes' League for boys from 11-16, with the Queens Park facilities playing a big part in the process. The Courier reported in February 1987: *"The availability of both the Queens Park and a large number of qualified officials has won Inverness Harriers a place in the Scottish Young Athletes' League and a home match in the very first season. At one stage the Inverness club was in danger of being placed in the East section of the league instead of the North East section which involves much less travelling. However when they came up with the offer of the Queens Park, its attendant grandstand and the squad of 20 or so officials on their club books, the league was quick to agree to their requested placing and accept the offer of a venue."*

At the initial North East section meetings, Inverness and Aberdeen had a first and a second each in Dundee, both effectively wrapping up semi-final qualification. So the North East title would go to whoever won the third qualifier at Inverness and that was the new boys by 556 points to 504. Absent that June day were John Wilson and Harry Lakeland, officiating at the Kodak Classic in Gateshead.

A superb second place behind Pitreavie in the semi-final led to a debut year final. Here there was the warm glow of a close-up fourth behind Pitreavie, Clydebank and Ayr. Individual winners were future Scottish senior internationalists David Allan (discus) and David Barnetson (hurdles and high jump) while Paul Williamson took the under 13 long and high jumps.

Domestic championship success continued and the top performer in the 1987 North Districts was Neil Munro with 11.0 in the junior 100 and 11.2 in the senior before completing his treble with the senior 200 in 22.6. John Bowman, moving down in distance, set a championship record of 1:54.6 in the 800 and then, just 12 minutes later, started the 5000 but understandably finished outside the medals.

For the fourth time in as many years, a major Scottish schools trophy went to an Inverness Harrier when Alison Edmonds won the Barker Shield for a 12.4/26.0 under 15 sprint double. This prompted a debate about whether the best interests of a developing athlete were served by receiving such a high award at such an early age.

Hugely powerful for a young girl, Edmonds, from Aviemore, had been thriving under John Wilson's guidance and over the next couple of years her string of precocious performances continued. As an Intermediate in 1988, she beat reigning British schools champion Kathleen Lithgow in the East v West 100. She then missed retaining the Barker Shield despite a senior club record-equalling 12.0 and a phenomenal club record 24.9 because both times she was second to Lithgow. A week later she also became sole 100 record holder with 11.9, helping a North team, heavily dependent on Inverness Harriers, win the Scottish Schools inter district match for the sixth year in a row. She had distinguished Schools and Celtic International performances and SWAAA titles as well and even represented Scotland at senior level both indoors and out. But she was never the same athlete again after taking up a sports scholarship at Strathallan School.

Also at the 1988 Scottish schools championships, Heather MacLeod retained her under 17 discus title with 35.50 and had the possibly unique distinction of international selection in both discus and long jump. Debbie Douglas' short athletics career included under 15 schools gold in the 100 (12.9), long jump (5.10) and pentathlon while David Barnetson won the under 17 high jump with 1.99. Hours later he was named, along with his sister, to jump in the same Scottish senior team against Ireland and Iceland at Grangemouth. But there was less luck for sprinter Colin Allan. By no means the first athlete to confuse the ambiguous track markings at Grangemouth he slowed down after 90 metres and missed a medal.

That year's Scottish Young Athletes' League campaign almost came to grief in the semis. Confusion over travel arrangements led to two Scottish champions being left behind in Inverness but the now twice North East champions still qualified in third place. Also during these early years Charlie Forbes, the main team manager along with George MacRae, realised late one Saturday night that he had forgotten to book a bus. However one was miraculously obtained and, although it broke down at one point, no harm was done.

The 1988 final saw further dramatic improvement to second behind Clydebank and the Inverness winners included Colin Allan, Peter Bissett, Paul Williamson and Calum Jack. It didn't end there. For the first time the Scottish

Charlie Forbes and Audrey Munro at the finish of the Highland Cross in Beauly.

champions were invited to the English auxiliary final in Birmingham.

Clydebank were obliged to turn this down because they had become notorious for scouring the highways, the byways and South of the border for recruits, and their large English contingent would not be eligible. The offer then passed to Inverness who gladly accepted, despite having to raise over £2000 at a time when the club was seriously strapped for cash.

Almost inevitably the boys finished last in Birmingham against the best of British but made a great impression, winning 13 medals, including an under 13 "A" string gold for Andrew MacRae with a 1500 club record of 4:48.7. After the meeting, SYAL Vice Chairman George Duncan of Perth wrote to the Courier thanking local businesses which had helped get these "excellent ambassadors" to Birmingham. He said that the impact they had made, including the distribution of 130 sprigs of lucky white heather and, for each opposing team, an Inverness plaque, had helped ensure that the invitation to Scotland would become permanent.

This was the pinnacle of a tremendous 1988 league season which also included both NEL titles and promotion back to Division 1 of the SWAL. What set the women's team on the way back up after relegation in 1987 was a last gasp opening match victory. Going into the last event, Inverness trailed Victoria Park by two points before Lorna Ross, Eilidh Johnson, Sheila Campbell (Gollan) and Linda Wilson won the 4 x 400 in 4:13.5, and the match by a single point. During a lengthy period with the club Lorna was a mainstay of league teams in hurdles, sprints, and jumps and even did the odd cross country race.

In the face of such a high level of activity, club finances came under strain late in the summer of 1988, ironically just as the additional burden of the first trip to Birmingham became apparent. Thanks to a several hefty bills, the bank balance had dropped to just over £1000, a very small margin of safety for a club of over 300 members. An emergency sponsored run was held and various public bodies and businesses were approached as potential sponsors. Fundraising had simply not kept up with the steady expansion of activities.

1988 saw the return of Audrey Grant, now Audrey Munro, after an absence of 17 years and the timing was significant since Audrey had turned 35 and become a veteran. With Colin Baillie as coach, she was an instant success and within months ran comfortably under 13 seconds for the 100 and became Scottish veteran champion in all three sprints, both indoors and out. The British W35 indoor 60 and 200 titles came at Kelvin Hall early in 1989 as a long veteran career progressed.

The Kelvin Hall indoor arena was proving a great asset. Apart from its role in Fraser's European selection, it helped Jayne Barnetson to a Scottish indoor record of 1.86. Meanwhile David improved there to 2.10 before clearing a Scottish junior record of 2.12 for senior AAAs bronze at RAF Cosford.

One of the main financial solutions was the development of commercial sponsorships, with a lot of work done by Turnbull. The 1989 open meeting was supported by Hugh MacRae the Builders to the tune of £1200. Welcome though the support was, the spirit of these deals did not sit comfortably with some of the club's volunteers who felt that ordinary club members were being sidelined in the face of sponsors. At one point the perceived incongruity of sponsors sipping wine and munching prawn sandwiches in the stand as sprinters thundered down the straight did receive some adverse comment.

At the beginning of the 1989 summer season, Mel Fowler made his first impact on the fortunes of Inverness Harriers. From the Glasgow area and a PE graduate of Jordanhill, Mel had just joined Northern Constabulary. He was already a GB junior long jumper but his versatility spread right across the sprints and jumps and even further. Among his first actions in a maroon and gold vest was to break the oldest club record, Ian Tasker's 13.67 triple jump set in 1967. Mel jumped 13.93 at the District Championships where Tasker happened to be jumps referee. He then went on to take the long jump record to a new level of 7.03. On a day when 51 medals, including 21 gold, came to Inverness, John Bowman had an excellent 3:54.2 in the 1500 while Grant McDowall, still a junior, had a 400/800 double of 50.8/1:57.5. Simultaneously the women took 11 medals, including four gold, in the East championships at Meadowbank.

That June saw two athletes steal the show in very different events. At Grangemouth, Edmonds became the third Inverness Harrier of the decade to make a senior international debut at just 16, against Ireland and Greece. She won the 200 in 25.12 after a Greek opponent was disqualified for a lane infringement. Nearer home, David Barnetson brought the South Highland Schools to an absolute standstill with a stunning display of high jumping. Everything simply stopped amid outbreaks of spontaneous cheering as he bagged height after height to clear 2.10 before three failures at the 2.13 European Junior qualifying. That was a target which remained unrealised after injury intervened.

Future senior internationalists like Fraser, MacMillan, Patience, Leighton, Devine and his own sister had gone through the South Highland schools before him, so Barnetson's performance was just the latest in a series of incredible meeting records by club athletes at this local school championship.

When she took her second and third attempts at 1.86 with a broken ankle in the 1986 Commonwealth Games, Jayne Barnetson had shown never-say-die qualities. These should have made it fairly clear that her declared retiral from serious high jumping would not be an end of it. Steadily, clearances in the lower 1.80s edged into the upper bracket as that Meadowbank nightmare become a more distant memory. Then on Friday July 7th 1989 she returned to that very same Meadowbank high jump area for the Miller Lite Grand Prix, one of several high profile events Meadowbank was attracting at that time.

She has always called the clearance "jammy" and the bar did rattle frighteningly, but it stayed on for a new national record of 1.91 and, for the first time, the native record as well. This also put the "ex-high jumper" top of the British rankings and gave her the single selection for the European Cup final in Gateshead. Here her fourth place with 1.85 helped the British team to third in the women's match.

During that July weekend, Jayne was one of no fewer than 11 Inverness Harriers in international action at three different venues. David Allan (hammer) and Heather MacLeod (discus) won their events for Scotland juniors/under 17s at Dumfries. Unfortunate fixtures scheduling created a clash with the Schools International in Dublin and two of a record eight team members there had to turn Dumfries down. The Inverness schools eightsome comprised Debbie Douglas (80H and LJ), Magnus Smith (100H), Ingram Murray (400H and 4 x 400), Duncan Hards (1500SC), Alison Edmonds (100, 200, 4 x 100), Sebastian Whyte (HJ), Colin Allan (200) and Darren Sutherland (4 x 400).

However the schools international results, headed by Whyte's third place with 1.95, produced a rare disappointment with most performances towards the back of the field. Perhaps the club's expectations had been exaggerated by the huge achievements of a slightly older, once in a lifetime generation. On the other hand to have eight members of one Scottish Schools team at all was a major achievement and contrasted starkly with the thin pickings of some later years.

The 1989 senior championships produced silvers for three Scottish senior internationalists, all with club records, either new or equalled. Devine threw the hammer 57.40, Fowler long jumped 7.23 and David Barnetson's first time clearance at 2.10 lifted him from sixth to second. One other club record was the junior 800 for Grant McDowall with 1:54.69. The man whose record he broke, Donald MacMillan now representing Durham AC, ran almost the equivalent of a 4 minute mile for bronze in the 1500 with 3:43.42.

It just got better and better in the SYAL where Inverness Harriers won the 1989 final at just the third attempt with 774 points from Pitreavie (722) in Glasgow. What no one foresaw was that this was the first of five titles in the six seasons from 1989-94. This was a formidable record for any club, never mind one based in a sparsely populated peripheral area, and a tribute to the efforts of George MacRae, Charlie Forbes and other team managers. It also created the annual need to fund the trip to Birmingham which competitively was always an uphill struggle.

Jayne Barnetson's 1988 dalliance with the 400 hurdles was only brief and later that year she developed her transition to the heptathlon, winning the Scottish title with 5331 points before a national record of 5606 in Prague. She rounded off the 1989 summer season with a further record of 5803 for Great Britain in Kiev. Jayne arrived there fatigued by a long journey after a late switch from Riga for security reasons, amid the death throes of the Eastern bloc Communism which had denied her two major medals. Her performances were: JT - 43.14, SP - 11.63, 100H - 14.50, 200 - 25.29, HJ - 1.85, LJ -5.87, 800 - 2:20.0. The first four were personal bests and the first three club records. Adding earlier efforts in high jump, long jump and 400 hurdles, between 1988 and 1989 Jayne set six senior club records, all of which but the shot still stand quarter of a century later. Her two days in Kiev ended in a medical room with an extremely scary looking Soviet woman doctor demanding a urine sample for a drugs test.

It was an injury-blighted year for Fraser who at one stage said: *"I'm really at my wit's end with this. I'm desperately keen to get to my second Commonwealth Games but I've had so many setbacks it's not true. There's no way I'm giving up though."* The Commonwealth qualifying standard of 14.00 was 0.11 inside his national record and his bid would now have to wait until the winter season. A mid-winter Southern hemisphere Games in New Zealand meant a chance to bid for separate standards indoors.

The prospects of a second Commonwealth Games tragically fell apart towards the end of 1989 for both Harriers. With standards of 1.88 and 5400 comfortably achieved, Jayne was selected for both events. Her indoor programme was a vital part of her Games preparation and it included a 60 hurdles at Bathgate in November. However the inherent instability of her left ankle caused a fall coming off a hurdle, creating further serious damage. She was hospitalised immediately and a fortnight later, Inverness Harriers' and Scotland's firm double medal prospect announced her withdrawal from the Games.

This is an appropriate point to conclude the tale of the athlete who is arguably the greatest Harrier of all time, because that race in Bathgate was effectively her last. In August 1990, at the age of just 22, she announced her complete retiral. Eight months after further surgery the ankle was still sore even to jog on, so the end of the road had come. Twice she had potential Commonwealth honours snatched from her by injury and had finished a galling fourth in the World and European junior championships. She must be among the best athletes never to win a medal at a major championship.

Fraser, meanwhile, had recovered from his hamstring injuries and was preparing for an assault on the 8.00 standard, 0.10 outside his national record, required over 60 hurdles indoors to go to the Games. As in 1986, selection went right down to the last race, the Scottish indoor championships at Kelvin Hall. Here a clash with the first hurdle caused a cut knee. Far worse still it cost him a team place because he crossed the line in 8.01. On the strength of that hundredth of a second - about three inches - the selectors declined to take him.

There is a supreme irony here. The 1980s had been a dream decade for Inverness Harriers, but it ended most tragically for the club's two greatest athletes so far, who had done so much to put the club where it was.

A very overdue development finally came in the spring of 1990 with entry to the SAL, the Men's League, which had been discussed on and off since 1982. Now, spurred on by the enthusiasm of Colin Baillie as team manager, this eventually came to pass. As with the women, there was a qualifying match for the bottom of four divisions and the club again produced a sledgehammer to crack a nut. On their books were five senior internationalists plus several junior and former schools representatives. This was more than enough firepower for the lower divisions at least.

One big problem was the extended uncertainty over the eligibility of some of the leading athletes. To obtain better competition, some of the top stars like Fraser and Dave Barnetson had joined British League clubs such as Edinburgh Southern and Edinburgh AC, but only second claim to maintain first claim status for Inverness Harriers. However English club politics intervened and the BAL decided to become first claim only. Given the importance of BAL competition, the Inverness athletes were, very reluctantly, forced to change their first claims. Then the process entered a period of much coming and going, brinkmanship and total confusion when Inverness Harriers didn't know whether they could use some of their very best athletes. Eventually the issue was satisfactorily resolved by a rule which allowed Scottish League clubs to use secondary first claim athletes, which the top names immediately became.

The incongruity of the overdue SAL entry was probably epitomised by Dave Barnetson's league record of 2.06 in the qualifying match in April 1990. He was one of six internationalists, three of them full, on a day when Fraser and Bowman were still to make their mark.

Another was Devine who won the shot (13.50) and discus (41.94) but, in a very rare incursion into the javelin, was almost defeated by his own team mate. Indeed it was only in the very last round that he threw 40.32 to better the 36.38 of..... that dying swan of the Edinburgh Commonwealth Games, javelin official and coach Brian Ross! By pure coincidence, Russell's throw exactly equalled Brian's club record. As winners of every single field event and totally dominant on the track, the team cruised into this league.

Inverness Harriers were by far the strongest team in Division 4 that summer and apart from the international athletes there were also very solid contributors like 400 hurdler Alistair Taylor and sprinters Sean Main and Mike Barron. In league conditions, good all-rounders like Taylor, Barnetson and Fowler were worth their weight in gold as the team progressed majestically to straight wins and the title.

The Queens Park provided the opportunity for home matches in national leagues, and the club hosted SWAL Divisions 1 and 2 as it moved between them. Something which never failed to amuse a host club for which the A9 had been a way of life for 15 years was the almost inevitable lateness of the team from Glasgow! One considerable asset at these meetings was a large squad of local officials, and not just performing basics. Leading officials, many capable of referee roles, included seasoned campaigners like Harry Lakeland, John Wilson, Ian Tasker, Brian and Trish Ross and Hilary MacLean. Of these, Brian also became a starter, Hilary the club secretary and John and Harry SAAA North District secretaries.

In 1990, David Barnetson cracked the world junior qualifying standard of 2.15, losing AAA junior gold on countback only to be denied a place by two athletes who had earlier jumped even higher. Meanwhile Fraser's injury bugbear at least gave him brief relief and 14.28 in the UK championships yielded his first outdoor GB vest against Finland in Helsinki that June. Then Devine, at the early age for a hammer thrower of 22, blasted through the 60 metre mark for the first time to win the Scottish title by four metres with 61.90.

By the summer of 1990 I was beginning to become concerned that performances in the main body of the club were showing signs of decline, albeit still minor ones. Only time would tell whether this was just a temporary blip or something more profound, but I did gently raise the issue in some Courier reports. School competition results are always a very good barometer and on June 8th I commented: *"In the wake of Saturday's low key secondary inter school sports, performances were also on the disappointing side in Tuesday's Milk In Action North schools championships at Queens Park."*

I then noted that just one female record had been broken at the North schools championships and that the fastest girls' 100 time across the two meetings had been an extremely modest 13.3. However attention had possibly been diverted by recent league successes, despite the criteria for such success being less dependent on the absolute quality of performances. I concluded: *"North schools officials are not looking forward with as much enthusiasm as usual to the Scottish Schools inter district match at Grangemouth on 21st June where they bid to maintain their seven year unbeaten record."*

And so, unfortunately, it transpired. The North, thanks largely to Inverness Harriers athletes, had won this match every year since its inception in 1983. But here for the first time victory had to be conceded to Dumbarton, with the weakness indeed on the girls' side.

En route to retaining their SYAL title, by 38.5 points from Ayr Seaforth, the team had to survive a bus breakdown. However another trip to Birmingham was finally secured at the end of a season which had produced victory in all five SYAL matches. The same day the men won 25 out of 33 events to add a clean sweep of all four SAL fixtures. Then the incredibly versatile Mel Fowler's 2:03.9 800 victory contributed to the men winning back their NEL title. However an alarming third in the North East women's contest and a less than inspiring SWAL campaign suggested that, even in leagues, there may be the beginnings of a problem on the female side in particular. On the other hand a complex ranking process made Inverness Harriers fifth top track and field club in Scotland that summer.

Sheila Gollan won the Hunter Cup for the top senior woman for her European Police 800 gold in Berlin in 2:10.35, a club record to add to her 1500 and 3000 of 1990. Also in Berlin was Fowler, now stationed at Dunvegan on Skye and with only a pavement and a primary school hall for training. This enforced a switch to sprints and writing his schedule proved an interesting exercise. He overcame these difficulties splendidly to finish fifth in the 400 and win silver in both relays.

There had been a midsummer crisis when Alan Hards, a central figure in the club, suddenly stood down as President for personal reasons. Vice President Kenny MacKay was working out of town and unavailable, so Harry Lakeland stood in for another term. That was confirmed at the 1990 AGM of a club which had now expanded to 335 members.

The new committee and office bearers were - President - Harry Lakeland, vice President - Colin Baillie, secretary - Ann Kemlo, treasurer - Liz Forbes, membership secretary - George MacRae. Sub committee conveners: coaches and officials - Brian Ross, finance and social - Lily Baillie, track and field - Charlie Forbes, road, hill and country - Paul Crowe, jogging - Maggie Roger, public relations - Robbie Munro. Committee members - Mel Fowler, John Findlayson, Audrey Munro, Mike Barron.

In 1988 the committee had created the club's first Honorary Life Members - founder Tom MacKenzie, past President and Treasurer George Bannerman and Walter Banks, the club's long time man at the SCCU. In 1990 it was decided to extend life membership to a tiny elite of eminent athletes who had become full GB internationalists. The first awards therefore went to Neil Fraser and Jayne Barnetson.

Financial woes returned over the winter of 1990-91 and Lakeland expressed his dismay that of 300 members, only 80 had taken part in a sponsored run. Worse still, two months later only 35 had returned a total of just £450 in the face of travelling expenses alone of £3500.

President Alan Hards hands over the club's first Honorary Life Membership certificates to Walter Banks, George Bannerman and Tom MacKenzie - 1988

Then the inability to find a sponsor caused the loss of an £11,500 District Sports Council grant towards a £45,000 administrative and changing room block. By now the District Council had added a small first aid and toilet facility. The only other accommodation was the original huts which, more than six years on, were showing their age. One very helpful intervention came from Highland Games heavy Bob Colquhoun who undertook a sponsored caber toss at all eight North amateur games venues in a single day.

At the 1991 open meeting, David Allan blasted through 50 metres with the hammer for the first time with 50.84 and Heather MacLeod returned to competition with 34.80 in the discus before progressing her club record up to 37.50. This followed a serious knee injury after landing in an over-hard Queens Park long jump pit at the previous year's Hunter Construction Cup match against Aberdeen. At 38, Audrey Munro set a "second career best" of 12.7 to beat husband Robbie by 0.2 in the 100.

On May 21st 1991 a very large Courier headline read **"Mighty Mel cops six of the best"** above a story beginning *"Inverness policeman Mel Fowler hauled five individual titles into protective custody at Saturday's Autosales North District Championships at Queens Park and then apprehended a sixth gold medal in the relay."* Performances on a wet and miserable day were unimportant but the individual titles embraced all three sprints and both horizontal jumps.

The Scottish schools' Eric Liddell Trophy came North again amid more unease about a principal award going to an under 15 athlete. This time it was a Tain based Harrier Stuart Sutherland - known as "Bubbles" because he was the younger brother of Darren Sutherland who went under the name of "Suds". Stuart won the under 15 400 by all of four seconds with a new record of 53.1. There was some relief that performances seemed to have improved again. The North, with Inverness Harriers leading the charge, won 12 gold, 10 silver and 7 bronze. However, in line with previous concerns, of these 29 medals, only eight went to girls.

The backbone of the North medal haul at the boys' championship was a 40 minute purple patch where members of the Gerry Barnes - Charlie Forbes group won two gold and two silver. Apart from the "Bubbles'" gold, Ingram Murray prevailed in the over 17 400 in 50.9 as he, Fowler and Barnetson vied to become the first Harrier to break 50. Stewart MacKay became the first under 17 to crack 9 minutes for the 3000 with 8:56.5 for silver, matched in the corresponding 800 by Mark Cruden (2:02.2). The top North medal winner was Scott Fraser who took gold in both the under 14 100 (12.5) and 200 (25.5) and soon came under the wing of coach John Wilson.

The throws were also progressing well and David Allan, in the hammer at the Welsh Games, became the club's ninth Scottish senior internationalist since Fraser's and Leighton's pioneering selections a decade previously. Heather MacLeod, who had missed out on four consecutive Scottish schools titles by going to Stirling University a year early, continued to collect junior discus selections. Meanwhile javelin thrower Elaine McQueen and shot putter Alastair MacKenzie were among six Harriers in the 1991 under 17 schools international. There was now an under 20 fixture against Wales where Duncan Hards false started once and only avoided disqualification by persuading the starter that his second premature emergence had been prompted by a camera clicking spectator! He went on to finish third in 56.8.

David Barnetson

David Barnetson became the club's first Great Britain internationalist in the new under 23 age group when another 2.15 sent him to Spain against the host nation, France and Germany. Another first saw Donald Tuach return from the Special Olympics in Minneapolis for athletes with a learning disability with a medal of each colour. The club's first disability athlete took 100 bronze, high jump silver and ran the decisive leg in the 4 x 400 relay. Sheila Gollan captained the women's East District team which defeated the west at Coatbridge.

The final Men's League match at Crownpoint, Glasgow secured the Division 3 title and extended the unbeaten run to all eight matches across two seasons. The cornerstone was a throws treble from Devine, including 57.22 in the hammer. However the occasion was marred when John Bowman, on his way home from holiday in Portugal, had his car broken into during the match and much of his holiday luggage was stolen. This brought home the harsh reality that the problems of this East End venue were rather more real than a few "mind yer moturr misturr?" jokes. To his credit, Bowman lifted himself to win the 800 "B" in a perfunctory 2:01.8 before making an early departure.

On another less fraught occasion, Bowman and MacKenzie had been embroiled in some trackside debate or other when they heard the gun go off. They looked up and saw the runners in their 5000 heading round the bend. Instantly fearful of the wrath of Baillie, they sprinted to the start, crossed the line and proceeded to pull in the entire field to salvage maximum points.

There now intervened a single glitch in the run of SYAL titles. In 1991 the honours had to be conceded to Ayr Seaforth despite four wins for Ross Ruickbie in the under 13 high jump "A" (1.40), shot (7.63), 400 (65.4) "B" and the 4 x 400. By now Kenny Kemlo was contributing unprecedented pole vault points, winning the under 17 with 2.80. The star effort came from Barry Smith who got very close to Thain's high powered under 17 100 hurdles club record with 13.6.

The Highland Games were continuing to fulfil a peripheral role with Inverness, Forres, Nairn and Glenurquhart the most popular. There has always been a special relationship between the club and the Glenurquhart Games which was a real favourite among the big hitters. In 1991 Devine, one of eight Harriers internationalists, won the heavyweight title. The Provost Fraser and Balmacaan Cups for the light events went to schools 400 internationalist Morven Fraser and Mel Fowler, but Fowler still wasn't finished. He started the 250m Auld Scottish Kilt Race off a distant back mark and still caught everyone. However this was not unprecedented since he once revealed that when called upon to chase villains, he would sometimes wait for a second or two *"just to make it a bit more interesting"*!

That year's club championships took a big step forward with a £1500 sponsorship from Tulloch Homes. Events took place across eight club nights after the schools returned in August, with a printed programme widely distributed. But in later years, as they declined, the championships shifted to the late season open meetings. More recently they have returned to the highly successful 1991 format as membership and motivation have recovered again. There was also a new award, the George Bannerman Memorial Trophy for the top performer in the club championships, and the inaugural winner was Ross Ruickbie in the under 13 boys' age group.

That Tulloch sponsorship, along with £2000 from fundraising, led to a much healthier financial situation and Treasurer Liz Forbes reported to the AGM that the cash balance had doubled to £5000. However it was not all upbeat since my concerns over performances had deepened and the Courier revealed that: *"In presenting his annual report, Charles Bannerman said that for the first time there was a significant note of pessimism in what he had to say, with definite evidence of declining standards - even against a generally declining Scottish scene."*

I went on to elaborate on a drop in performance levels in some events and some junior age groups and, for the first time in years, in membership. That was partly due to a decrease in Joggers' numbers and Black Isle now vigorously recruiting athletes from Ross-shire. Regarding performances, I emphasised some external factors but also internal ones such as a shortage of coaches, especially in the jumps. These early signs of decline were also predominantly on the female side, and we now know that what was delaying a corresponding trend with the men was a bubble of talent which was beginning to move up through the system.

However I also went out of my way to highlight what was still very much right, and that it was a very high peak from which patchy declines had now become apparent. With the benefit of hindsight, there were also two factors which were not realised at the time. These were that club had been benefiting from a generation of talent which might never be repeated and the effect of the reduction in athletes from Ross shire with its highly efficient schools set up.

It seems unfortunate to end a chapter on such a note of pessimism, but history has to reflect reality. What I had highlighted was the very beginning of a long period of relative decline from the probably unrepeatable days of the 1980s. However in many areas, the 1990s still had a lot to offer and celebrate in track and field.

CHAPTER 8 – THE BUBBLE BEGINS TO BURST – TRACK AND FIELD 1992-97

Despite apprehensions about a fall in some standards, the senior men remained a formidable force. In 1991, Inverness Harriers' men commanded 18 of the North's 21 Scottish top 20 listings. These included top place in the hurdles for the injured Fraser with 14.51 and runner up spots for Devine (60.28 in the hammer) and Barnetson (2.11 in the high jump). Early in 1992, all three were named in the Preparation Squad for the 1994 Commonwealth Games in Canada. Allan, Fowler and a few others were also highly ranked.

In contrast, several senior women had departed. Apart from Barnetson's enforced retiral, Alison Edmonds had gone and Sheila Gollan's availability was limited. Soon after, she moved to Edinburgh Woollen Mill for UKWAL competition. The two fastest female sprinters now were the veteran Audrey and near-veteran Dianne.

A club like Inverness Harriers also suffers from athletes becoming students and leaving the area for much of the year. It was fortunate that a nucleus of men had remained in the North to lessen the effect of the departures. Then there was growing concern over declining standards among the young athletes, initially the girls and some boys' field events, with attendant serious implications for future senior prospects.

The indoor highlights of 1991-92 predictably came from Fraser and Barnetson. Neil rubbed shoulders with Commonwealth champion Mark McKoy and world champion in waiting Colin Jackson to record a fast 8.02 in the 60 hurdles at the Prudential Classic at the Kelvin Hall. Soon after Dave, who had cleared 2.15 in Norway, took his Scottish indoor record to 2.16.

The summer of 1992 was paradoxical because it produced the greatest league positions to date in parallel with a worrying decline in many performance levels.

The men's and women's teams began on the same late-April Sunday, in Macbeth-like conditions of "thunder, lightning or in rain". By the end of the season the men, previously champions of Divisions 4 and 3, were runners up to Falkirk Victoria in Division 2. Just like the women nine years earlier, this was a transition from Division 4 to Division 1 in straight seasons. Meanwhile the women pulled off three straight wins in Division 2 to bounce back up to the now fairly familiar top flight. Unsurprisingly the President's Trophy that year went jointly to the men's and women's team managers Colin Baillie and John

Wilson because league success is often as much due to management as to athletes.

The boys cruised through the earlier stages of the SYAL for a third national title in four years. Although last in the English final once

Men's League Team 1992
Rear – John Bowman, Graham Laing, Alan Kemlo, David Barnetson, Cammy Roger, George MacRae
Front – Colin McClean, Charlie Forbes, Colin Baillie (Team Manager), Stan MacKenzie.

Photo Ewen Weatherspoon

again, they won 17 medals, but just two in the field. Pride of place went to the rapidly improving Scott Fraser who won the under 15 100 and 200 in 11.62/23.53. Timmy Black was second in the under 17 100 in 11.34 and made a rare step up to win the 400 B in 51.59. In terms of national leagues, Inverness Harriers could look forward to 1993 as members of Division 1 of both the men's and women's leagues for the first time, and as defending SYAL champions.

Individually, Dave Barnetson broke Geoff Parsons' Queens Park record and the North championship record with 2.17 before missing a Scottish native record of 2.19. At the same meeting, Grant McDowall, just 20, neared his 800 best with a championship record of 1:53.6.

Fowler won four senior titles to raise his four year haul to 16. However, despite a bigger programme, the club's overall medal haul of 21 gold, 11 silver and 9 bronze was its lowest for seven years and the field events suffered especially badly. Barnetson later missed the Olympic trials due to injury, but took his first Scottish senior title along with the native record of 2.19. This meant that brother and sister now held the two high jump native records. This was a remarkable achievement which must be unique in the annals of athletics in Scotland.

The barometer of the Scottish Schools, which has always tended to give an accurate reading both of where the club is and is likely to be in the immediate future, told a mixed story. The boys took 17 medals, including 7 gold, but the girls won just four bronze. A second generation Harrier, Iain Wallace son of Mike and Maureen, gained a second international selection, taking the under 17 100 in 11.2. He was the club's only selection for the schools international where he ran a very fast 11.0. There was a corresponding under 15 Scottish schools success for Scott Fraser (11.6) before his international debut at the Celtic Games.

Another warning came when the North team, critically dependent on Inverness Harriers athletes, lost the schools Inter District match for only the second time since it began in 1983. This again was due to a weaker girls' side although Elaine MacQueen took the javelin with a throw of 30.66.

Then at the SAAA/SWAAA age group championships the boys won three gold, four silver and two bronze while Janice Forbes' under 13 discus gold was the only female success. The boys' winners included javelin thrower Alan Kemlo in the under 20 age group. He had recently become the first Harrier to throw over 50 metres and this time reached 48.38. This gained him selection for an under 20 international in Antrim where his pole vaulter brother Kenny was in the under 17 event.

Late in July the long arm of the law extended to Whitehaven in Cumbria where an all-international trio of Harriers from Northern Constabulary scooped four golds in the British Police Championships. Gollan won the 800 and, by 14 seconds, the 1500. The other two successes came from Grant McDowall in the men's 800 and Fowler who, despite the restrictions of Dunvegan, returned to long jumping with a very healthy 6.92. That he was able to do this in such a restricted athletic environment on Skye was a major achievement and a tribute to the versatility of one of the greats of Inverness Harriers track and field.

Late in August 1992 I wrote a piece in the Courier under the Blytonesque headline **"The mystery of the missing sprinters."** By now, women running sub-13 for the 100 had gone from commonplace to a rarity. I also observed that *"It is an even sadder fact that the only sprinter in the North to have broken 13 seconds with any consistency over the last three seasons is veteran champion Audrey Munro of Inverness Harriers who will be 40 years old next January."* Another athlete of an earlier era, Linda Wilson, despite virtually no training due to nursing shifts, was more or less the only other. A short lived attempt by Jayne Barnetson to return as a sprinter in 1993 saw her run 26.3 for the 200 – the fastest by a Harrier for four years.

Jimmy Neil, Audrey Munro and Bill Arthur at the Scottish Vets' Championships around 1990

Committee and Officials – 1992.
Rear – _Cammy Roger_, John Findlayson, Charlie Forbes, John Sinclair, George MacRae.
Middle – Kerry Wheeler, Lorna Benson (Ross), Julie Wilson, Phyllis Law, Mairi Wheeler, Maggie Roger, Ann Kemlo, Kenny MacKay.
Front – Alan Hards, Andy Law, Liz Forbes, Monica Findlayson, Harry Lakeland (President), Colin Baillie, Walter Banks, Tom MacKenzie, Brian Ross.
Photo Ewen Weatherspoon

The Queens Park was closed for several weeks that summer for an upgrade so the club had to decant temporarily to Millburn. The track still hosted the Scottish Veteran Championships where Audrey won the 35-39 400 in 67.8, raising her tally of gold to "around 20" (she had actually lost count). Other champions were Bill Arthur in the over 60 sprints and Highland Games heavies Ally Munro and Bob Colqhoun in the throws.

A relatively low key indoor season saw Gollan make her indoor debut in an international 3000 against Wales in February 1993 at the Kelvin Hall. Neil Fraser won another indoor hurdles title and Scott Fraser took medals in the under 15 sprints. When the 1992 outdoor rankings came out that February, the only top 20 Scottish entries by senior women were Heather MacLeod, 6th in the discus with 39.46, and Gollan 12th in the 800 (2:13.6), 11th in the 1500 (4:28.84) and 14th in the 3000 (9:46.1). The men had 13 entries, a drop from 18 in 12 months, while the young athletes' showing again proved patchy.

New boys' age groups, moved from 1st January to 1st September in line with the girls, were introduced in the summer of 1993. This meant that the boys' under 13, 15 and 17 club records could no longer stand and it proved impossible over the years to amend them. Consequently, under 17 marks like Devine's superb 59.72 hammer and 16.95 shot and Barnetson's 2.06 high jump, and several others of similar quality, have been in limbo ever since.

By now Devine, after emigrating to Australia, had effectively been lost to the club, but he remained a member. His massive 63.00 hammer throw in Melbourne in December 1992 therefore became the first club record set in the Southern Hemisphere. This put him right into contention for the 1994 Commonwealth Games in Canada. He was joined in Australia for six months by David Allan who returned home to win the inaugural SAF North District hammer with 55.04, an effort challenged by the shock of an extreme weather change! These were the first official joint North championships for men and women and the combined medal haul was 47 gold, more than half the total, 25 silver and 18 bronze.

Allan threw 56.46 in the second Men's League Division 1 match but the team still dropped to joint bottom. He then dashed off to Glasgow Airport to join Fraser and the rest of a Scottish team for Tel Aviv. By now the Men's League team ranged from youngster Paul MacIntyre in the steeplechase to veteran Cammy Roger in the hammer. But it was a short stay at the top, with an immediate return to Division 2 in 1994.

Despite the individual performance decline being so far more marked on the female side, the women stayed in Division 1 for the first time ever. This was not the only time league results would appear insulated from individual shortcomings. The likely reasons are that the rest of Scotland was also in decline by now and that a still relatively large club could simply fill places "for the point(s)" with quality no longer all that vital. The apparent buoyancy of league results probably helped delay the realisation that a real performance crisis was biting.

A first ever SWAL home match in June 1993, thanks to a reduction of the division to the six teams the Queens Park could accommodate, also helped survival. Predictably the central belt clubs showed their customary reluctance to travel. By now the men's and women's teams were both boosted by second claim athletes from the rest of the North and that home match produced an unprecedented fourth place. This was also the placing in the next match away from home and for the season. That a team which was now seriously struggling for quality should be able to achieve this posed serious questions about standards in Scottish women's athletics.

Meanwhile the boys registered a fourth SYAL victory in five years by their biggest margin to date, 76 points from Minolta Black Isle, with Aberdeen a further 50 adrift.

1993 saw the local introduction of two initiatives which arguably accelerated the country-wide decline which was already in its early stages. Sportshall Athletics was an indoor variant, using a range of customised equipment. This included foam javelins and "reversaboards" to allow races to be run between games hall walls. Sportshall did help provide competition in remote areas such as Shetland and Argyll, and for very young children. However there was the concern that it promoted a dumbing down of the sport at a time when fitness and conditioning were already suffering from a lower and lower priority. Sportshall also claimed to be a means of club recruitment, but in Inverness at least this worked in reverse. Rather than youngsters joining the club from Sportshall, the club was being called on to bail out local Sportshall teams in regional and national competitions.

The other buzz word was "Fun Athletics" which led to a further dumbing down through a serious undermining of training methodologies. "Fun Athletics" was being promoted by SAF development officer Graham Ross and my personal view is that it was precisely the wrong methodology at the wrong time. Dubbed "beanbags and hulahoops" by some of its many opponents, "Fun Athletics" saw levels of physical activity in clubs drop alarmingly. This was just at a time when more sedentary lifestyles needed compensated for by a more rather than a much less rigorous regime.

At Inverness Harriers, the mid 1990s saw a serious drop off in work ethic and commitment to sound conditioning, just when quite the opposite should have been an urgent priority. This would have devastating implications for performance standards for years to come.

1993 also saw a relaxation of the strict Corinthian rules of the last 110 years. Amateurs were now allowed to compete in so-called "professional" meetings, if they had SAF permits, and the "pros" were accepted into amateur competition. Clearly this would principally involve the Highland Games although Inverness athletes did not depart their own code to any great extent.

Fowler, still in Dunvegan, did however want to do the 1993 Skye Games and the club ensured that the promoters had the necessary permit. Mel duly came off traffic duty in Portree and proceeded to wipe the floor with the professionals with a string of wins. This apparently did not go down well in pedestrian circles and, miraculously, the following year's Skye Games somehow omitted to acquire that permit.

Fowler then wrapped up the amateur circuit with a flourish when he cleared 13.79 to break Tasker's Glenurquhart Games 1967 triple jump record of 13.67. He had improved this figure as a club record in his first act as an Inverness Harrier in 1989, but took four more years to do it at the Games. This was one of his six wins that day and Tasker was first to congratulate him.

Scott Fraser had a great year and at just 15 set a club under 17 100 record of 10.86 to win the invitation race alongside the GB v USA international at Meadowbank that July. His 1992 best was 11.5 and the previous record was Ronnie Sharp's highly respectable 10.9. Fraser was also one of a disappointingly sparse crop of Scottish schools medallists, and the only Harrier in that year's under 17 international where he ran 10.99 in 6th place.

Tiny 60 pupil Kilchuimen Academy in Fort Augustus achieved its first Scottish schools gold through Alastair Watson in the over 17 hammer (35.92) with a triple input from Inverness Harriers. Julie Wilson was now the PE teacher there and enlisted help from Harry Lakeland and technological studies teacher Brian Donaldson, who was now poised to make a very telling contribution to the club.

One other outstanding schools performance came from David Cotter of Nairn who ran secondary first claim for Inverness. He won the under 17 100 hurdles in an impressive 13.5. This instantly put him straight into the same bracket as Andrew Thain and the young Neil Fraser and he soon claimed a GB junior vest. David Allan meanwhile got closer to 60 metres with 58.42 for his first Scottish senior hammer title.

There was a more gratifying 4 gold, 3 silver and 3 bronze at the now combined under 13 and under 15 boys' and girls' championships in Grangemouth. Of these, 2 gold, 1 silver and 2 bronze went to the Broadbent twins, under 13s Adam and Oliver who were fine all-rounders.

At the end of July, David Barnetson thought he had made a wise choice of Moscow with the GB under 23s rather than Belgium with Scotland. But, apart from a season's best of 2.13, his decision to visit Russia soon after the collapse of Communism wasn't such a good idea. He said: *"Our hotel was meant to be one of the better ones in Moscow and it was incredible. There were cockroaches everywhere! The room was teeming with them and they were even coming out of the fridge. We just had to hope and pray that the things weren't in our beds as well. But we weren't prepared to take too many chances so nobody got too much sleep. The place was disgusting. The food was inedible so we ended up resorting to the MacDonalds they've got in Red Square - at least you can be more or less sure of what you've got there. A big Mac with fries and a Coke cost 2300 Roubles which is dirt cheap at about £1.50 in our money but half a week's wages for some people there."*

This is a good illustration of how attitudes have changed. In the 1990s, the Young Athletes' League was actually sponsored by these very same world's biggest purveyors of foodstuffs of questionable wholesomeness. The sponsorship, with its club McDonalds banners and the distribution of free vouchers, was clearly designed to get these sporting youngsters into the habit of a diet which was less than conducive to sporting performance.

Scott Fraser moved indoors with equal effectiveness and won the Scottish under 17 60 in 7.07. He then gave a number of seniors a big fright when he took 0.01 off Elliott Bunney's Scottish under 17 indoor record with 7.01 in an invitation race at the GB v USA, also at the Kelvin Hall. This was only broken again in 2014.

Inverness was very fortunate in the early 1990s to have a Sports Injury Clinic run by Munlochy GP, and sometime runner, Colin Fettes. Colin very quickly received invitations to accompany Great Britain athletics teams, including to the 1993 World Championships in Stuttgart. It was Colin Fettes who was with Colin Jackson at his mandatory drugs test after winning the 110 hurdles and breaking the world record. As a souvenir, Colin Jackson gave Colin Fettes the name panel from the front of his vest and this remains one of his prized possessions.

That 60 metre hammer throw remained tantalizingly elusive for David Allan and at the North championships he had the frustration of reaching 59.84. The club's haul of gold dropped by over 30% despite a slightly bigger programme and Barnetson returned from a serious knee injury to clear a modest 2 metres. Among the Harriers' other senior champions was 1986 Commonwealth 400 hurdler Moira

MacBeath who had switched clubs from Caithness to see out her career. She won the 100 hurdles in 15.9.

The creation of a women's North District now meant that the Inter District match was East v West v North. For the North, this was always going to be a complete mismatch for a team inevitably a long way short of viability. Holding the event at the Queens Park in 1994 did nothing to alter that certainty, although Kirsten MacKay, with 2:19.9, joined Margaret MacDonald in the sparse ranks of junior female athletes to break 2:20 for the 800.

Of course no national meeting in Inverness would be complete without a central belt travel catastrophe. This time it reached comic opera proportions for both the East and the West buses. Their dramas ranged from getting lost in darkest Kinross to a lengthy standstill in the massed ranks of the Dunfermline Half Marathon and a breakdown. The two buses arrived 15 minutes after the scheduled start of a match which did not finish until well after 6pm. There were then repeat performances by City of Glasgow travelling to the SWAL in Aberdeen and the Glasgow team getting to Grangemouth for the schools inter area match.

Inverness Harriers official John Findlayson raised a big laugh when he observed: *"That's three times they've been late now – presumably they get to keep the bus."* By now John Findlayson, another entrant to the club as a parent, was playing a big part in administration and team management. This would continue for many years, particularly in the convening of events, both club and championships.

The 1994 Scottish Championships were immediately followed by the Commonwealth Games team announcement. Devine, now 26, came home from Australia to compete and won the hammer with 62.70, somewhat short of his best of 65.36. This was due to a shoulder injury for which he had treatment from Colin Fettes, who also provided the selectors with medical confirmation of the problem. Allan struck silver for an Inverness 1-2, albeit with just 55.80. Despite the injury, Devine was selected and joined 1986 pioneers Fraser, Patience and Jayne Barnetson in the ranks of Inverness Harriers' Commonwealth Games athletes. Unfortunately he underachieved in Victoria and finished 11th with 61.90.

However there was to be no second Barnetson in the team since David's ongoing knee problem reduced him to 2.05. These championships also gave a superb platform to young Scott Fraser, still under 17, who excelled with a modestly wind assisted (3.2) fourth in the 100 in 10.70. This followed a much more strongly assisted hand timed 10.7 at Grangemouth.

Fraser also won the Scottish Schools in 10.9 at a meeting where the Broadbent twins scooped three under 14 golds. Again the girls' pickings were thinner with Janice Forbes the only champion in the under 14 discus (23.84). There was also an early medal for Kirsty Roger, bronze in the under 17 high jump with 1.55, in advance of a successful multi events career.

Forbes added the under 15 discus at the SAF championships where Kenny Kemlo set a new club senior pole vault record of 3.55. Mark Cruden, who had recently run 1:55.6 at the AAA under 20s, took 800 bronze in 1:59.2. Scott Fraser, now with a "legal" best of 10.79, beat future national hurdles record holder Ross Baillie in the 100 before moving on to the schools international. Here he came within a whisker of becoming Inverness's first winner, missing out by 11.03 to 11.06 – to one Dwain Chambers!

In the leagues the men, like the women previously, bounced straight back up to Division 1 as Division 2 champions. The women's league incredibly produced another fourth place for the season, despite Inverness performance levels continuing in freefall.

The boys were going for their fifth SYAL title in six years but on Tuesday August 2nd the Courier headline read **"Black Isle beat Harriers to lift Scottish title".** This was far worse than defeat, it was defeat by their nearest neighbours and closest rivals – even if it was just by 17 points. Then it emerged that Black Isle had fielded an over-age athlete.

The athlete's points were deducted and a 25 point penalty applied. Inverness Harriers were declared the winners and got another trip to Birmingham. Black Isle appealed and while the penalty was cancelled since they had reported the offence themselves, Inverness still led and the altered verdict stood. Again the star of the Birmingham trip was Fraser who retained his under 17 100 and 200 titles (11.03 and 22.63) and played a decisive role in a relay victory in 45.95.

That fifth SYAL title masked the fact that the decline in quality which had begun on the women's side was now spreading and this time couldn't be absorbed by the parallel weakening of opponents. Black Isle ran out convincing winners of the following year's final at Crownpoint on August 6th 1995 by over 100 points, with Inverness third, a further 50 adrift. The Courier reported: *"As for the Harriers – champions in five of the previous six years – their ever deepening lack of quality finally caught up with them. The Inverness club took six golds in the "A" events and of these three went to Steven Smith who lives in Glenmoriston and is seldom able to attend club training, while two more went to Scot Thompson who is coached at Queens Park but is a first claim member of Nairn.......there were no under 17 medals, offering little hope of reinforcements for the Men's League in the foreseeable future."*

The clear conclusion was that the Queens Park was producing markedly less than previously and that there were also longer term implications. Scot Thompson, like Cotter, aspired to GB level but always remained secondary first claim.

On the same day at Meadowbank, a backs to the wall effort secured survival in Division 1 of the Men's League for the first time. However, despite the inevitable euphoria at what was a massive achievement for the men's team, there was a changing picture here too. Fowler single handedly contributed 55 points – one fifth of the team's total. Multiple contributions like this from Fowler and Barnetson were becoming an increasingly prominent feature in this league where replacement for natural wastage failed to materialise from the junior ranks. The happiest man that day may have been Graham Herbert whose 5000 pb was returned as 14:59.99!

Meanwhile the SWAL situation became even more bizarre. An Inverness team which was a shadow of those which had been relegated in earlier years finished a record third in the final match of 1995 to secure yet another season in Division 1. Significantly, for the second year in a row the Hunter Cup for the top female performer went to one of the Caithness athletes who had joined the club for league competition, hurdler Kathryn MacKenzie.

In all three national leagues, viability was becoming increasingly dependent on secondary first claim athletes as the club produced less and less. Apparent buoyancy in leagues produced an illusion of ongoing health and success. The ability of "bums (of any standard) on seats" to deliver team results disguised the decline in standards, and even team results were now to a large extent a product of external athletes.

There were even problems in the North East League when the club pulled out of the June match. Numbers became too small to travel following the decision to support the North team in the Inter District match against which the NEL was bizarrely scheduled. Enthusiasm for the NEL was waning and it was no longer the Holy Grail it had been in the 1970s. There was a reluctance to travel for what had become a low level of competition. In a first step towards adopting the Grampian League as a local outlet, the club duly left the North East League which soon became defunct. Until now, the Grampian League had been regarded as too small beer to bother with but the club was now descending towards this league becoming a more suitable competitive medium.

One piece of sad news, which almost epitomized the decline, was the injury-enforced retiral, at 31, of Neil Fraser who had been right at the cutting edge of Inverness Harriers' entry into big time athletics. A variety of problems had blighted his career since the early 90s. In April 1995, 14 years after his first big senior breakthrough at the 1981 east districts, he called it a day. This was an athlete who had no senior international role models to benefit from in the club because he was the first. He was the original role model and his contribution had been massive in all areas. On announcing his retiral he said: *"I've persevered with this for a very long time, but it gradually took its toll to the extent that over the last few months my heart hasn't been in it. It's desperately sad, but there it is."*

Two weeks later, the club faced a further crisis when Barnetson announced that injury had forced him to give up high jumping and turn to 400 hurdles. However this was premature in the extreme and seemed to have the effect of reviving his high jump. A superb season included several clearances above 2.10, including 2.17 to win the Scottish championship. Controversially, despite Barnetson heading him by 4cm in the rankings, the place in the Five Nations international went to national record holder Geoff Parsons. Although Dave did persevere further with the hurdles, the necessary heavy endurance work did not appear to suit a man clearly well supplied with fast twitch muscle fibres.

The Scottish Schools championships produced over 17 gold for Scott Fraser (10.8) and high jump silver for Kirsty Roger (1.55). Both were selected for the over 17 schools international in Wales at a time when Kirsty also became the first home Scot in the SAF under 20 heptathlon championship.

Janice Forbes, with a pb of 29.78, won her fourth consecutive SAF age group discus title and there was an under 13 high jump gold for Iain Ramsay (1.45). The top medal winner was Steven Smith with an under 15 100/200 double which came with little input from the club's coaching.

By the mid-90s there was also concern, especially from Tom MacKenzie and Ian Tasker, that Highland Games entries were falling away. This was despite the best efforts of the North of Scotland Amateur Highland Games Association who held an emergency meeting in September 1995. Nairn, Inverness and Forres were among those affected, although there was a big club presence at the Golden Jubilee Glenurquhart Games at the end of August. The club's Games regulars included the ever present Fowler, along with Dianne and Audrey who had been very much brought up in that tradition.

A radical Queens Park upgrade took place in two stages in 1996. This kept the track out of use from mid-May until early August and training was transferred to the Bught. Apart from a new administration block and clubrooms, the £270,000 project also included an extension of the outer ring to eight lanes and the installation of fully automatic timing. As well as allowing more space at busy times, this also enabled the facility to host eight competitor events such as the Men's League. There was an irony here too though. In the face of this extra space, club membership had declined to a 15 year low of 202, down by over 40% compared with the peaks around 330 at the start of the decade.

Lack of numbers hit hard in the Men's League where the team was reduced to eight for the third match and just seven for the final one in Glasgow. Reliance on Barnetson and Fowler had become so acute that these two contributed two thirds of the points that day. Barnetson equalled his personal best and club record of 53.0 for the 400 hurdles and, in the face of parallel national decline, this shadow of a team stayed up in Division 1.

The same day, Inverness Harriers finished last in two age groups and second last in the other two in the women's cup final at Coatbridge. But still in the SWAL, another fourth place in Division 1 was achieved by a team desperately short of senior and under 17 athletes. Survival was secured by a shrinking club, with secondary first claim help, still being able to fill places better than Pitreavie and Central Region. In the Young Athletes' League it was another third place, this time behind new champions Ayr Seaforth and Black Isle.

The District Championship on May 11th 1996 was the last meeting at the Queens Park before the final part of the upgrade began. 58 medals, including 26 gold, were about par for the course. But given that Shetland ran Inverness very close, there wasn't much left for the rest of the north. Some new names appeared when javelin specialist Linday Loades threw 29.18, before taking the Inter District event with 31.90. However this thrower also emerged as the North's top under 17 sprinter with 13.9 and 28.6. Lesley Clarkson won the corresponding under 15 sprints with 13.2/27.1 while in the same age group, Vicky O'Brien did a 75 hurdles (13.3) and long jump (4.27) double

That July, there were five North athletes in the schools under 17 international - but none was from Inverness Harriers. The club's leading school athlete was Kirsty Roger who won the over 17 Scottish schools pentathlon and took a gold and two silver in hurdles and jumps. She upped her high jump to 1.65 at the SAF under 20s but the top medal winner here was Iain Ramsay with gold in the under 13 75m hurdles (13.71) and a Scottish age group record of 1.60 in the high jump. "Skinner" went on to clear 1.91 as an under 17. Barnetson arrived at the senior championships intending to focus on the 400 hurdles where he was fifth in 53.28 but in between the heats and final he ended up successfully retaining his high jump title with 2.10. Graham Herbert was 8th in the 5000 in 14:47.

The 1996 Forres Games saw cash prizes at SAF events in the North for the first time. Three years after amateurs were admitted to SGA professional events, the practice of the amateur meetings offering vouchers now largely disappeared and most changed to cash. The typical first prize was around £20 and Fowler went home with over £100 from Forres.

By the end of the season Barnetson had taken his 400 hurdles down to 52.6 and became the first Harrier to break 50 for the 400 with 48.8. That won him the MacKenzie Cup while the Charles Hunter went to Kirsty Roger for her series of national medals and an under 20 international outing in Antrim. Simon MacIntyre (2:05.4 under 15 800) and Steven Smith (6.32 under 17 long jump) shared the Post Office Cup for juniors. Jacqui Findlayson won the corresponding Mrs D. M. Duncan Rosebowl as the club's only female Scottish age group champion with 28.94 in the under 17 hammer. Linday Loades took the Allan Trophy for the most improved junior, having gone from 22 metres to 31.90 in the javelin while Iain Ramsay's 1.60 high jump made him the most promising under 13.

These awards were presented at a somewhat tense AGM at Millburn Academy on Friday 20th September 1996. Clearly the club, along with the sport as a whole, had been in broad decline for some time and there was now also a degree of internal friction. Before the meeting Colin Baillie told the Courier: *"The Harriers' marketing is not as good as it should be. The club is not following up recruitment through the schools and we should be trying harder to attract these people. There is talent there that can be recruited and after that it's what we do with them that counts too."*

In a blunt acknowledgement of the club's declining status, the meeting decided to withdraw from the Women's Cup and join the Grampian League. However the sharp end of that 1996 AGM was the election of the new committee where a block vote among the Joggers' interests secured a completely new regime as Inverness Harriers went into its Golden Jubilee year.

No record of the precise composition of the 1996 committee can be traced, but virtually the same committee was re-elected in 1997 and comprised - President - Cammy Roger, Vice President - Graham Whyte, Secretary - Nancy Hamilton, Treasurer - Liz Forbes, Membership secretary - Marie Wheeler, Coaches and officials - Mel Fowler, Track and field - John Findlayson, Road, hill and country - Graham Whyte, Joggers - Maggie Roger, Finance and social - Richard Chester, Public relations - Ann MacLean, Committee - Corinne Gordon, John Grant, Ian Fleming, Kerry Wheeler.

The highlight of the ensuing indoor season was Kirsty Roger's fistful of championship medals in a variety of events, both club and university. With her under 20 penathlon gold she became the club's second 1.70 high jumper and for a time even shared the Scottish under 20 record in the embyonic women's pole vault with 2.40.

The official re-opening of the refurbished track was performed by Provost Allan Sellar who fired a symbolic round from the starter's pistol at the Open Meeting on April 16th 1997. The star turns were under 15s. Vicky O'Brien recorded 12.34/4.86/13.49 in the 75 hurdles/long jump/100, Kate Grainger threw 29.80 in the javelin and Ewan Sime reached 11.70 with the shot. It was just as well that the new timing system was in action since just 0.03 separated the top three in the under 13 100 which was won by Lewis Danby.

March 1997 brought disaster when Inverness District Council claimed not to have received the Men's League's track booking for that May's Division 1 match and let the facility out to another body. This was to have been one of the cornerstones of the Golden Jubilee season. This was possibly an omen because 1997 saw the more or less inevitable relegation of a men's team where numbers had now slumped to as low as six. Club officials attributed the slump to the lack of high quality athletes coming through the ranks to replace those who had departed.

However Inverness Harriers didn't go quietly. At the last meeting at Grangemouth, Barnetson signed off by improving his Scottish native and club high jump records to 2.20. He had swung back towards high jumping from 400 hurdles and, with the next Commonwealth Games in Kuala Lumpur just a year away, this was an important performance. Later he took AAA bronze, losing silver on countback with 2.15, and British bronze with 2.17.

It was a similar picture in the SWAL. The only surprise was that such a badly depleted team should only be marginally relegated to Division 2. The Young Athletes did manage to move back up to second behind Ayr in their final. However the biggest shock came in the club's debut season in the Grampian League where Inverness Harriers came very close to a complete wipe out by Black Isle in the north qualifiers.

The Ross shire club won all four men's matches and the first three women's, with only a last gasp Inverness success preventing a clean sweep.

In mitigation, a minimum membership age of 11 meant that Inverness under 11 teams were very sparse and this affected the overall standings. But this crushing defeat in a local competition – which concluded just days before its Golden Jubilee celebrations - fully demonstrated the recent descent of a club which nationally had ridden so high for so long.

Individually, the North District championships wrote a further essay on the wall. Despite overall entries being down to only 160, a tally of just 20 golds meant that Inverness Harriers, for the first time in the championship's 20 years, had to concede top of the medal table to Elgin.

The under 17 javelin throwers were in good form though, with John Mitchell from Skye recording 54.54 in men's event while Lindsay Loades did 29.90 in the women's. Vicky O'Brien performed the, by then, rare feat of a sub 13 100 with 12.9, hand timed due to an automatic timing failure. That same week, Kirsty Roger was named in the GB under 20 heptathlon squad following a personal best in the United States. Kirsty, now with City of Glasgow for UKWAL competition, also struck gold in the Scottish under 20 heptathlon with a personal best of 4778 points, 60 better than the senior winner. Shortly after, her brother Neil won the Scottish schools over 17 hammer with 38.90 to gain selection for the over 17 international. Lindsay Loades' javelin silver made her the first Inverness athlete since 1994 to be selected for the British schools international.

In 1997, for the first time in 20 years, there were no Inverness Harriers vests at the Scottish senior championships. Barnetson was there, but obliged to compete for City of Edinburgh, and won his third consecutive title with 2.10 in poor conditions. That range of downbeat statistics perhaps epitomises much reduced fortunes as Inverness Harriers approached its Golden Jubilee.

CHAPTER 9 – OFF-TRACK ROLLERCOASTER – 1986-97

By the mid-1980s the club had a more or less comprehensive stranglehold on North cross country, apart from the very competitive men's events. More intermittent success here had depended on the comings and goings of major players like Axon, Kenney and MacMillan. The main challenge usually came from club or RAF athletes from Moray, which was also reflected on the road where, for instance, the team result in the 1986 Ness Motors "10" read Forres 23, Elgin 27, Inverness 35.

The winter of 1986-87 saw an unprecedented domination of North cross country by Inverness Harriers. The relays at Muir of Ord produced an overwhelming boys' and women's 1-2-3, the winning trios being Duncan Hards, Stuart Jarvie and Andrew Chalmers alongside Roma Davidson, Jenny Rankine and Sheila Campbell. Only the men's team title proved elusive among seven at the District Championships in Elgin, which also individually yielded four gold, five silver and six bronze. In the league it was six, five and four individual medals plus five firsts and two seconds across the team contests.

Julie Wilson finishing fourth in the Scottish Inter District and Universities' match – St Andrews 1988.

This was a time when Campbell and Julie Wilson were in fine form, picking up Scottish international and select outings. Wilson was in the shape of her life that autumn, finishing third and sixth in senior SWCCL races, seventh in the East v West and narrowly missing a full international. Former Millburn Academy runner John Bowman also returned from service in the Navy to win the men's North league and launch a spectacular career.

This led to greater impact on the much tougher national scene. Roma Davidson became the first Inverness athlete to win a national cross country title, the Scottish Schools under 13 by 100 metres. This sent her to Ireland as Inverness Harriers' youngest ever internationalist. Stuart Jarvie's under 17 bronze got him there too so the destinies of the Banks awards were not difficult to determine in the spring of 1987.

Under 13 boys' Scottish cross country bronze medallists 1988. Front – Ian Fraser, David Shand, Neil Forbes, Andrew MacRae, Ewan McHattie. Rear – Archie Forbes

The SCCU championships yielded Junior Boys' and Senior Boys' team bronze.

The running boom continued to inspire new races and the Black Isle Marathon had a 10K and a Half Marathon added. The 10K was especially popular since it ran from the top of the Black Isle down to Fortrose Academy. Runners therefore had two 10K PBs - their real one and their "Black Isle PB", typically a minute or more faster.

Inverness Harriers' "Caledonian 8" along the canal to Dochgarroch and back was another newcomer. In 1987 it highlighted a major difficulty originating from there being two kinds of races. Mainstream events had been around since the sport began and were restricted to club members and unattached runners of less than one year's standing. But now there were also "People's" races, products of the running boom and open to all-comers and hence the only option for anyone running unattached for more than a year.

The Caledonian 8 fell into the club runners' category. It quickly emerged that most entrants were unattached and it was impossible to determine for how long. Here was a huge anomaly which was resolved by events eventually becoming open to all, but with an extra levy for non-members of Scottish Athletics.

April 1987 saw a "Man versus Horse" competition between the Harriers and the Highland Long Distance Riding Club. The riders, with the first 11 places, won "neigh bother" over a 9 mile course which was probably better suited to them. The runners also noticed that their equine rivals received the very best of veterinary assistance at the finish while they themselves were simply left to lie exhausted at the roadside!

Just one year can make a big difference in an amateur club and 1987's record haul of cross country league awards was reduced to just one team, the Junior Women's, and four individual successes in 1988. One mitigating factor was that several club athletes were now running for Culloden Academy.

Championships turned out to be a different story. Heading a list of four team and four individual successes in the Districts at Fairburn House in November 1988 was a clean sweep of the top three places in the Youths' race for Stewart Jarvie, who was also unbeaten league champion, Finlay Everitt and David Bell. Julie Wilson, in advance of fourth place in the Scottish Select v Scottish Universities' match, just edged Sheila Campbell for the women's championship. At the Hydrasun meeting in Aberdeen, individual winner Ingram Murray, Darren Sutherland and Duncan Hards dominated the Senior Boys' event.

The summer of 1988 was unusually quiet on the road but the cross country season started reasonably well. There was further District Relay domination by the women and the boys who then came within 10 yards of another breakthrough - a national relay medal. Andrew MacRae put the team into fifth on the Junior Boys' lap (12:54) and Ingram Murray improved to fourth with 12:30 before schools internationalist Calum Jack from the West coast (11:37) just missed raising that again to bronze.

The District Championships produced a mixed bag, with the positives including team and individual wins in the Women's, Youths' and Senior Boys' age groups. Sheila, now Mrs. Gollan, Calum Jack and Ingram Murray were the individual champions. These were also the three age groups which yielded success in a somewhat improved 1988-89 league season compared with the previous one.

Earlier in the decade unprecedented clusters of talent had produced outstanding results in several sprint relays and for the Senior Boys' national cross country team. Now it was time for another influx to start producing results, many of them in the Senior Boys' and Youths' endurance events. Scottish schools track medallist Ingram Murray had an excellent cross country season where he was only pipped for inter-district gold in the last 200. Also on the way up, sometimes intermittently due to football commitments, was Stewart MacKay who took an under 15 Scottish schools silver and was an outstanding, close up 9th in the 1989 international in Wales.

Andrew MacRae, Calum Jack, Grant McDowall, Mark Cruden and Duncan Hards were also developing as Charlie Forbes established himself as an endurance coach. Early successes included fielding an all-international trio of Jack (1st), Jarvie (2nd) and McDowall (4th) to retain the North District Youths' cross country title in November 1989.

In Julie Wilson's absence at PE college, Sheila Gollan was the top North woman by a distance, with the leading man. Originally from Oban, Gollan had trained as a PE teacher but joined Northern Constabulary and had also been doing well in Scottish and British Police competition. She was awarded the Banks Salver with the Rosebowl going to the rapidly improving Murray.

In North women's road running, 40 minutes has traditionally been something of a 10K "gold standard". Although comfortably achievable by Wilson and Gollan, and often by Maggie Adamson as well, Ann Smart also joined the club, breaking the Dornoch 10K record with 39:19. Stan MacKenzie only finishing third in 31:20 is perhaps a reminder of men's standards.

After three years' absence due to lack of finance, the 10 mile road race returned in September 1989 with sponsorship from Delmore Cars. MacKenzie defeated a field of 126 in 57:48 with George Mitchell the first veteran in 59:37.

Incredibly, the Alves to Forres had survived on the A96 until Forres Harriers replaced it with a new 10K on much quieter roads from Dallas to Forres as late as 1989. MacKenzie was fifth in that 10K in 31:52 and Gordon Ewing was top over-50 with a highly commendable 35:08.

Triumph blended with controversy at the North cross country relays at Muir of Ord. The men returned their first win for five years thanks to Colin McClean (13:11), Grant McDowall (13:09), John (12:28, the fastest in the race) and MacKenzie (12:56). This followed the rejection of a vigorous Harriers protest that a Black Isle woman runner, who had crossed the finishing line with a three second lead, had cut the course.

In October 1989, the national cross country relays came to Inverness for the second time in less than a decade and were again organised by Walter Banks at Kinmylies. On a foggy afternoon the furthest travelled club, Teviotdale Harriers, became men's champions while Victoria Park took the boys race, with Inverness 21st and 15th respectively.

Bowman had to concede the individual District Championship in Dornoch to Banff's Alan Reid. On the day before the first Sunday in Advent, Bowman angrily, but seasonally, reflected *"I ran like a turkey!"* The women's championships, unusually, went ahead three weeks later in Elgin with what the Courier described as *"disastrous Inverness results"*. In the absence of Gollan, racing in Glasgow, all three team trophies went to a briefly resurgent Fraserburgh.

Forres Harriers' men started the final league race with a four point lead so host club Inverness desperately needed their top four to run. No fewer than 30 Harriers lined up but, as the Courier reported, with one worrying omission: *"Ian Gollan, who was due to come off shift with Northern Constabulary half an hour before the*

The joggers in the original Club Hut – early 1990s.

start of the race, still had not arrived when the athletes were being assembled. Inverness officials were anxiously hoping for the whine of a siren, the flash of a blue light and a last minute appearance – and a last minute appearance they certainly got when Gollan appeared with just seconds to go....on a bike!" Bowman won while MacKenzie (5th), the vital Gollan (8th) and McClean (10th) successfully finished the job. Three other team titles also came to Inverness.

Club handicaps were thriving with turnouts often topping 30 men alongside throngs of youngsters. The final race in the spring of 1990 yielded a narrow victory for me over Peter Thompson, described thus in the Courier: "... *the flame of burning ambition on the part of the leading two was almost extinguished by the Highland and Islands Fire Brigade. Just outside Telford Street Park, the proceedings were engulfed by the roaring of engines and the whining of sirens. Thompson's evasive action almost took him through B and Q while Bannerman saw 50 gallons of water land three yards in front of him as the machine charged through a roadside puddle. The whole incident may just have been stage-managed by Gordon Fraser* (club member and senior fireman).... *but perhaps not."*

The club championship results show that Stan MacKenzie won by just six seconds from George Mitchell. However this obscures the full story, as related by Stan who already had something of a reputation for navigational aberrations: *"To be quite honest I lost my way and had to wait for the rest to catch up on me so I could find out where to go."* The other club champions were: Youths – Nigel Cox, Senior Boys – Stewart MacKay, Junior Boys – John Colquhoun, Women – Ann Smart, Intermediates – Mary Ann Loughrey, Juniors – Shelley MacRae, Girls – Alison Findlayson. The Joggers' championship went to Mark Wilson.

That winter ended in a bang for Banks Trophy winners Stewart MacKay and Sheila Gollan. Now that the four home nations had lost their individual status, Gollan was invited to the GB trials for the World cross country championships. Already East District champion and fifth in the Scottish, she was 30th

Sheila Gollan in Action

among the best of British. MacKay struck silver in the national Senior Boys' championships with further contributions towards team bronze from Darren Miller, Neil Forbes and Andrew MacRae. The Scottish schools then yielded MacKay further silver, and a second international selection.

By 1990 Graham Laing, a 2:13:59 marathon runner and seventh in the 1982 Commonwealth Games, had settled in Inverness as manager of the BT shop. He very quickly changed his first claim to the Harriers from Aberdeen and his first success was in the Ord Hill Race at North Kessock in August 1990, over a new 5.5 mile course.

The 1990-91 winter season remains unparalleled in the history of Inverness Harriers but the District Relays in Fort William created one of its most chaotic moments. Once again Ian Gollan, now policing Lochaber, was due off duty during the afternoon and once again was vital for victory. So the men took something of a gamble by declaring a team with Gollan, returning from a road accident in Glencoe, the last runner.

Grant McDowall (15:32) put Inverness "A" third before Bowman, whose 14:29 was the fastest, took the lead on a Fort William course which, not for the first time, created some disquiet. When MacKenzie (15:41) set off there was still no Gollan and this time there was no blue light and no wailing siren - not even the last minute appearance of a bicycle. The reason was that Constable Gollan had been called away to a second road accident and there was no way he was going to make it this time. Consequently there was no-one waiting to take over from MacKenzie, who is probably best not quoted, and Inverness Harriers' finest remained incomplete. But at least WPC Gollan posted the fastest lap of the women's race to secure that title and Stuart Sutherland (14:04), Stuart MacKay (12:17) and Neil Forbes (13:45) were followed home by their own silver medal winning B team in the boys' race.

That year's downhill Black Isle 10K also had a following wind which helped Julie Wilson win the women's race by over a minute in a remarkable 35:24 while Stan MacKenzie's third in the men's came in an equally unique 29:52! Graham Herbert famously described this course as *"the kind which gives you the chance to put your elbow on the bar and tell the world what your best time is."*

Willie Aird and Alf Leslie replaced Kenny MacKay as men's club race handicappers and had a superb debut. The opening race is always difficult and while handicap winner Bowman set a new Holm Mains record of 20:55, the middle 20 in a 35 strong field finished within just 90 seconds. Bowman had a further record in the Craig Dunain race (19:04) and even took four seconds off Kenney's 1983 Balnacraig time with 25:17. The Craig Dunain men's field of 37 runners was a record which still stands. The boys' and women's winners were Alasdair Thomson and Dianne, now a mother of two but returning to competition.

Bowman, really at the top of his game now, got his first full Scottish international at Irvine in November. The following month he was in the Scottish select at Cumbernauld and, in January 1991, the senior team at the Home Countries international in Northern Ireland. He even became second claim for Derby's Omega AC to finish 20th in a field of 500 in the Midland championships, contributing to team gold. Then 52nd in the English Inter Counties championship gained him selection for the world championship trials in Basingstoke in February. But, with the Scottish runners already at Glasgow airport, this was cancelled due to heavy snow and never rescheduled.

January 1991 saw the first competition for the Peter Thompson Memorial Quaich, donated by his work colleagues after the death of the club's Past President. Because Peter had been so adept at fooling the handicapper in the Bught club handicap the Quaich was awarded to its winner. On this first occasion it went to someone almost as skilled, although Andy Law was better known within the club as a coach and especially as an official where he aspired to London 2012 after he left the area.

The club handicaps, which were eventually switched from Saturdays to Sundays, provided a lot of valuable competition. For the men, opportunities to compete at distances below 6 miles/ 10K have traditionally been difficult to access in the North so the club races filled an awkward gap. They also greatly enhanced the club's social side.

By now Bowman, MacKenzie, McDowall, Sheila Gollan, Robert McHarg and a few others were training with highly experienced endurance coach Gerry Barnes. Retired and living in Nairn, Barnes had a long and distinguished pedigree and his Inverness group thrived. But it wasn't just senior athletes who were gaining international recognition. January 1991 saw MacKay, unbeaten in domestic competition, finish third for Scotland under 17s against Wales and Ireland in Limerick.

That busy month also saw what the Courier described as *"a devastating show of force"* from the men's team at their home league match at Kinmylies. For the first time in the league's history, and not matched for another two decades, a maximum 394 points was achieved by a 1-2-3-4. Bowman (35:00) won from MacKenzie (35:56) and Laing (36:11). McHarg (36:51) then pipped Lochaber's David Rodgers at the death to complete the clean sweep. This also converted an overall six point deficit into a 38 point lead, allowing the team, two matches later, to retain their title.

It really is difficult to determine the outstanding moment of that memorable 1990-91 cross country season but the SCCU championships in Dundee in February must rank very highly indeed. MacKay dominated the Senior Boys' race, now designated under 16 in an age group realignment. The Courier reported: "The 15 year old Scottish schools captain's personal triumph, achieved by an almost casual parting company with the opposition with just 300 yards to go, gave his club their first individual Scottish cross country gold and set up a team success where they picked up the J.D. Semple Trophy - last won by the Harriers nine years ago."

Winning under 16 boys' team Scottish cross country championships 1990 with Tom McKean – Andrew MacRae, Stewart MacKay, Matthew MacKenzie, Mark Cruden (and non-counting member John Colquhoun.)

Matthew MacKenzie (6th) and Mark Cruden (25th) soon followed. Andrew MacRae then overtook six runners to finish 37th and secure a repeat of the 1982 victory, by just three points from Edinburgh AC. McDowall, Craig Stewart, Nigel Cox and Nicky Cruden added under 20 team bronze after a double tiebreaker. As one of just four clubs with teams in all five age groups, Inverness were contenders for the overall award, the A.T. Mays trophy, but lost out to Cambuslang. At the presentation Walter Banks was *"on his feet in undisguised delight."* This was also a triumph for Charlie Forbes who coached many of the junior athletes and later that year became Inverness District Sports Council's inaugural Service to Sport winner. Fittingly MacKay and Bowman shared the Rosebowl while schools international debutante Shelley MacRae won the Salver.

Absent from the men's team that winter had been Colin McClean. Believing that his athletics career was over due to work commitments, he had competed in and won the mile at the professional Braemar

Games, which compromised his amateur status. Soon after, his circumstances changed and he had to apply to the SAAA for reinstatement, which was granted.

The summer of 1991 was quiet on the roads at a time when the composition of the men's squad began to evolve due to arrivals, departures and work commitments. Sheila Gollan was now also finding police shifts a problem to the dismay of Gerry Barnes. Bowman raced relatively infrequently on the road, preferring the track.

Stan MacKenzie found himself in the thick of controversy at the Moray 10K early in September. About 200 yards from the finish in Cooper Park and in the lead, he responded to a gesture from an official which resulted in a wrong turn and once this was rectified he crossed the line in third place. He was eventually declared the winner but without a time. However the real talking point was his subsequent allegation that he had been deliberately misdirected.

He told the Courier: *"I was absolutely disgusted at what happened and when I tackled the official about it he just turned his back. Apart from winning the race I was on course for a good time and although they offered to give me first place anyway I told them I was not interested, although I have nothing against the Roadrunners club as a whole."* However that wasn't the end of the matter. Race director Dr. Donald Brown then wrote to North District secretary John Wilson, accepting that an error had been made but insisting that they were not willing to accept MacKenzie's allegations of cheating, which Dr. Brown said were unwarranted and slanderous.

At the following month's District Relays at Nairn, MacKenzie found himself at the centre of a carbon copy of the previous year's Fort William misfortune. This time it was McClean (12:48), Laing (13:00) and Bowman (12:17, fastest lap) who did the early spadework after a call to MacKenzie's mother-in-law raised hopes that he would arrive on time. The unfortunate reality was that Stan had actually slept in and dashed on to Nairn East Beach 10 minutes too late. At least he got a break two weeks later when a Courier headline declared **Black Isle victory ends 'Dozy' Stan's run of nightmares"**. "Dozy" was the nickname coined by Bowman post-Nairn and the headline heralded a half marathon win in 71:57.

The 1991-92 cross country season fell apart somewhat. The women's and boys' relay titles were conceded to developing clubs Moray Roadrunners and Black Isle. The Roadrunners' improving men cashed in big time on the presence of just five Harriers at the second league race in Caithness. Never a cross country runner at the best of times, I even found myself having to count for the first time in a dozen years, finishing 30th in horrendous, sleet-lashed conditions at Scrabster Farm.

My misery was compounded by visions of sharing the fate of the dead sheep I passed on each lap. I then became so cold at the finish that I couldn't remember going back to my car. The final ignominy was having to walk in bare feet through the gents' urinal both to and from the spout of freezing water which was the only means of removing layers of thick mud.

The women, against mounting opposition from the Roadrunners and Fraserburgh, retained their District title at Elgin and although Bowman won the men's race, the Roadrunners were the top team here. After the 10K controversy, this had become something of a grudge match, so when Stan and his fellow counters went up for their silver medals, he found the victorious Roadrunners playfully pointing him in the wrong direction!

In the dying days of 1991, Bowman stepped up another gear to finish 43rd in a world class field including several Kenyans in a televised international race at Beamish near Durham. Accessing this kind of competition inevitably meant absences from the bread and butter races and a week later the Courier reported: *"Inverness Harriers' defence of their Keyline North League men's title took its expected terminal nosedive at Saturday's third meeting at Elgin. But with champions elect Moray Roadrunners packing their four counters into the top seven places and the Inverness club only managing to put one runner in the top 20, the damage was much worse than expected. The Harriers' deficit quadrupled to 100 points at a stroke."*

This was less than a year after the club's greatest cross country triumphs and events were beginning to resonate with my then somewhat controversial AGM warning on standards. There were still positives. Bowman received another World Championship trial, albeit at the expense of hitting black ice and crashing on his way home and the trauma ruined his next few weeks. The women's North league title went to Ann Smart just four days after her son Bobby's first birthday.

Into April, Sheila Gollan again hit the headlines with silver in the European Police cross country championships in Guildford. Only a very good Danish runner stopped her from holding the cross country and 800 titles simultaneously. Meanwhile Shelley MacRae and Alasdair Thomson contested the most Northerly international ever held in the UK which brought the British schools teams together in Alness.

The summer of 1992 was barren in the extreme on the road. Laing won the Newtonmore 10 miler (53:30) and the Cooper Park "6" (30:42). Apart from a number of veteran awards for George Mitchell and the Inverness "10" team title, that was about it. The "10" also saw the return to Inverness of winner Simon Axon, now with Hunters Bogtrotters. His 52:20 took him home more than two minutes clear, but the real story was his arrival at the Delmore rail crossing at four miles where he spotted an oncoming train.

"To start with I thought it was one of these great long goods trains that would take ages to pass and I certainly wasn't going to lose time and break my rhythm by stopping," he explained. "So I put on a bit of a sprint and managed to dash across the line about 10 or 15 seconds ahead of the train. There certainly wasn't any danger, but in any case it turned out to be a much shorter train than I first thought."

That unravelling 1991-92 season was the prelude to a sudden, dramatic and extended cross country slump in most age groups, especially in the North league. This was particularly marked on the male side where, in their local league, Inverness Harriers won no team titles at all in the 13 years between 1992 and 2005, and very few individual ones. The senior men's 23 year team drought was only ended in 2014, after just a single, shared, individual title in 1994. Other competitions such as the relays would not always be quite so unproductive.

In complete contrast, 20 of the 27 senior women's NDCCL team awards between 1987 and 2013 came to Inverness. But if it had not been for four or five strong performers across the millennium divide, the girls might have been as severely challenged as the boys. This awards drought was only partly explained by improved performances by Black Isle and Moray Roadrunners since some of the factors were to be found within the club itself.

The opening 1992 league race at Peterhead yielded no individual or team wins at all across the seven races. The Courier reported that "a disastrous performance in the prestigious men's team contest had the local squad fifth, 65 points behind defending champions Moray Roadrunners."

The following weekend's District Relays in Forres brought better news with a Young Athletes' win for Ian Gunn (12:06), Stuart Sutherland (10:56) and Mark Cruden (11:06) and runner up spots in the other two races. Clouds of gloom do tend to be punctuated by silver linings and the same three boys later took national relay silver.

A desperately poor league series saw the only overall first place going to the women's team and two meetings yielded total blanks. The inaugural SAF North District championships in Fraserburgh similarly saw individual champion Ann Smart lead home the winning women's trio, and that was it.

That year's Banks awards went to Mark Cruden, top finisher in the unprecedented winning under 17 North inter district team, and to Shelley MacRae who was third for Scotland in a match in Northern Ireland. She was pressed for the salver by Margaret MacDonald who followed up some fine 800 performances with a schools cross country international debut in Llanelli.

Ann Smart also became the first SAF North road champion in March 1993 with the 10K title at Nairn in 40:59 on a windy day. Bowman (31:43), second overall to Peterhead's Reid was the best of 12 men in the top 40, ten of them inside 36:30. These included Andrew Farquharson with 33:48 just 24 hours after completing a 50K (31 miles) race in 3:21, and 17 year old Stewart MacKay who ran 35:43 just 24 hours after playing football for Nairn County. However Dunfermline club Carnegie packed their four into the top nine to win the team honours.

For the men, the road had suddenly become much more productive than the country and Nairn was a relatively rare team defeat in 1993. At the Glen Nevis "10" Alan Murchison (53:42) led home a winning squad which also comprised Farquharson (57:07) and 47 year old Mitchell, the first veteran in 57:14. Murchison had by now become something of a club legend due to his regular training runs with his Siberian Husky tied by a long lead to his waist.

There are not many short road races in the North, but into May the Newtonmore Mile appeared as a prelude to the village's "10". Again Murchison was the first Inverness finisher in 4:32 on a slightly uphill course. The other winning team members were Charlie Forbes (4:54) and myself (4:57).

There were further successes at the Muir of Ord 10K. Then at the much faster Dornoch 10K in July, there was an unbeatable 2-3-4 for Murchison (31:42), Brian Fraser (32:10) and MacKenzie (32:45). This was an era when Mitchell could be top vet on 34:08 but still almost a minute and a half adrift of a place in the winning team.

The next success looked a lot better than it really was. The Scottish 10 mile road race championship was at the club's annual Delmore fixture, but that success had to be tempered by there being only 93 runners. Herbert (5th in 54:32), Farquharson (9th in 57:37) and Paul Garner (12th in 58:48) produced the goods.

Into October Murchison won the hilly Forres "6" in 32:10 while MacKenzie (33:46), Paul Garner (35:03) and Mitchell (35:15) successfully backed him up. Then in the very last Black Isle festival, 10K runner up Herbert (30:26), a not fully fit Bowman (32:02) and Brian Fraser (32:45) retained that title.

Club group before Inverness 10 mile road race –early 1990s.
Back- Steve Worsley, Alastair MacDougall, Dave Ewan, Stan
MacKenzie, Martin MacLean, George Mitchell, Ann MacLean. Front
– Ian Thomson, Charles Bannerman, Graham Herbert, John Grant.

October 1993 also saw the start of a golden era in the 66 mile, 6 runner, 12 stage Great Glen Relay where Paul Crowe, Ian Wheeler, Peter Fletcher, Mark MacLeod, George Mitchell and Graham Whyte recorded 6:31:36 to beat Wolves of Badenoch by eight minutes. Crowe, as road hill and country convener, and Whyte were doing a lot of good organisational work with adult off-track running which was vibrant.

However this success wasn't repeated over the country. A special dispensation was given to hold the opening league meeting in Thurso as early as September 25th due to fixtures congestion. The course was as muddy as ever, but at least runners enjoyed a rare fine day.

The men's race was a personal triumph for Murchison. He set off even faster than the eccentric Reid, who once famously led the Kenyans in the first half mile of a televised road race. Despite a late challenge from the Peterhead man, Murchison held on. Stephen Cook was a good sixth but there were only three Harriers there, so the team challenge nosedived at the first hurdle. Given that no fewer than 16 men had contributed to the summer road successes, a furious Murchison said: *"It's a complete disgrace that a club of our size couldn't raise four men to go to Thurso. We've a huge squad of runners and a lot of them knew the event was on and in fact I was led to believe that several were going to be there."*

Internal club issues were largely to blame for the overall poor turnout. In Thurso, there were only two complete Inverness teams in what had now become nine age groups with the addition of under 11 boys and girls, although the club's age structure excluded contesting these new races. The long trip to Thurso for a race over a course which was usually far from conducive to running was a big disincentive for many.

Murchison's outburst did help galvanise efforts for the District Relays at Muir of Ord which produced the first men's win since 1989, albeit not without the now familiar panic. At least this time Bowman, who had had a puncture returning from a Fire Services course, did manage to dash into the car park five minutes before declarations closed. Sixteen weeks in North Berwick relegated him to third on the opening lap (13:24) but Herbert (12:48), MacKenzie (13:35) and Murchison (12:50) secured victory by 61 seconds over Moray Roadrunners. The boys took the first two places, while under new SAF arrangements a new senior women's championship produced second place but no girls' team could be raised.

Kinmylies hosted the North championships in November 1993 and produced the first men's team victory for eight years with the six counters in the top 15. Murchison was third behind Alan Reid and was closely followed by a now partly resurgent Bowman, with Herbert, Brian Fraser, MacKenzie and Farquharson the other counters. This was only the men's second ever District championship and District relay double and flew in the face of the league debacle.

By now Sheila Gollan had shifted her first claim to Edinburgh Woollen Mill so there was a stewards' enquiry about her eligibility for Inverness here. The green light was given and the Scottish internationalist won by 90 seconds, with Maggie Adamson and Julie Wilson confirming that the team title would stay in Inverness. But alongside the senior double, results in the young athletes' races were alarmingly poor with a number of incomplete teams on a day when Minolta Black Isle dominated.

One favourite local race is the Boxing Day Nairn Turkey Trot. This began as a modest handicap in the 1980s but nowadays attracts over 200 and the increase has prompted two changes over the years. The Turkey Trot eventually had to become a scratch event with a predictor competition when numbers made handicapper John Wilson's job impossible. Later, in 2013, there was a venue switch to Nairn Dunbar

Golf Club after fears that the upper floor of Nairn Sailing Club might not be strong enough to support the mass of humanity!

There has always been a big presence of maroon and gold and while cooks usually get a rest on Boxing Day, in 1993 five of them, all from the same family, were extremely active. Local GP Malcolm Cook had five sons, including schools internationalist Stephen, a major player for Inverness Harriers who was handicapped out of contention but the other four boys - Richard, Chris, Colin and Andrew - finished 4th, 6th, 8th and 9th in a remarkable race.

Despite the men's championship double, the cross country personnel problem increased as standards continued to plunge in the younger age groups. 1994 started particularly badly with no winners of any kind in the North league at Elgin and no senior women at all. Turnouts had by now become so bad that the committee was forced to withdraw the traditional club bus because of the losses it was making. Inevitably this had the synergic effect of further reducing numbers due to lack of transport. Presence at national championships, already in decline, was further compromised when distant Irvine became the only venue able to accommodate the new SAF joint men's and women's event.

The 1993-94 cross country season reached a depressing end. The only league success of any kind was Murchison's share of the men's title with Reid. Ultimately what had cost the men's team award was the incomplete squad at the Thurso opener. However the Banks awards still went to internationalists since Stephen Cook and Margaret MacDonald had both run for Scottish schools in Cork, and Cook won the Scottish under 20 title.

Roy and Lorraine MacDonald and their committee of volunteers were well into organising the Inverness Half Marathon which now finished in the Queens Park. The increasingly popular fun run had become a 5K but a request from the Harriers' men to make this an official race couldn't be met. The request itself indicates that the male athletes were moving away from cross country towards shorter road races. So in addition to a big club presence in the Half, several of the better runners did opt for the 5K - fun run or not - with a predictable Murchison - Herbert 1-2.

Summer 1994 was singularly unproductive, although Herbert won the Glen Nevis "10" and Murchison the Dornoch 10K at the head of successful teams. Then in September Harry Young (61) collected a Connochie Plaque, the coveted official award for completing 21 Ben Nevis Races. There has never been much of a presence in ultra-distance races, but in the mid-90s Andy Farquharson did tackle a number of them, although heavy rain reduced his effort in the 1994 British 24 hour championship to 83 miles.

The return of cross country produced an early quadruple blank in the District Relays, the men losing their title to a Lochaber side which included four times winter Olympic biathlete Mike Dixon. Controversy erupted at the second league meeting at Nairn where a number of men ran on the much firmer and faster sand further down the East Beach, well below the course markers. Those who followed the more powdery marked route at the top lost up to 300 metres. The Harriers, who had narrowly won the season's opener, believed their men had been disadvantaged by this and lodged a furious protest. A letter went to the league, but the result stood on a 6-5 vote against declaring it null and void. A 4 point lead was hence converted into a 29 point deficit behind Moray Roadrunners.

That race was almost an allegory of that entire cross country season which sank into anonymity just as the runners had sunk into the soft sand on Nairn Beach. One emerging force was under 17 league winner Kirsten MacKay who was also the club's only individual North champion in Thurso where Margaret MacDonald and Shirley Lipton successfully backed her up. In the various women's events, Gollan's availability had considerably reduced and Wilson's form was not at its best. The men remained reasonably strong and won the final race, but were usually no match for Moray Roadrunners.

None of this was for lack of effort from Graham Whyte who had carried on the high standards of Paul Crowe's convenership of off-

Club run – apparently not competitive and possibly the traditional New Year's Day event – heading from the canal, very probably towards The Mast. Early 1990s.

track running. There simply weren't the young athletes about any more. One possible analysis at junior level is that the decline hit slightly earlier in endurance than in track and field because of the more fitness dependent nature of endurance.   A large group of senior men was still training hard but had lost runners like Bowman for work reasons and Herbert to the USA for six months. Meanwhile an increasing number of others such as Paul Crowe, Peter Ferguson, Charlie Jarvie and even the evergreen George Mitchell were edging further into the veteran category.

One winter institution of the mid-90s was the Tuesday "Leachkin Brae" session. For some, like Neil Black, this was a weekly "must do" but for most, with Mitchell a natural leader, it was interspersed by a paarlauf or mile reps at the Bught or a track session.

The Leachkin session's first effort was a progressively accelerating 6 minute dash up the A82 to Craig Dunain West Lodge. A couple of minutes' rest there, including a bladder-emptying for some, preceded a 700 metre ascent to the hospital duck pond. The jog through Craig Dunain Hospital which followed evolved into a furious, slightly downhill scramble to the bottom of the eponymous centre-piece of the session. The gold standard for that half mile-odd of hell up the steep Leachkin Brae was five minutes. Finally, after a long jog back down, there was a mile effort past Charleston Academy to Torvean Golf Club, with the incline switching viciously from down to up over the last 400.

The Leachkin Brae ascent seemed to have a particular effect on Crowe who, even at the best of times, could be called "a grunter". There was one famous mid-effort riposte from Ian Thomson which could not be reproduced in this family book. Even in the pitch dark you were well aware if Paul was on your tail. Paul's grunts combined with the even more strident banshee wails of Hamish Cameron of Forres led Peter Ferguson to describe them jointly as "the rhythm section."

Since 1977, the Christmas Relay had been run from outside the BMX track. By 1995, with the Sports Centre now open, traffic had increased markedly so there was a switch to Charleston Community Centre. That was short lived and a further change took the race to Canal Field and then to the Bught, with teams reduced to four as numbers fell away into the new millennium.

The winter of 1995-96 was exceptionally cold with Inverness experiencing -20C at least once, making endurance training very difficult. Christmas Eve saw the annual Man v Bike race from Peter Ferguson's house near Castle Heather in brilliant winter sunshine but Arctic temperatures. Deep powdery snow made the underfoot conditions difficult enough but created a nightmare for the cyclists who got off to the worst of starts when four of them shot over their handlebars in the first 200 yards. Needless to say the runners dominated, with George Mitchell, Graham Whyte, Peter Fletcher and Laurie Redfern taking the first four places.

A few days later there was an improvised extra club race in similar conditions but without the sunshine. The route went up "Vomit Brae" (no explanation needed!) and back down the Craig Dunain zigzags and again Mitchell, now 50, had the fastest time. The handicap winner, by a massive three minutes, was Neil Black who apparently had made a better recovery from flu than he had seemed to imply when he discussed the matter with the handicapper! The Courier headline read **"Black Magic on White Hill"**.

Around this time a number of the older runners also began a longstanding weekly Saturday night ritual of meeting up in Nico's bar for a race post mortem or a general chat about running. This soon became a club institution which lasted for several years and contributed a great deal to the social cohesiveness of the senior distance runners.

The previous winter's near wipe out in the North league had served as a wake-up call. Alongside track and field problems, it prompted a review of coaching arrangements and increased efforts to field teams, including the restoration of some buses. After the final meeting at Muir of Ord, the Courier reported: *"Inverness Harriers' list of prizes was greater than last season although still rather less than their much enhanced efforts this winter deserve. However it was all a far cry from the corresponding Muir of Ord meeting, almost 10 years ago to the day, when the Inverness club won the team contest in every single section."*

The improvement really only amounted to a few more single-race team successes while across the season Rhiannon MacLean, Inverness's only North schools champion, Kirsten MacKay and Richard Cook impressed individually.

The Walter Banks Rosebowl in March 1996 came as a slightly belated 50th birthday present for Mitchell. His bronze at the Scottish Veteran M50 championships in Elgin opened the door on an amazing series of national veteran medals of all colours. These led to repeated selections for the British and Irish international in a career which stretched from 1984 right through to 2013, by which time he was 67. Rhiannon took the Salver.

With Murchison out of contention through illness, Herbert was the top Inverness man and won the club championship – only because he read in the paper that it was on.

The previous year he had turned up at Glen Nevis 24 hours too early! During that summer Herbert was always thereabouts on the road and Brian Fieldsend was now making a return to the sport. On Herbert's departure, Fieldsend become his successor as the top Inverness man and became senior club champion in February 1997. When the Senior Boys won the Scottish title in 1982, Fieldsend had finished well outside the counting team – in 156th place.

Graham Herbert

There was some further cross country improvement in 1996-97, especially on the female side. A girls' district relay success from the very credible trio of Jennifer Main, Rhiannon MacLean and Alison Campbell was followed by three team wins out of four in the District Championships at Nairn. The senior women were especially resurgent and took the league title with the main contributions from Jenny Rankine and the under 17 and veteran champions Alison Campbell and Ann MacLean. But there was, for the moment, more or less no presence in national cross country, a situation which would last for several years.

March 1997 saw the men's run of Glen Nevis team titles halted at seven while the following weekend's Craig Dunain Hill Race had a new award for the winner, the Hugh Calder Memorial Trophy following the death of the original benefactor. That went to Englishman Dave Neill (34:41) with Fieldsend third, 41 seconds behind.

So as the Golden Jubilee of 1997 approached, the 11 year rollercoaster experienced in track and field was matched by a broadly similar cycle in road, hill and country. Once again the background was a complex one. There were changing values in society and within the club as well as more competition from within the local area, and all that against the backdrop of a decline in the sport as a whole in the latter years of the cycle.

CHAPTER 10 – JUBILEE AND BEYOND – 1997-2005

The Golden Jubilee celebrations were not without their uncertainties. For a start, no one was sure about the precise date of formation, until Tom MacKenzie and an old Courier article fixed it at September 3rd, 1947. The official celebration in September 1997, comprising an afternoon track and field meeting followed by a dinner in the Lochardil Hotel, was hence arranged for Saturday 6th. A public plea went out for former club members to attend. Dianne suggested including attempts on the British women's veteran 4 x 100 and 4 x 400 records of 55.2 and 4:24.6. Once Midlands-based Sandra MacDonald (formerly MacLaren) confirmed she would make it back from holiday, the

Line up for the Golden Jubilee marathon relay. Mel Fowler is second in the queue.

quartet for both attempts was named as Sandra, Dianne, Audrey and Janice MacKinnon.

The next uncertainty emerged from a car crash in the Pont de l'Alma in Paris in the early hours of August 31st. Diana, Princess of Wales' funeral was fixed for September 6th and the country was set almost to close down. A minority view that the celebrations should be postponed drew little support. However the programme had to be altered since the track would not now open until 1pm and the dinner began at 7. In the 4 x 100, amid a carnival atmosphere, the baton hit the deck at the second change but the solution was simple. A second race yielded a triumphant 54.25 and the women then completed the British record double with 4:19.77.

The afternoon also included the miracle of a sub 2 hour marathon - albeit by a 21 strong relay of both genders and all ages running 400 metre laps after an idea by Paul Crowe. The journey of 105 laps and 195 metres was started by President Cammy Roger completing the 195 metres and handing over to Dave Barnetson. The honour of the last stretch went to Mel Fowler who brought the team home in 1:54:52, some 12 minutes inside the world record. David Allan, who had spent so long pursuing a 60 metre hammer throw, had the crowd on its feet when one effort sailed out to a personal best of 60.58.

Record breaking women's relay team –
Dianne, Janice, Audrey, Sandra.

Tom MacKenzie said: *"It makes me very proud to be here today, 50 years on, to see the Harriers still going strong on this special occasion. Back in the early days the facilities were nothing like this and I'm also pleased to have been involved as a District Councillor with getting the sports centre and track here."*

The dinner, where Neil Fraser wore his 1986 Commonwealth Tartan kilt and a number of other exiles also returned was as huge a success, with Tom among the speakers.

The euphoria did not last long since at the AGM on September 22nd, Cammy had to warn of possible withdrawal from some leagues while Liz Forbes reported that an £1800 loss had wiped out half the club's reserves. Graham Whyte expressed fears for the men's distance group.

These alarm bells did provoke something of a bounce in the cross country season which began with Mhairi Spence, Jennifer Main and Rhiannon MacLean landing the girls' District Relay. The District Championships in Alness in November produced four female team awards and the under 17 boys', plus the under 17 women's title for Alison Campbell. That female domination was repeated in the fourth league match on the club's new course in Torvean Quarry which included three tough ascents of Torvean Hill.

At the final match in Nairn, Ann Smart led home a female team clean sweep for the season while Alison had to share the under 17 award after losing both shoes in thick mud at Elgin. The under 13 girls - Alexina MacArthur 5th, Michelle Milne 9th, Mhairi Spence 14th and Liusaidh Matheson 57th - took Scottish championship bronze and there was further success for Jennifer Main, whose 7th in the Scottish schools gave her an under 15 international.

Indoors, Barnetson, now fully restored to high jumping, won the Scottish with 2.20. This put him right into the Commonwealth Games frame and in April he went for 17 days' warm weather training in South Africa. At the veteran championships Dianne, fresh from a national 40-45 400 record of 62.23 in the Scottish, won the British in Glasgow on a day when Audrey Munro took the 45-49 200 in a Scottish record of 27.78.

Into the spring of 1998 Fowler achieved what Rangers just missed in the SPL - "10 in a row" North District long jump titles with a virus-affected 6.33. An encouraging new generation of youngsters began to appear with the Scottish schools again the catalyst. In the younger age groups, Alan Pearson had an under 14 100/200/LJ treble with 12.38/25.01/5.23 while Kate Grainger became under 15 javelin champion with 32.95. In the under 17 long jump, Vicky O'Brien struck gold with 5.63, a 48 cm advance on the previous year. This followed 11.83 for 80 hurdles silver, 0.01 inside one of the few club records still surviving since the 70s. Her international debut gave her third with 5.60.

Vicky's success left me with a dilemma. At a time when the club's specialist coaching for juniors was very limited I had, through the Royal Academy, taken her on that May. But this was intended as a six week school effort aimed at international selection and here was a major breakthrough. Then at the end of June Lesley Clarkson, who had also been underachieving, asked if she could join us too. The upshot was that I returned after a 12 year absence to do a complete four year Commonwealth Games coaching cycle which started with both athletes becoming GB junior internationalists by early 2000.

Specialist coaching provision began to improve and Cammy was progressing as a throws coach with Kate Grainger while Maggie was turning towards multi-events with Scottish schools medallist Maureen MacKinnon. Brian Donaldson was developing a pole vault squad despite having to travel from his new base in Plockton, with Anna Watson and Iain MacKenzie to the fore. Charlie Forbes' coaching had the additional challenge of his working away from home, and apart from Mhairi Spence and Jennifer Main he had Simon MacIntyre who had controversially been left out of the Schools international but later won the schools Inter District 1500 in 4:08.1.

Then disaster struck for Barnetson. He had twice cleared the Commonwealth "consideration" standard of 2.20 and only had to prove his fitness to board the plane for Kuala Lumpur. However ankle and hamstring problems, made worse on his very first day in South Africa, meant that he simply ran out of time. *"I'm just absolutely devastated. It really is very difficult to express just how I feel,"* he said.

Although some talented youngsters were coming through, numbers continued to plunge. As membership headed towards a 20 year low of around 120, one summer training night in 1998 attracted just 12 athletes. This was the reverse of a few years earlier when lack of quality rather than lack of numbers had been the problem. Shortage of athletes also made the Men's League predicament even worse. Even eventually getting a home match failed to prevent relegation to Division 3. Then the boys recorded their worst SYAL performance in 11 years, finishing fifth with 268 points behind winners Black Isle (405). Yet the women still led a charmed life when the late addition of two Elgin athletes helped them back up to Division 1.

That final match at Coatbridge also had a non-counting under 17 pole vault where Anna Watson set a Scottish under 17 record of 3.02. She improved this by a Bubkaesque single centimetre at the Grampian League final in Inverness where the club hugely upped its game to win four of the nine age groups. The turnround was most marked among the women where Lesley Clarkson made her 400 debut with a club under 20 record of 59.07. The title was finally secured in the 4 x 400 by the chronologically diverse quartet of Vicky (15), Audrey (45), Dianne (40) and Lesley (16). Kate Grainger further upped her under 15 javelin record to 35.73.

The 1998 AGM made the realistic decision to scrap the sub-committee structure which originated from the expansion of the 1980s but activity levels now no longer justified it. There was also a pledge to try to overhaul the coaching arrangements. Pole vaulters Anna Watson and Ian MacKenzie claimed the two principal awards with MacKenzie sharing the MacKenzie cup with disability athlete Donald Tuach. Huge progress by Scottish under 17 1500m champion Simon Macintyre and Kate Grainger won them the junior equivalents while Vicky O'Brien's big long jump advance won her the Allan Trophy. There was a financial improvement where losses were reduced to just £254, in advance of a vital £4000 from Awards for All.

By the late 1990s, North cross country had entered a massive slump. At the 1998 relays in Forres, the only two girls' teams were from Inverness Harriers who were not represented at all in the boys' race. Alison Campbell, Ann Smart and Julie Wilson won the women's title from two Moray Roadrunners teams while the Inverness men could only manage fifth.

Torvean Quarry hosted that year's District Championships which were a reprise of 1997 with a female clean sweep and thin male pickings. This was effectively repeated in the league. The under 15 girls took Scottish championship bronze and had Jennifer Main as North league champion while sisters Fiona and Mhairi Spence tied for second. Also two future Commonwealth Games athletes, discus thrower Kirsty Law and high jumper Rachael MacKenzie, both began to make their mark at this time – in the unlikely guise of North cross country league individual champions in 1997 and 1998 respectively!

That indoor season produced a clutch of pole vault medals for Watson and MacKenzie, matched by O'Brien in the long jump and Clarkson in the 300 and 400. It also saw Maureen MacKinnon in the Scottish schools team for the indoor pentathlon international at Kelvin Hall.

The first Grampian League match of 1999 saw Clarkson claim the 18 year old club 400 record with 57.4 in just her second run over the full lap. The previous holder, now 41, had little time to reflect since Dianne was preparing to win the B race.

The club had endured a difficult few years but here now was another bubble of talent moving through and producing several international selections in various under 20 age groups. Alison Campbell and Simon MacIntyre went to the schools' over 17 cross country international while Anna Watson (PV), Ewan Sime (HJ and JT), Vicky O'Brien (LJ), Lesley Clarkson (400), Kate Grainger (JT) and Alan Pearson (sprints) were all in a new junior track and field match in Ayr in May. By now Ian MacKenzie, who had scaled 3.80, had switched first claim to Inverclyde for Scottish League competition but was still coached by Donaldson.

The mid-summer of 1999 was a purple patch for O'Brien and Clarkson who had been training hard together for some months. A foot injury almost kept Vicky out of the Scottish schools, but a below par gold medal with 5.39 got her into the Schools international. Here she made history as the first Inverness athlete to become British schools champion, by 15cm with 5.63 in poor conditions. In between the Scottish schools and the international she posted an astonishing 5.95 at the Scottish under 17 championships to go second on the all-time list. In just two months from late June to late August 1999 she also took AAA silver (5.78), won the Celtic International (5.77) and jumped 5.85 on her GB under 19 debut at the age of 16 in Berlin.

Lesley meanwhile won the Scottish schools over 17 400 in 56.74, just half a second outside a very tough record. The SAF under 20 title was followed by progress to the AAA under 20 final at just 16.

Removing a full second from the 28 year old North Schools 200 record with 25.5 gave her the British Legion Trophy which was presented to her by the previous record holder, Audrey Munro. Soon after she broke Edmonds' senior club 200 record with 24.87 in the SWAL at Meadowbank. Five improvements of her 400 best saw that come down from 59.07 at the start of the season to 55.7 in the Grampian League final in September.

MacIntyre produced a spectacular but alarmingly delayed finishing burst to land the over 17 Scottish schools 1500 in 4:04.94. With Grainger (36.94) and Ian MacKenzie (4.00) also in gold medal form, it was a good championship for Inverness Harriers, leading to seven call ups across the two schools internationals. These were also the athletes who would contribute to a large Inverness presence in the new Bank of Scotland national training squad which meant regular trips south for training days and competition.

International success just kept coming during that summer which saw 23 separate selections. Grainger (38.22), O'Brien (5.77) and Clarkson (39.86 in the 300) were all Celtic international winners. The Scottish team also included Alan Pearson and Ewan Sime, whose 1999 international appearances spread across SP, HJ, JT and LJ, where he improved to 6.52 as an under 17. Kirsty Roger set a heptathlon best of 4866 for GB under 23s in Stuttgart while MacIntyre advanced to 3:58.02 in the 1500.

Then there was the older generation. The 1999 world veteran championships in Gateshead included Dianne and Audrey in the sprints and Cammy in the throws. This was a triumph for Dianne who came home with a medal of each colour - bronze in the 40-44 400 in 60.09, silver in the 4 x 100 and a magnificent world gold in the 4 x 400. Despite a knee injury, Audrey reached the

```
WAVA - Europe                                           Hy-Tek's MEET MANAGER
07/08/99 15:43 PM   XIII World Veterans Athletics Championships          Page 1
              Gateshead, England - Thursday 29/07/99 to Sunday 08/08/99

                         Event 52 W40 400 Meter Dash

               W World: 53.68 Sara Montecinos (CHL) 20/03/94

                   Results - Finals - Saturday 07/08/99
                          Compiled By Time

RANK COMP# ATHLETE NAME             AGE TEAM ACTUAL TIME    AGE-GRADED TIME
-------------------------------------------------------------------------
  1  6208 Verhoef, Tilly C          W43 NED      57.61      52.26   91.67%
  2  3643 Brown, Jenny A            W40 GBR      60.05      55.79   85.38%
—  3  5829 MACKENZIE, Dianne J      W41 GBR      60.09      55.38   86.49% —
  4  6189 Oost, Sonja               W42 NED      60.42      55.25   86.69%
  5  5952 Smith, Margaret           W43 GBR      61.20      55.52   86.29%
  6  5641 Brown, Alison J           W40 GBR      61.56      57.18   83.77%
  7  5668 Colebrook, Katrina J      W41 GBR      61.91      57.06   83.94%
  8  5923 Roe, Edna F               W44 GBR      63.12      56.81   84.33%
```

semi-finals of both 45-49 sprints and struck bronze in the 4 x 100 while Cammy was 7th in the 50-54 hammer. The two women were made life members at that year's AGM.

However this top level success concealed a decided malaise throughout the greater body of the club which could no longer be obscured by league performances. By the skin of their teeth the men avoided relegation to Division 4 while there was no advance for the young athletes on 1998's worst ever fifth place. The women did finish fourth in Division 1 of the SWAL but that was in such a dreadful state that it was discontinued in its current form. From

Dianne after the 1999 World Veteran Championships.

2000, the four division competition which the club had joined in 1981 was reduced to a single league of eight teams, some single-club, others composite.

There was better news in the Grampian League final in Aberdeen where under 11, 13, and 17 boys' wins bucked the trend. Maureen MacKinnon, Vicky O'Brien and sisters Jill and Lesley Clarkson set a women's 4 x 100 league record of 50.2. The developing under 11s were largely a product of the 10 year old group which Colin Baillie had been running for some years on Wednesdays. This final was followed by a somewhat more optimistic AGM than the previous year's. However in the face of facility rents going up from £1600 to £3000, membership fees increased by £5 to £20 for juniors and £33 for adults.

The winter season opened with Stan MacKenzie (32:32) winning the Forres "6" from Andrew Wright (32:54). With MacIntyre 7th in 35:06 and Ann MacLean (41:25) the necessary female member, this produced a team success. In the Golspie 10K, the MacLeans came within 23 seconds of a "his and hers" double when Ann won in 41:32 while Martin (37:16) was men's runner up.

The start of the cross country season revealed further decline across the North in the junior age groups where some of the fields were down to only two runners. At the relays the women and girls only had one other team to beat while the men performed heroically to overcome all-conquering Keith. The now familiar travel drama this time delayed MacKenzie's arrival but after Simon MacIntyre (14:01),

Dougie Flynn (14:50) and Andrew Wright (14:13) built up a 49 second lead, MacKenzie was there to hold off North number one Simon Pride for a 15 second margin of victory.

A healthy 8 in the top 11 at the District Championships kept the women's award in Inverness but there were no complete club teams in any of the junior age groups. There was a similar pattern across the series of league races and this lack of results in junior cross country was arguably a legacy of the abandonment of endurance and conditioning on the advent of Fun Athletics. It was possibly no coincidence that the club's two best under 13 endurance runners at this time were swimmers who adopted athletics as their secondary sport.

On Saturday 16th October 1999, BBC Radio Scotland's six o'clock news announced that a climber from the Inverness area had been rushed to hospital after a fall on An Teallach in Wester Ross. It soon emerged that the victim was Paul Crowe who had been walking the mountain with some Harrier friends. The club was stunned as Paul, who was unconscious for three weeks, battled to recover in hospital from serious head injuries. By New Year's Day 2000 he was well enough to act as starter for the traditional run up to The Mast and attend the town centre Millennium Mile which was won by Simon MacIntyre.

Paul battled slowly back into running and by May 2000 was fit enough to complete the Ben Romach 10K, a remarkable achievement. His clubmates regrouped after crossing the line themselves and applauded him in over the last 100 metres. Paul continued to run and was instrumental in bringing parkruns to Inverness in 2011.

The 2000 indoor season began somewhat controversially when a request from Vicky and Lesley for traditionally standard club support for attending championships was turned down. As a result they decided to appear in their national rather than club vests, starting at the West Districts in January. Competing as seniors, they both won their specialist events and then went head to head in the 60 which produced a 1-2, with the faster starting Vicky having the edge. The finish was caught on film by Inverness photographer Gordon Gillespie who was contracted to SAF to do championship PR photos. When that photo reached the local press the athletes' kit did not go unnoticed.

Just three weeks later, both became AAA junior silver medallists in Birmingham. Despite 4 inches of snow not being ideal for run up practice, Vicky jumped 5.63, losing gold, and another GB vest, by one centimetre. Later that day Lesley overcame the most difficult of qualifying conditions to post two indoor pbs in 90 minutes, both behind Jenny Meadows and improved to 56.08.

This gave her a GB debut in the winning 4 x 400 relay against France and Germany early in March. By now she had been told informally by national coach Meg Stone that she could be short listed for Scotland's proposed relay squad at the 2002 Commonwealth Games in Manchester. Vicky, meanwhile, had the compensation of her Scottish senior debut indoors in Cardiff, although it transpired that this effectively was the swansong of a short but highly successful top level career.

After the SWAL became a single division Inverness Harriers appeared reluctant to become involved with any of the composite arrangements. Consequently some of Charlie Forbes' and my athletes, including internationalists Clarkson, Main and Spence, made their own private arrangement through Bill Walker to form a Lothian and Inverness team. This paid off instantly for Clarkson who, in April 2000 at Scotstoun, shot straight to the top of the Scottish senior 400 rankings with 55.2 at just 17.

Coach and athlete - Lesley Clarkson, Frances Baker Shield winner, June 2000

This immediately placed her at the centre of a tug of war since she was wanted by both Scotland seniors and GB Juniors for the annual Loughborough International. GB eventually got the nod so they could try out athletes for a possible 4 x 400 in the World junior championships in Chile. This placed athlete and coach on opposite sides of the divide that May Sunday afternoon since I was sprints coach for the Scotland team where Charlie Forbes was team manager. For many years Charlie managed Scottish teams at all levels and a GB team at a match in Scotland.

Lesley was on a roll and her next outing was the Scottish junior international in Cyprus with Kate Grainger although Simon MacIntyre was again controversially left out. In June 2000 Lesley brought a major Scottish schools trophy, the Barker Shield, back North again. Her 55.99 wasn't one of her better efforts but it still removed *0.24 from what was regarded as one of the toughe*st championship records so was voted the best performance. The SAF under 20 championships yielded her more gold but over 200 with 25.07. The same day Grainger retained her javelin title and Martin Davidson won the triple jump with 12.37. Grainger and Davidson were also in the under 17 schools international.

The medal-rich summer of 2000 moved on to championships at opposite ends of the age range. The Scottish vets' in Aberdeen produced seven gold medals, including 40-44 records of 27.0 and 61.9 in the 200 and 400 for Dianne. Audrey completed a 45-49 short sprint double with 14.1 and 28.6. The President lifted the 50-54 hammer and discus with 44.62 and 36.14 and Dorothy Bannerman made her veteran championship debut in the 100 hurdles with the first of several golds in 17.4. A few weeks later, Dianne produced possibly the performance of her life when, at 42, she broke the minute for the 400 with 59.98 in the Grampian League.

In July 2000 the Queens Park played host to its first national championship, the SAF under 13s and 15s, which produced two local under 15 successes. Calum Scott-Woodhouse took the 400 with 54.35 while Alexina MacArthur powered away at the end of the 800 for a fast 2:19.19. Scott-Woodhouse and fellow sprinter Grant Burnett gained international debuts when they joined Grainger in the Celtic Games.

A few days later it was tug of war time again for Clarkson who had to turn down the Scottish schools over 17s to contest an EAA Permit meeting in Budapest. This produced another major breakthrough with 54.80 on July 22nd, just days after her 18th birthday. It was her seventh club 400 record in 15 months, but disaster was not far away.

Lesley had been named as captain of the Scottish team at the inaugural Commonwealth Youth Games at Meadowbank. On Thursday August 10th, whilst warming up for a final training session before the weekend's competition, she caught her ankle on the kerb and damaged ligaments badly. Clearly she was out of the Youth Games and captained the team from crutches.

The huge irony was that the accident occurred 14 years almost to the day and just 20 yards away from where Jayne Barnetson had exited the 1986 Commonwealth Games, also with a damaged left ankle. The undivided attention of the team physios accelerated Lesley's return and just three weeks later she managed fifth in the AAAs junior, but in 56.39. A place in the World Junior relay was always a long shot and that was the chance gone.

That year the SYAL was extended to cater for girls and both Inverness teams, struggling for numbers, finished seventh in the final at Scotstoun. This was a worst ever for the boys and the club withdrew from this league altogether. After a decade and a half which had included five national titles in six years, this was another low point. Problems were further highlighted when the men struggled for viability in Division 3 and the only success in the Grampian final was Colin Baillie's under 11 girls. The issue of "social athletes" was raised again but no positive solution was found then or since.

Over the country the senior women had the addition of Mhairi Spence as an under 17 and she also gained a Celtic International. The women's fifth consecutive league title came at Forres with a clean sweep of the first three places with Julie Wilson (18:59), Jennifer Main (19:18) and Ann MacLean (19:37). This completed a grand slam of the league and both championships for 2000-01 with contributions also from Katie Boocock and Mandy MacIver.

The men had a sometimes dramatic but still inconsistent resurgence. They retained the District Relay, took the District Championship for just the third time in 15 years and at Nairn won their first North league race for seven years. Stan MacKenzie (13:02), Eric Riddle (12:47), Andrew Wright (12:47) and Simon MacIntyre (12:45) delivered the goods in the relay at Inverness's Canal Field before Mark MacLeod replaced the unavailable MacIntyre in the league race. Steve Worsley and Brian MacKenzie then joined the successful league quartet to make a District Championship six. MacIntyre gained another Scottish under 20 vest for the Reebok Cross Challenge in advance of an under 23 selection the following winter.

The last weekend in February 2001 saw new ground broken twice. Lesley Clarkson became Inverness Harriers' first ever AAAs champion, in the under 20 400 in 56.34 in

Birmingham. Nearer home there was a first ever women's national cross country team title in Irvine. Jennifer Main got the individual

bronze and the Spence sisters, Mhairi and Fiona, were 7th and 18th. Internationalists Jennifer and Mhairi later shared the Rosebowl in a week when Clarkson, the only Scot in the GB junior indoor team, became Bank of Scotland athlete of the month for March.

The Foot and Mouth outbreak of early 2001 wreaked havoc with the distance programme. The Inverness Half survived but the Nairn 10K and the Craig Dunain Hill Race were cancelled along with the Scottish schools cross country championships, a particular blow for Jennifer Main, Mhairi Spence and Alexina MacArthur.

That spring Clarkson went to San Diego, California for warm weather training with the Commonwealth Games Preparation Squad. She returned in top form for the British Universities at Scotstoun where a sparkling run saw her race through 200 in 25.1 to edge fellow Scot Carey Easton by a yard in 54.44, with the rest of the field well adrift. Equally importantly, this was inside the European Junior qualifying standard of 54.55. However, two other British athletes had run even faster and got the individual places while Lesley was named in the relay for Grosseto in July. At the venue, just two days before the final and selected for the second leg, she came down with a stomach bug and had to withdraw. The reserve replaced her and Team GB still took first place. A first international championship medal proved as elusive as ever.

Around this time two of the club's leading male sprinters began to make their marks. Ali Beaton was the classic 100/200 runner who learned from a single 400 that this was not for him. However it was that same move to 400 which made Grant Burnett. In a career which has lasted over a decade and a half, Ali has made the North District championships his own at both 100 and 200 and also tasted Scottish championship triumph.

Ali has epitomised the ultimate Inverness Harriers club man for his entire senior career with a string of performances in leagues, championships, open meetings and Highland Games. He won his first North title in 2001 with a championship record of 11.13 but was hit by cramp in the 200. This was a problem which was often not far away and almost

Ali Beaton

cost him his finest hour at Scotstoun in 2003 where his Scottish championship weekend began with 11.00 in the 100 heats and a windy pb of 10.92 in the semis. Then cramp struck in the final so the overnight remedy before the 200 was a stiff dose of salt water. This kept the problem at bay and Ali ran superbly for silver by 0.01 in 22.77, becoming the first Inverness man to win a Scottish sprint medal since Ian Young in 1935.

Burnett meanwhile began his transition to 400 in 2001 with SAF under 17 gold in 52.18 and 200 silver in 22.68. At the Scottish schools he went one better with a double in 23.29/52.61 while Calum Scott-Woodhouse booked the second international place in 53.58. Grant also gained Celtic selection before ending the summer top of the Scottish under 17 rankings with 11.37/22.68/50.80. He lost 2002 to a stress fracture in his foot but was soon back.

The 2001 AGM saw a complete change at the top with Ashley Woodhouse taking over as President, Ian Fleming as Vice, Fiona MacKintosh as Secretary and Rob Deakin, who was an accountant, as Treasurer. Rob's first task was a cash flow analysis and he reported that there was an imminent danger of the club running out of money, prompting urgent fundraising. Maureen MacKinnon was awarded the new Duncan Memorial Trophy for multi-events.

In the early 2000s, much of the junior coaching burden was undertaken by Ian Fleming and Bett McAllister who, as Bett Robertson, was a former club athlete. Bett did especially well with the precocious talent of Briony Swanson. At the age of 12, Briony, whose father Dennis did much work in the background, had an incredible 2002 with 4:59.9 to win the Scottish schools under 14 1500 and 2:22.02 for 800. In cross country she took the Scottish under 13 title and the Banks Salver plus a clean sweep of all six under 13 North league races. This spearheaded the only team success that winter where the MacLaren twins, Jade and Danica, were the other main counters. Brian Fieldsend got the Banks Rosebowl and then ran 2:35:02 for second in the Scottish championship at the Lochaber Marathon.

That 2001-02 cross country season's failures were usually due to lack of runners which at times was acute, but there was an early peak in October when four relay titles out of five were retained in a single weekend. The men failed to hold on to theirs at the Districts but the women (Jennifer Main 15:10, Katie Boocock 16:09 and Julie Wilson 15:01), boys and girls all came out on top at Nairn. The next day the second fastest time ever in the Great Glen Relay, 6:10:21, was set by Kenny Riddle, Eric Riddle, Craig Preece, Brian Fieldsend, Steve Worsley and Stan MacKenzie.

The latest veteran arrival was Kathryn Nicholson, formerly Kathryn Urquhart, whom we last met as the under 15 relay reserve in 1980. On her veteran debut she took the Scottish indoor 60 title by a whisker in 8.51, the 200 in 27.86 and just missed the 400 with 64.03. Next it was British bronze in 8.33 and 27.75 before outdoor success in a veteran career which was brought to a premature end by a foot injury.

The main event of 2002 was the Manchester Commonwealth Games with the prospect of Lesley Clarkson being selected for the 4 x 400. The winter season saw her win her third UK-level title in 12 months at the British Universities indoors. Despite the Kelvin Hall not being the fastest, her 55.49 was only 0.08 outside the championship record.

This led to her GB senior debut in the relay at the annual Kelvin Hall international where she was invited to share the pre-event publicity with European indoor 60 champion Jason Gardiner. Never the fastest starter, she was horrified to be handed the difficult opening leg since she was reckoned to "know her home track". She ran 55.3, effectively another indoor best, establishing the team in its eventual third place.

A bronze at the Scottish trials in June (55.12) followed by 54.85 in Geneva kept her well on course. She was duly named in the six woman Scottish 4 x 400 pool for Manchester, becoming the fifth Harrier to be selected for the Commonwealth Games. However this was at a time when permanent residence in Glasgow led to her joining a Coatbridge based training group. Unfortunately she then suffered a form dip between selection and the Games at the end of July and missed out on a run in the competition itself.

Other highlights included Kate Grainger progressing to 39.52 in the javelin at the open meeting which had shrunk considerably from its earlier 300 athletes. She set a senior North District javelin record of 38.56 and was selected for the Cyprus junior international. Beaton went sub-23 in the 200 for the first time and Kirsty Law added 6 metres to the under 17 discus championship record with a rankings-topping 37.60.

Kirsty had begun with Black Isle AAC but moved to Inverness Harriers to obtain discus coaching and became Cammy Roger's latest success. A poor 2002 Scottish schools only yielded bronze. Some negotiation was therefore required with the SSAA to get her an international discus berth at Scotstoun where she was already doing the shot as champion, as was Mark Deakin. It was just as well the SSAA took this on board because with 37.94, as a first year under

17, Kirsty became the second female Highland athlete after Vicky O'Brien in 1999 to win the British Schools International.

So it was with some dismay that no SAF selection letter for the Celtic Games arrived the following week but it emerged that this had gone to the wrong Kirsty Law and once it was sorted out she went on to win that as well before SAF under 17 gold produced her fourth major success of the summer.

The Halliburton (formerly Grampian) League final at the Queens Park was mired in controversy when an overnight downpour created travel difficulties although the track was usable. The meeting went ahead despite the absence of a disgruntled Aberdeen team. Inverness Harriers retained their women's crown, rounded off by a 4x100 success from a half-veteran quartet of Maureen MacKinnon, Dianne MacKenzie, Dorothy Bannerman and Lesley Clarkson in 53.3. Beaton's 11.24 made him the top male track performer for the second year in a row. Again in this league the women were stronger than the men who, in the North, lagged well behind Black Isle.

Brian Fieldsend's summer road successes included the hilly Forres Games 10K (32:27) and the Moray Marathon (2:38:48) while veteran Graham Laing ran 92 minutes in the Inverness to Drumnadrochit road race, just 17 minutes slower than his record of 22 years previously.

As a GB senior internationalist, Lesley Clarkson received her life membership at an AGM where Maggie Roger inherited the Presidency from Ashley Woodhouse. The hope was expressed that a rebounding junior group was sowing the seeds of a recovery from the recent 20 year membership low. The meeting agreed a cut price senior "non-track" membership for just £20 to attract adult distance runners.

The 2002 North cross country relays produced only silver for the women and bronze for the girls. Lochaber's Dawn Scott ran all three women's legs consecutively as a non-counter and beat all the teams. The Inverness women took yet another District championship with Fiona Dahl 3rd, Mandy MacIver 4th and Katie Boocock 6th. The North league produced top placings for veteran Julie Wilson and sisters Alexina and Charlotte MacArthur in the under 17 and under 13 age groups. There never was going to be any chance of junior team honours since the club sent no youngsters to the opening match due to concerns about the safety and suitability of the courses in Thurso.

The 2003 Scottish veteran championships were at Grant Park, Forres where George Mitchell's track sessions paid off in the form of a four second gap on Aberdeen's Colin Youngson in the last 300 for the over 55 title. Sixth in the British vets' at Irvine was followed by another over 55 international. The club championships had a nailbiting finish with a tie for second place between two members of the medical profession, dentist Tom McWilliam and doctor Calum Urquhart. Indoors, Kathryn Nicholson retained both Scottish veteran sprint titles and took British 60 silver and 200 bronze.

There was a Craig Dunain double for Brian Fieldsend (35:01) and new Scottish hill running champion Fiona Dahl (46:52). Fieldsend next moved well down distance to take the Halliburton 1500 in 4:15.53 and extended his run of 10K successes at Ben Romach in Forres with 32:26 on a course particularly susceptible to windy conditions.

At the outdoor District championships Law's under 17 discus record of 38.56 was matched by Rachael MacKenzie with 1.64 in the high jump which she improved to 1.65 at the North schools before a promising 1.70 in the Halliburton. At the North Schools Burnett's wind impeded 11.30/22.81 got him the British Legion Trophy for the second time in three years.

Kirsty set the 2003 Scottish schools alight with three under 17 titles leading to a triple international outing. She retained the shot with a 10.67 pb and atoned for the previous year's discus debacle with 38.54 after taking the hammer with 36.43. Burnett (22.61) and Eleanor Richardson (26.06), who frequently travelled to training from Gairloch, did an over 17 200 double.

Kirsty blasted through 40 metres for the first time at the following week's Ross shire schools. The throw was properly measured, but was not allowed to stand. Completely unpractised manual timekeepers were returning track times in hundredths, which implied they were fully automatic. The statisticians predictably queried a clutch of half-second 100 metre pbs and the organisers responded by cancelling all results, field as well.

Kirsty rapidly put that disappointment behind her and the following month, as Scottish captain, became the first north athlete to retain a British schools title before winning the Celtic Games by 4 metres with 39.59. Then to cap another momentous season she became the club's first AAA outdoor champion with 39.80 to remain unbeaten in Great Britain. Maggie Roger awarded that year's President's Trophy – deservedly – to Kirsty's coach, her husband Cammy.

Beaton's 200 silver was not the only one to come North from the 2003 Scottish championships. Now first claim City of Glasgow for league purposes, Clarkson matched it in the 400 (55.58) before finishing third for GB under 23s against France with 55.28. In the Loughborough International she was joined in the Scottish 4 x 400 by Kathryn Evans from Lossiemouth who eventually joined Inverness second claim for the Halliburton League and ran the 4 x 400 in the 2010 Delhi Commonwealth Games.

Then there was the 2003 Newtonmore Games. Here a 14 year old novice called Jamie Bowie finished the 100 behind endurance coach Charlie Forbes and the 800 behind sprints coach Charles Bannerman. It is not clear how influential these defeats were in young Master Bowie turning away from both distances towards the 400 but both coaches have frequently dined out on the tale!

2003 must go down as the club's least successful league season ever because it drew a complete blank across the ten age groups of the only league it contested in its own right, the Halliburton. Dundee was a controversial choice of venue, leading to Nairn boycotting the final altogether.

The women's North cross country championship run continued that November, with help from

Glenurquhart Games 2003. Rear – Dianne, myself, Lesley Clarkson, Charlie Forbes, Rachael MacKenzie. Front – Lynsey MacIntosh, Kathryn Nicholson.

newcomer Eleanor Reid. This at least was progress from the previous month's relays where the only Inverness Harriers presence was a single, unplaced men's team. The women, after struggling for three runners at the final match, also won the league. Otherwise it was almost a complete blank in this local competition. That season Tom McWilliam and Mandy MacIver were awarded the Banks trophies. Lesley Clarkson signalled her move up to 800 as first woman in the Nairn Turkey Trot where the overall winner was her former GB team mate Andrew Lemoncello who was visiting family. Two months later she took Scottish indoor bronze in 2:08.95.

Katie Boocock devised a new 5.3 mile course for the 2004 Craig Dunain Hill Race. The A82 crossing had been a constant worry and the zigzags, like much of the rest of the area, were seriously eroded by bikers. Katie's out and back solution involved the Great Glen Way from the new start at Torvean Bridge before cutting on to forestry tracks for the final ascent to the mast. The race produced a Forres 1-2 from international hill runner Kyle Greig (33:03) and former Ben Nevis Race winner Graham Bartlett (33:52), with Steve Worsley first for Inverness in 6th place (35:18).

In May 2004 the club held a dinner to mark the combined service to athletics of 105 years by Tom MacKenzie (57) and Walter Banks (48). Both had now retired completely but a few weeks later, Walter appeared at the South Highland Schools secondary meeting and sat, watch in hand, in the seats formerly occupied by the manual timekeepers. I went to sit beside him and realized that he was testing his timekeeping skills against the official electronic results. Unbeknown to Walter, I did my own comparison between what he was recording and the electronic timing. It emerged that, at the age of 83, he had taken all four times in a 400 with an average error of 0.04 seconds!

The summer of 2004 was so sensational for Kirsty Law that the whole tale needs told at once. Having wintered well, this huge Caley Thistle fan returned from warm weather training via Hampden without a pre-purchased ticket, so was refused entry to her team's 1-1 Scottish Cup semi-final draw with Dunfermline. So she may have been taking out some of her frustration at the following day's Harriers' open meeting with a huge discus pb of 42.07. That this was her first year as an under 20 didn't stop her from winning another AAA title at Bedford, leading to her GB junior debut in July in Manchester against Australia and Scandinavia. In a moment of inspiration, she winged the 1kg implement out to a massive 46.40 to go top of the UK under 20 rankings.

She said: *"I was completely overcome at such a huge improvement and I think a lot of it is because I have been learning to focus a lot better in competition which means I can get closer to what I'm really capable of."* Unfortunately she didn't quite follow this through to the Commonwealth Youth Games in Australia at the end of the year and 41.30 left her in 6th place, short of the medal which a more realistic effort would probably have obtained.

It was also a great year for Rachael MacKenzie who equalled her 1.70 pb for fifth in the senior championships, where there were no Inverness medals. In her own age group she had a treble in the Scottish schools (1.68), the national under 17s (1.65) and the Celtic Games (1.65).

Meanwhile Lesley Clarkson improved her 800 to 2:06.74 and won AAAs under 23 silver, leading to her only GB international over two laps. By now she was Inverness Harriers' most capped GB internationalist by some way but at the end of the 2004 season she decided to retire from the sport after five years at the very top.

Elsewhere there was ongoing concern. The North Schools produced what the Courier called *"the poorest set of results in living memory"* and in 2005 the qualifying standards had to be relaxed by between 10 and 20%. Even against diminished competition, Inverness schools in 2004 took only 13 gold from a huge programme. This prompted the vastly experienced Colin Baillie to observe: *"It is very worrying indeed to see standards falling as much as they have. Some performances are very poor indeed. Unfortunately this seems to mirror a general decline in athletics and we are going to have to work very hard to reverse that trend."* He also deplored Scottish Atlhetics' slowness in providing the development officer which they had promised more than a year previously.

All the same there were up and coming prospects. Danica MacLaren took Scottish schools under 17 javelin silver with 28.95, while her twin sister Jade brought the club 300 record down to 41.94. And the young lad who had been beaten by the two coaches the previous year at Newtonmore did finally opt for 400 where he posted 54.28 at 15.

The league season — in other words the Halliburton — was marginally better than 2003 with final wins for the under 17 women and men. However 50 individual events yielded only three Inverness "A" winners - Rachael MacKenzie (1.65), Ali Beaton (11.70) and Kirsty Law...... with 24.86 in the javelin!

At the end of her phenomenal season, this was Kirsty's final competition under coach Roger since Cammy and Maggie were taking a step back from athletics. Maggie stood down as President and Andrew Mackintosh stepped up from Vice. Maggie's valedictory gesture was to award the President's Trophy to Joggers stalwart Sylvia Main. Predictably the main women's trophies went to Kirsty and Rachael while Grant Burnett, now consistently sub-50 in the 400, got the MacKenzie Cup.

The cross country season gave a now familiar women's treble, albeit against very limited opposition and with Eleanor Reid by far and away the North's top individual. The team successes included a tenth consecutive North District title over the club's new course at Fairways. This was also the early stage of a run of ten consecutive league titles which only ended in 2014.

By this point domination of North women's cross country by the club had become so well established that further repetition can be avoided from now on by assuming success unless otherwise stated.

On the other hand different individuals led the charge as Eleanor Reid and Morag Ross were succeeded by Melissa Whyte, Sheila Gollan and occasionally Jenny Bannerman, with evolving supporting casts.

2004-05 yielded limited junior successes which included the under 13 and 15 girls' championships and the under 13 girls' league. Murdo Traill led the under 13 boys to the club's first male league team success for 14 years. National cross country participation was now effectively a distant memory although junior numbers did creep up in the club handicaps.

The women also shone among a record field of 1136 in the 21st Inverness Half Marathon in March 2005. Lorna Bennie (92:15), Lesley Clarkson, now reincarnated as a semi competitive road runner (93:55) and Jennifer Main (95:41) took the team title. Shortly after, Siggy Gould led a men's trio which won the corresponding award at Craig Dunain.

That summer saw an attempt to return to the Men's League by forming Highland Athletic Club, a separate body existing solely for that purpose, and some Inverness Harriers were involved in this pooling of North talent. However matters had now descended to such levels that not even the whole of the North could sustain a Men's League team and Highland Athletic Club lapsed after two seasons.

One further indication of the depth of that descent was the Courier reporting, after the opening Halliburton League meeting, that (at a local league match!) *"There was a breakthrough for the club when they won the under 13 boys' contest."* Ross County continued to lead the way in the Halliburton North male contests and in a final which had few Inverness individual winners, the only Inverness title was in that under 13 boys' age group.

Much of the club's credibility therefore depended on the likes of Grant Burnett, Kirsty Law, Rachael MacKenzie and a fast improving Jamie Bowie, with telling performances also from Ali Beaton. Burnett and Law made their Scottish senior international debuts at Loughborough with, respectively, a 48.2 flying relay split and a throw of 44.47 for fifth place. They were also winners in the under 23 Derby international. Scottish under 23 champion Burnett was regularly sub-49 now and ended the season on 48.02 via North District championship records of 21.81 and 48.44. However his season was interrupted by an injury – from high jumping at the Inverness Games.

MacKenzie cleared 1.70 again and won the over 17 schools international while Law had 10 throws above 44 metres but could not quite match her 2004 best. Beaton roared back from injury with a 22.39 behind Burnett, and an 11.17 to win the 100 at the North championships before a late season legal pb of 10.97. Bowie had a great Scottish Schools silver in 51.56, was selected for both Schools and Celtic internationals and improved to 50.68. Along with Jade MacLaren, now on 41.34 in the 300, Bowie became another new entrant to the Bank of Scotland squad.

That summer of 2005 saw Dorothy Bannerman set a Scottish veteran 40-45 record of 13.09 for the 80 hurdles while there was another tentative attempt at a summer distance race series with one or two events held. Beaton and MacKenzie took the premier senior awards while the under 17 trophies went to MacLaren and Bowie.

However this time the donor did not present the MacKenzie Cup at the AGM. Tom MacKenzie had died that February, severing a vital link with the club's origins. There was further disappointing news for that AGM. Membership had been recovering from its 20 year low of 120 but 2004-05 saw another drop from 188 to 172. There had been very slight rises among the juniors to 50 girls and 32 boys while the men dropped from 44 to 38 and women from 22 to 18. The biggest fall of all was in senior non-track, from 20 to just 5.

Despite an attempt to introduce "standards awards" for the youngsters, there had been another loss of momentum in a club which was seriously stagnating again. The main area of optimism was a small number of top performers, including a nucleus of emerging young athletes, three of whom in particular now need to be properly introduced.

CHAPTER 11 – MAJOR MEDAL AT LAST! - 2005-2011

Since this is not a crime novel, there is no need to conceal the identity of three of the main suspects until they reappear in the final pages. It therefore suits the narrative to summarise the careers of Kirsty Law, Rachael MacKenzie and Jamie Bowie from late 2005 until just before the end of this chapter which gives an account of the club's first major medal in 2011.

Kirsty first breached 50 metres with 50.89 in July 2006 before a huge 52.30 the following month. By 2011, unfortunately a year too late for the Delhi Commonwealth Games, that improved to 55.17 at the Loughborough International for third place in the UK senior rankings. The intervening years saw a move to Loughborough and further changes of coach as well as surgery on her back. She won the 2006 AAA under 23s before retaining that as part of a trio of major titles which also comprised the Inter Counties and Scottish championships.

Kirsty Law

Her only real low point in 2007 was underperforming in the European under 23s and only 2010 failed to produce Scottish senior gold. By now third in the Scottish all-time list, Kirsty was never out of the annual UK top six after 2005. However she still loves to return to the Queens Park where she has delighted spectators with a number of 50 metre throws. With huge reluctance she changed her first claim to Shaftesbury Barnet and then Sale Harriers for UKWAL competition but was made a life member of Inverness Harriers in 2006. Her desire to compete for Inverness even extended to offending officialdom by wearing the club vest out of place at a championship.

The same six seasons were, literally, somewhat up and down for Rachael who increased her personal best to 1.76 in 2007 and matched that in 2009. Coached throughout by Dianne, with some technical support from outwith, she took four Scottish senior silvers and a bronze and, in 2007, AAA under 23 silver. A number of Scottish selections followed, including her senior debut at the 2007

Loughborough international where she was third with 1.74. However for Rachael, the best was to come after 2011.

Jamie is the youngest of this trio by 16 months so although his 400 dipped into the 48s in 2007 and 2008 from his under 17 best of 50.86 it was 2009 before he really began to develop. That season, under Polish coach

Rachael MacKenzie

Piotr Haczek, there was a big improvement to 47.26 en route to fifth in the AAA under 23 championships and relay selection for the European under 23s. This followed a Scottish senior silver in 47.87. He

Jamie Bowie

then left for a university year in Paris where he qualified for the French elite indoor championships and came home to take his first Scottish senior title, the 2010 indoor in 48.54.

In complete contrast, the club was otherwise suffering from a decided lack of profitable activity and low overall performance standards. Some have blamed a hangover from the fun athletics ethos and methodology of the 1990s, such as when youngsters could be seen at training sessions sitting round a bucket throwing beanbags into it.

Cross country age group successes in 2005-06 were

largely limited to under 13 and under 17 girls. Inter district representation was even more limited, partly due to the sensible decision to restrict this level of competition only to the small numbers for whom it was realistic.

Just days before his 95th consecutive club handicap, Jim "The Postie" Davidson was knocked off his bike and injured. Undaunted, he negotiated an extra 20 minutes' start and walked round the Kinmylies course to maintain his record. A year later he received a presentation from the club on completing 100 handicaps, a sequence begun in 1987.

George Mitchell won the 60-65 Scottish vets' cross country championship at Forres and was later selected for a veteran mountain running international in Switzerland. However SAF failed to tell him and the first he knew about it was from the Courier the day before the race by which time it was too late. Former Highland League defender turned distance runner Billy Skinner became organiser of the Craig Dunain Hill Race in 2006. In seventh place, he also headed the winning club team, accompanied by Mitchell and Jim Meehan. This was matched by the women's trio of Karen MacLeod, Katie Boocock and Muriel Fuller.

There was controversy over the Nairn 10K when Moray Firth Radio promoted it as a charity fundraiser. This prompted a huge influx of joggers, forcing the organisers to impose an entry limit late on. As a result a number of club runners, including one of the leading Harriers Tom McWilliam, were unable to contest an SAF permitted race which was part of a competitive series. In the end the race was postponed by snow, which caused a knock-on postponement of the club cross country championships – bizarrely until July 25th!

There was snow on the track too for the April open meeting which produced little. The late season meetings, which included the club championships, were very thinly subscribed. North District championship gold medals were restricted to 16, a total almost matched by both Orkney and Shetland.

In the Halliburton League, the men finally began to edge in front of Ross County in the North section, hence removing a source of some embarrassment. In the final, Ali Beaton scorched to 10.93. There were team wins for the under 13 girls and the women whose only individual success was Danica MacLaren with 30.28 in the javelin.

2006 saw the return of both boys and girls to the SYAL but the club failed to reach the final. To make things worse, a downpour at the final qualifier at uncovered Caird Park, Dundee forced the youngsters to acquire dry clothes from a local supermarket.

Scottish schools medals were few and far between and comprised a 400 silver for Jade MacLaren, who went on to win the SAF under 20s with 56.94, and three bronze. One of these, and an international relay place, went to Donald Ferguson in the under 17 400 (53.14). By now Bett McAllister and Ian Fleming were operating team coaching and Donald was their first internationalist.

Ali Beaton and Jamie Bowie decided to try the "pro" games, so off they went to Halkirk. Like Grant McDowall who contested Tain a few years previously, they returned battered, bruised and spiked while Bowie was knocked over in the 200. The typically mild mannered Beaton merely commented: *"Let's just say it was different!"*

The Hunter Cup went to Jade MacLaren, now down to 56.82 and an under 23 internationalist. It was presented to her by her own coach Kathryn Nicholson, Charles Hunter's niece. Beaton got the MacKenzie Cup while the junior awards went to sprinters Donald Ferguson and Celtic international debutante Sarah Smith.

The 2006 AGM sent the club into its diamond jubilee season with a new top table of: President – Angus Dick, Vice President – Charlie Forbes, Secretary – Hilary Cameron, Treasurer – Fiona MacKay, Membership Secretary – Alister Cameron.

This AGM also welcomed a surplus of £2000, partly due to increased fundraising and partly to reduced levels of activity. Moves were initiated to address this latter issue through attracting more youngsters and more ambitious, competition orientated training programmes.

There had been intermittent controversy for years over conditions and courses for cross country in Caithness and Lochaber which resurfaced in Thurso in November 2006 in weather which had seen a tanker swamped in the Pentland Firth. Some athletes were bruised by the impact of hailstones and even the indestructible George Mitchell was forced to drop out for the first time in 20 years. Jackie Mair (formerly Lyall) collapsed during the women's race and had to be hospitalised with a low core temperature.

Afterwards she said: *"I think the main problem was exposure. The weather really was dreadful and there's absolutely no way I'll be going back up there for cross country. My 12 year old daughter was also running and I wouldn't let her go again either. It certainly wasn't suitable for kids and the races should never have gone ahead in the first place."* What saved Jackie an overnight stay in hospital was that she could travel home with team mate Dr. Eleanor Reid.

2006-07 also yielded increasing but still limited awards in the younger age groups where a major revival was beginning across all club activities. Craig Campbell, Catriona Fraser and Chris Fife were the pick of these juniors.

The Women's League was providing good individual opportunities. Jackie Mair's daughter Charis high jumped 1.56 at the age of 12 in the April 2007 meeting and a year later improved to 1.67. By now the Petrofac North qualifying matches were going completely Inverness's way, albeit in the face of very low overall turnouts. Donald Ferguson, with 1:59.37, posted the club's first sub-2minute 800 for several years. Trophies in the Petrofac final were again limited to a couple of junior age groups.

A more successful SYAL campaign produced a very close North East section battle between Aberdeen, Arbroath and Inverness. A chapter of disasters at Dundee, ranging from no shelter to no results, led team manager Janice MacLeay, that year's President's Trophy winner, to describe the organisation as *"a complete shambles"*. In the end the club missed a place in the national final on the strength of points docked for not having a full quota of officials but it was clear that a steadily expanding club would be a prime candidate for future finals. Meanwhile the men returned to farming themselves out to various clubs for SAL competition.

A North District tally of 25 gold, 18 silver and 12 bronze against mainly island opposition included a 100 championship record of 11.10 for Ali Beaton while Bowie and MacKenzie impressed with 50.54 and 1.70. That same week MacKenzie and Law were named for the Loughborough international, sending a positive ripple through the club. MacKenzie got another senior call up for the Celtic Cup.

The club's three top performers went to the AAAs under 20s and 23s in Bedford where it was discus gold for Law (50.37) and high jump silver for MacKenzie (1.70) while Bowie got his first sub-50 timing of 49.97 in the 400 semi-finals. An attempt to revive attendances at national championships saw a dozen competitors at the under 15s and under 17s come home with three silver and four bronze.

2007 saw the long awaited appointment of the Highlands' first Athletics Development Officer, Julie Wyatt. This post was partly funded by the clubs and she also, for a time, became a coach and a committee member at Inverness Harriers along with Tracy Tamijmarane. A new body, Culloden Harriers, came into being and for a time worked as a feeder for Inverness Harriers.

Meanwhile Scottish Athletics introduced Regional Squads but, along with other aspects of the sport in the North, a Highland Regional Squad was not viable. There were neither enough athletes capable of reaching even reduced standards nor coaches experienced enough to run the squad. Within the club the vastly experienced Harry Lakeland returned to oversee the under 13 age group which was where his coaching career had begun 30 years previously.

The 2007-08 cross country season produced major progress as numbers, boosted by the restoration of club buses, and quality of performances improved among the juniors. There were three young athletes' team titles in the league, making Inverness Harriers the top club for the first time in many years. This should, however, be tempered by a lot of other clubs having incomplete teams. Inverness's weakness was the men who twice failed to raise a full league side.

However the overall tide was very much on the turn and another step back in the right direction was a return to the national cross country championships at Falkirk. A party of 26 Harriers included under 13 boys' team silver medaliists Craig Campbell (7th), Patrick Urquhart (11th), Patrick Kelly (31st) and Alexander Thorne (66th).

There was still a slump in indoor competition but Kirsty turned to shot putting and even gained an indoor senior international in Cardiff. She improved to 12.63 and became Scottish senior champion with 12.22.

Although participation and performance levels had begun to rise, so had tensions within the club. In the face of ongoing internal problems, President Angus Dick resigned after 18 months in office and Vice President Charlie Forbes took over. Angus told the Courier: *"Over the period I've been in office, we've gone from one minor crisis to another. There have been things happening that have not made life easy as President. I would not want to name any particular individuals but it has not been easy over the last 18 months."*

Difficulties had been mounting and some of the club's longer standing members were at odds with a minority faction on the committee. By now there were frictions across an appreciable range of the club's activities. Possibly the biggest controversy related to the SYAL and this played a significant part in the resignation of five committee members. The committee rejected a proposal that the club should give up its individual SYAL status to become part of a new body called Team Hippo under the umbrella of a pan-Highland development organisation. However, this was unexpectedly brought back to committee and squeezed through.

So at a time of major expansion, and with every chance of reaching the national final in the club's own right, the number of competitive opportunities for Inverness athletes was suddenly slashed in a composite team. This also meant that Inverness Harriers' coaches had to surrender to Hippo their selection rights over their own athletes. There were further fears that this might be the thin end of a much more sinister wedge which could become a regional club. However membership of Team Hippo only lasted for 2008 and a prompt U-turn saw Inverness Harriers apply for and regain its separate status while Hippo also continued. The other benefit here was to double at a stroke the number of SYAL places available to athletes from the North.

A clear top spot in the 2008 District medal table was this time largely due to the rapidly growing junior ranks. Leading Inverness performances included Sarah Smith's 12.33, the fastest 100 by a club member since Alison Edmonds. This gained her a senior selection for Loughborough and for the under 18 Celtic Games, both in the 4 x 100.

Sarah was coached by Dianne who had by now retired from competition. Apart from Rachael's successes and Sarah's progress, Charis Mair (HJ) and Donald Ferguson (4x400) also reached the Celtic Games. Now that Bett McAllister and Ian Fleming had completed their spells of coaching, Charis and Donald had moved to Dianne's group. Charis won the Scottish schools under 15 high jump with Ian Coghill the boys' champion. She also took the Scottish under 15 high jump whilst reducing the 75 hurdles club record to a very respectable 11.38.

The Petrofac produced the club's best results since joining, with successes in the under 15 girls, under 13 boys and under 11 girls,

Donald Ferguson, Jamie Bowie and Sarah Smith at the 2006 Celtic Games.

plus five good second places. The club championships reverted to late season club nights and entries soared to over 100. Rachael and Jamie received the Hunter and MacKenzie awards while Charis and sprinter Stuart Laing took the Duncan and Post Office trophies.

Road running had been very quiet but Andrew MacRae, David Gallie and Michael Bond sowed the seeds of a revival with a Golspie

10K team win. A few weeks later in October 2008 there was yet another belated but incredibly successful return of a former Harrier to the ranks when 44 year old Melissa Jeans (now Melissa Whyte) rejoined after 25 years. In a second career which lasted three and a half years before it was interrupted by injury, Melissa took Inverness Harriers' women's long distance running to unprecedented levels.

Her only two defeats by North athletes were by Lochaber's Nicola Meekin in the District Championships and Dawn Scott in a league match, both during the first two months of her return and she steadily embarked on a wider stage. Between 2009 and 2011 she took the club records for 10K to 35:05, 10 miles to 58:57 and the half marathon to 77:26. At 47 she became Inverness Harriers' oldest Scottish senior internationalist with road and cross country selections. She also became the backbone of a club team which, both on road and country, would soon field the top three runners in the area.

Melissa Whyte

Her individual 2008 District Championship silver also came alongside 3 gold, 1 silver and 2 bronze from eight team contests. Another improving distance runner, Mhairi MacLennan, was top under 15 girl. There was the further boost of a win in the final men's league race on a Forres course shortened due to a thick covering of snow. Alec Keith (5th in 27:31), Andrew MacRae (6th in 28:01), Jonny Muir (8th in 28:21) and Graeme Campbell (20th in 30:34) were the counting four.

Melissa made her road debut in the 2009 Nairn 10K with 37:04, a time only previously bettered within the club and the North by Julie Wilson (36:47). This took North women's road running into a completely new era, where it would stay as other runners began to swell a strengthening Inverness women's team. These included Jenny Bannerman who won four consecutive local road races in the early summer of 2009 before a rapid improvement across the 800 to 10K range. Melissa was the unanimous choice for the Mary Banks Salver, with the Rosebowl going to one of its youngest ever winners, Craig Campbell.

At the 25th Inverness Half Marathon inaugural 1985 winner Graham Laing was given competitor number 1 although injury reduced him to a token 80:58. The 2009 race saw the introduction of the Graeme Moffat Memorial Quaich following the death of one of the race's stalwarts. This is for the first Inverness Harrier to finish and the inaugural recipient was Jonny Muir (78:16). On the hills, individual winner Alec Keith, David Gallie and Dan Dickens took the honours at Cioch Mor near Dingwall.

One big track and field highlight of 2009 was the club's return in its own right to the SYAL. This created an instant rivalry with Team Hippo, the 10 club combine from the rest of the North. Brian Ross and Harry Lakeland were among the officials assembled to guarantee no repeat of the shortage which had cost a final place in 2007. A 50 seater bus and a minibus were needed for the opening match in Dundee, a reflection of a rising membership which was now well over 200 once again.

Defeating Hippo by 519 points to 487 on the club's return was a huge morale booster. Successes included Ian Coghill in the under 17 high jump (1.82) and Callum Green in the under 15 100 (12.3). The second match went marginally Hippo's way, sending Inverness into the final qualifier as narrow North East section leaders on event points. That also went narrowly to the 10 club select but both teams progressed to the final. Here a delay at SAL in advising registration numbers for new athletes led to the loss of their points, consigning Inverness to seventh place.

In the other league, the Petrofac, there was an increase from three to four of the ten trophies – under 11 boys and girls, under 13 boys and under 17 men. Rachael MacKenzie (1.76 HJ) and David Smith (under 15 sprint double) both won best performer awards.

Further evidence of local progress came at the 2009 District Championships where 31 gold, 12 silver and 15 bronze represented a 30% increase in titles over 2008. The usual suspects had a busy day with a sprint double for Beaton and another high jump title for MacKenzie.

Stuart Laing received the British Legion Trophy at the North Schools for an 11.21/22.87 sprint double. Inevitably the link – or lack of one! – was made with the fact that his father Graham had had a distinguished athletics career as a marathon runner. These two extremes re-emerged later that year when Lesley Clarkson supplemented her 200, 400 and 800 club records with a fourth one –

in the marathon! She recorded 3:35:22 on her debut in Berlin and improved to 3:08:37 in Turin in 2012.

For six weeks in the middle of the summer training was switched to Charleston Academy to accommodate work on a £125,000 track upgrade, allowing it to host more elaborate meetings. This included repairing worn areas, new pole vault and steeplechase facilities and equipment to time races on the back straight, with the prevailing wind. However, to my knowledge, this facility has never been used so the track's productivity remains diminished. Indeed its amenity was further reduced by the installation of barriers blocking off the inside three lanes outwith competitions and club nights. I would suggest that the resulting reduction of wear is zero, so the only effect at times when they are in place has been to reduce the track's usefulness for doing long intervals.

This unavoidable closure, which actually saved the club £1000 in rentals, did not help those working towards internationals. Top of the pile was Bowie whose fifth place in the AAA under 23s (47.26 in the semis) won him a relay place in the European under 23s in Lithuania. The team was sixth in 3:06.18 and Bowie ran a superb 46.3 split and made a very notable mark on the race. The club responded with a life membership.

Bowie and Law, along with Kathryn Evans who was then making fairly regular second claim appearances for the club, were all in the senior Loughborough team while there were four juniors in the Celtic Games. Here, James MacPhail won the 400 hurdles with 54.5 over 2'9" barriers before setting a club junior record of 55.23 over the full 3' hurdles. Craig Cameron was in the long jump while Stuart Laing and Eleanor Briggs contested their respective 4 x 100 relays.

There was more good news when the under 13 boys won the national Superteams contest. Paula Gass and Connel MacDonald took national age group multi-event titles and Highland Games involvement experienced an increase, especially among the youngsters. At the Nairn Games half marathon, Melissa made her debut with 82:08 in a dreadful wind. David Gallie broke two hours in the Ben Race with 1:57:06 for 65th out of 400.

The season ended well into September with the final open graded meeting. These events had now been passed by the club to the Hippo organization and Rachael MacKenzie contributed to breaking one of her mother's records. 30 years previously in 1979, Dianne had anchored the Women's Cup 4 x 400 team to 4:06.3. To round off 2009 Rachael, along with Jade MacLaren, Sarah Smith and Katie Munro, revised that to 4:04.04.

However it was for her 1.76 high jump that Rachael again won the Hunter Cup while Bowie took the MacKenzie Cup following his European selection. The Post Office Cup went to Callum Green, Scottish schools under 15 400 champion in 53.93, while Charis Mair got the Duncan award for a 12.03 80 hurdles. At that same 2009 AGM, Charlie Forbes was re-elected as President with Dianne again, like her mother before her, Secretary, Donnie Fraser, Treasurer and Dougie MacDonald, Membership Secretary. Cohesion was now returning to club administration.

It was also around this time that the club's stock of beanbags and hulahoops, arguably a symbol of its darkest years, was quietly disposed of to a children's playgroup. Another development was the recruitment of part of the next generation of senior figures within the club. Duncan Flockhart, whose family had longstanding athletics connections, joined after his daughters had become involved with Culloden Harriers. Keith Geddes had been a promising young sprinter in the 80s and came back when his sons became members, while a further important recruit was another parent Stephen Graham. All three were deeply involved in the radical progress which was imminent in the organization and training methodology within the junior age groups.

There was an interesting head to head at the District cross country relays in Dornoch in October 2009. The women's entry was so poor that their 3 x 4K race was combined with the men's 4 x 4K. By the time Melissa Whyte, Jenny Bannerman and Eleanor Reid had finished, they were ahead of the Inverness men's A team. But there was an even deeper comparison. Adding the fastest time in the women's B team from Sheila Gollan, who was now back first claim, meant that the top four women had a faster combined time than the male quartet!

Although Eleanor was soon to depart, this was still an indicator of an evolving strength in depth in women's distance running not seen since Gollan and Julie Wilson were at their peak in the early 1990s. Julie was still competing quite regularly so this meant that four of the club's top senior women distance runners of all time were then all in maroon and gold together.

In practice Jenny's cross country appearances steadily reduced in favour of the road, a medium on which Sheila very seldom competed, while Melissa never ran on the track. But, with other athletes like Julie, Jackie Mair, Alison Wilson and Sarah Liebnitz to call on, and with more soon to arrive, here was a pool of distance runners who could mix and match and win any women's team contest in the North. Indeed

Melissa, Jenny and Sheila took the top three places in cross country league races twice in six weeks early in 2011.

This was also the trio which delivered the 2009 North cross country championship on home ground at Fairways. Organised by the club, the meeting incorporated the Scottish Universities championships and in the women's race Melissa finished a good second to the student winner, former European junior 1500m champion Morag McLarty. It was an even more significant day for the men where Alan Murchison, now a veteran, returned to take the individual silver and lead the team to a much improved second place. Melissa went on to 7th in the women's inter district cross country, 3rd in the inter district 10K and 8th in the national cross country championships – at the age of 46.

The winter of 2009-10 was exceptionally hard and postponed events included the club's Christmas relay, which did not return until 2011. A markedly lower weather threshold for track closure than in earlier years compounded the difficulty. Dianne partly solved her group's problem by hiring the Highland Football Academy in Dingwall while Duncan Flockhart used Nairn Beach. However it often wasn't easy for distance runners to get the miles in. The need for an indoor athletics training facility was becoming more and more pressing.

The District cross country championships produced three team titles and individually 4 gold, 4 silver and 1 bronze. However the league was even more successful with five team and six individual winners. The individuals were Melissa, veteran champions Julie and Sheila and young athletes Craig Campbell, his sister Heather and Mary Flockhart.

The men, most of whom had at some point been beaten by Melissa, were becoming decidedly worried that a woman might win the Moffat Quaich at the 2010 Inverness Half Marathon. But in the end Donnie MacDonald had a breakthrough race to record 78:37 while Melissa was unperturbed that her new pb of 80:09 missed a milestone by a narrow margin.

The 2010 summer championships got off to a flying start with 34 gold, 30 silver and 17 bronze in the new Highlands, Islands and Grampian regional championships. These also included Aberdeen who were next on 17, 10 and 4. The highlights were doubles for James MacPhail with a 49.62 400 and an under 20 championship 200 record of 22.37 and Rachael who high jumped 1.74 and triple jumped 10.84.

Kirsty temporarily lost her Scottish discus title to Nav Daliwal while Jamie reduced his club 400 record to 47.24 in the B final of the UK championships. A tiny representation at the Scottish under 20s and 23s created short lived dismay. This departed again after four golds at the Scottish Schools, including the under 15 high jump from Anna Nelson. Anita Evans (38.96 in the under 15 hammer) and Ian Coghill (1.85 in the under 17 high jump) both won SAL age group titles.

After an appeal to SAL, which got as far as Chairman Frank Dick, Sam Freck was eventually selected for the 4 x 100 at the Celtic Games. Then Craig Campbell made his Scottish international debut in the Home Countries hillrunning event in Ireland in September 2010.

There was another leap forward in the SYAL with a clean sweep of all three qualifiers by 122, 11 and 72 points from Team Hippo. However the sheer size of the 10 clubs told in the bigger programme in the final where Hippo were fourth and Inverness Harriers fifth. The season finished with a real bang with eight of the ten team titles in the Petrofac League final on home ground. The meeting ended with a huge improvement of the women's club and league 4 x 400 records when an all-international quartet of Kathryn Evans, Rachael MacKenzie, Sarah Smith and Jade MacLaren ran 3:54.25.

Early that August the club made the presentation of a quaich to Jayne Barnetson to mark her 25 years as Scottish national record holder in the high jump.

Selecting the MacKenzie, Hunter and Bannerman trophy winners was easy that year and the respective winners were Jamie Bowie, Rachael MacKenzie and Melissa Whyte who also retained these the following year. Two high jumpers, Ian Coghill and Anna Nelson, won the junior awards.

The winter of 2010-11 was almost as hard as its predecessor and struck earlier. At the end of November, thick snow and a ferry cancellation conspired to postpone the North cross country championships in Stornoway. The event finally took place at the original venue on February 26th. This was now sandwiched between the national championships and the Nairn 10K so the women made a collective decision not to travel. So despite having one of the strongest teams ever seen in the North, Inverness Harriers' run of women's titles ended at 15.

There was never much chance of raising a men's team, but the original plan to mobilise a large number of young athletes for a hostel stay paid off handsomely. From seven age groups, six team and six individual titles came back to Inverness. League performances were almost as overwhelming with individual titles for Melissa Whyte, Sean Chalmers, Mhairi MacLennan, Gillian Gordon and Josie Steele. Once again there was quality back in the ranks because, apart from Whyte's exploits, Mhairi MacLennan and Sean Chalmers both had seasons to remember. Mhairi's 6th place in the national championships gave her an under 17 Celtic international debut in Dublin. And Sean added a tremendous fourth in the Inter Counties to runner up spots in the under 15 Scottish inter districts and national championships. It had been the most successful cross country season for many a year.

That was also reflected in attendances at club handicaps where Billy Skinner performed the almost unprecedented feat of winning back to back long course races. Billy was just returning to competition after an extremely unpleasant attack of Lyme Disease, a tick borne infection which is a potential hazard for off-road runners. It had initially looked as if he would need a heart pacemaker but that was avoided. On his return to training he won the Holm Mains race before outsprinting Charlie MacLennan in the Craig Dunain. That same day Stephen Graham, in his debut season as short race handicapper, achieved the closest of finishes, especially among the top three, Craig Wilson and Charlie's sons Finlay and Gregor. When Stephen had to step down from club duties for work reasons he was greatly missed.

A combination of Inverness Leisure's decision to close completely over the festive season and bad weather hit training plans hard, especially for those competing indoors. The club was ultimately given a track key but initially Bowie had to prepare for the successful defence of his Scottish indoor title (47.87) without a track while Law, who was also home for the duration, was unable to throw. President Charlie Forbes commented: *"It's been very difficult indeed for the whole club to get training done for several weeks now and the track being closed was a big blow. The whole club is buzzing just now and we really need to get things back to where they were before all these problems began."* Buzzing indeed it was, with a further boost from London 2012 still to come.

Whyte had already posted road victories in the Nairn 10K (35:50) and Inverness Half (80:31) when she received another international call-up for the Home Countries cross country international on the last Saturday in March. After finishing 16th she hopped straight on to the plane and arrived home in time to defend her title in the Moray Roadrunners 10K on the Sunday, albeit in a modest 36:45. She later made enormous progress to 77:26 in Edinburgh in May 2011.

The second Highlands Islands and Grampian Regional Championships in 2011 turned out to be the last before the event reverted to its North District format, but not before Kirsty Law upped the Queens Park discus ground record to 51.17 and Ian Coghill high jumped 1.94. Anna Nelson took Scottish schools under 17 high jump gold and, although unavailable for the main international, did later compete in the UK School Games.

Progress among the young athletes was typified by a national team double that summer. First of all the under 14 boys (this was the first season of a three year experiment with even age groups) won the national Superteams competition. A week later at Wishaw a mixed team from the club, representing the Queens Park, took first place in the Scottish Inter Facilities Challenge. Successes included a shot putt double for George Evans (12.09) and Katie Stark (9.13). The younger athletes also began to make significant inroads at Scottish championships.

This was therefore a period of significant progress, but the major feature of 2011 was that it was very much Bowie's big breakthrough year. Indoors he became British Universities champion (47.65) and retained his Scottish title (47.87). An Inter Counties victory and 46.78 in Belgium were the ideal prelude to the AAA under 23s. Bronze in that gave him another place in the British 4 x 400 at the European under 23s in the Czech Republic. He teamed up with Nigel Levine, Thomas Phillips and Luke Lennon Ford and on the third leg in the final ran an inspired flying split of 45.33. This was the fastest of all four British runners and made a major contribution to a gold medal in 3:03.53, by 0.09 sec from coach Haczek's Polish countrymen. Jamie Bowie came home to a hero's welcome.

To round things off, he had hoped to run in the Petrofac Final in Aberdeen that September, but was denied by a thigh injury. He did, however, attend the meeting as "non-playing captain" and was certainly an inspiration to some of the junior athletes on a day when there was a repeat of the previous year's eight out of ten team titles.

So in 2011, after a wait of more than a quarter of a century, Inverness Harriers at last had its first major medallist. Jayne Barnetson had come desperately close in 1985 and 1986 and was very possibly further denied by injury. Then in 2001 only the late intervention of illness had snatched almost certain European Junior 4 x 400 gold from Lesley Clarkson who, Jamie later revealed, was his earliest role model.

The title of this final chapter leaves little doubt about where it is heading but, during a period of resurgence, there is also a lot more to relate, even before the start of the Commonwealth Games qualifying period in April 2013.

During a brief spell with the club, Paul Raistrick contested the Commonwealth ultra-distance mountain running championships in Anglesey on the same September weekend in 2011 as Craig Campbell represented Scotland in the UK junior hill running international at Llanberis, also in Wales. One of Craig's contemporaries, Stephen MacKay, became an unusually young 10K winner when at Golspie he ran 34:19 at just 19. David Gallie had a nasty fall in the Ben Nevis Race and the upshot was eight stitches in his head although he declined to be helicoptered off the mountain. It is not clear whether this was because he is a reluctant flier or he was apprehensive about what some of his training partners might have had to say!

That very same day, September 3rd 2011 which also happened to be Inverness Harriers' 64th birthday, the inaugural Inverness 5K parkrun took place over three laps of the Bught. This route, especially when the grass is soggy, produced times up to a minute slower than runners' road performances. These free events were not organised by the club but club members such as Billy Skinner, Paul Crowe, Tim Cooke and Dougie and Averil Lamont turned out to be absolutely central to this venture. The first parkrun also produced an Inverness Harriers double victory for Tom McWilliam (19:06) and Ann Smart (22:45).

Club members continued to play a prominent in these Saturday runs. Members of the Wednesday night Joggers group became especially regular participants while some of the more serious competitive athletes also used them as an occasional part of their programmes.

In the absence of an African presence at the Loch Ness 10K, Melissa Whyte won by three and a half minutes in 35:45. Harley Davidson was awarded the Gerald Cooper Memorial Trophy for the first Highland finisher in the marathon.

At the cross country relays in Dornoch, Melissa, Sheila and Jenny were a massive nine and a half minutes clear of the field and produced the three fastest 4K splits in the race. There was a great 1-2 for the girls' teams and the winning trio was Hannah Fraser (12:13), Lauren Fraser (10:17) and Mhairi MacLennan (10:28) while Ali Velzian (9:37), Scott Lisle (9:47) and Sean Chalmers (8:47) won the boys' race.

However Craig Campbell, with 8:44 for the B team, had the fastest time.

Melissa (W45), Sheila (W40) and George Mitchell (M65) were called up for the British and Irish veterans' cross country international in Glasgow that November. Melissa excelled by winning the combined women's race against younger athletes while George was third in his age group. A date clash meant that they all had

Jenny Bannerman

to miss the North District cross country championships at Forres. However Jenny Bannerman stepped into the breach and won the women's title in what was her last serious cross country race as her career moved towards road racing. Junior champion Emma Atkinson was third and Roma Davidson fifth to complete a successful team. There were even more emphatic placings for the under 17 boys when Sean Chalmers and Craig Campbell took the top two spots and Finlay MacLennan was fourth. For the second time in three years the men's team got the runner up spot.

The Olympic year of 2012 started brightly both indoors and out when Sean won the under 17 Inter District cross country race in Edinburgh by 4 seconds while Mhairi MacLennan was 6th in the women's contest and Ian Coghill cleared 2 metres in the high jump in Birmingham. Later, Bowie retained his Scottish indoor 400 title with 48.48.

At the cross country league in Evanton, three Campbells all raced simultaneously with father Graeme and son Craig in the combined under 17 and senior race while mother Doreen was in action elsewhere on the course in the women's event. Heather and Connie were also signed up Harriers and five members from the same family must be a record.

Melissa moved up another gear in February and, in the W45 category at the Scottish Vets' cross country championship in Kilmarnock, headed the entire field, including runners as young as 35. Among them was W40 winner, former leading world mountain runner

Angela Mudge. Melissa also led a dominant Inverness quartet at the Kinloss to Lossie half marathon. Although British Athletics' Power of 10 listings do not accept this race for ranking purposes, she ran 76:30. Sarah Liebnitz was second in 83:05, Roma Shepherd (formerly Davidson, who had made a return after many years) third in 88:06 and Lesley Clarkson fifth in 88:31.

This race took place just days after Melissa's 48th birthday and turned out to be her last major effort before what, at the time of writing, has turned into an absence of almost two and a half years. Inverness Harriers' most accomplished female distance runner developed a pelvic injury and although she managed to struggle through the Inverness Half in just under 80 minutes, the injury was long term.

She left behind a considerable depth of talent in women's distance running and in her absence from the Nairn 10K, Jenny Bannerman ran 37:54 to win. This race also had three Harriers women under 40 minutes for the first time when Sarah Liebnitz did 39:14 and Roma Shepherd 39:45. Then, in Bannerman's absence from Elgin, there was yet another team success from Liebnitz (the winner in 40:33), Shepherd and Jackie Mair. By now domination in North women's road and country was such that Inverness were even winning team events with two or three leading runners absent. With a further improvement to 38:59 at Ben Romach, Liebnitz won the Moray and Nairn three race series.

The women were just one of four successful teams in the 2011-12 cross country league, although rising distance club East Sutherland did take five junior titles. Inverness's 16 individual medals were headed by seven gold, including one for Mhairi MacLennan who also won the Scottish Schools over 17 title and gained selection for an international at Rouken Glen. Meanwhile Chalmers (under 17) and Scott Lisle (under 15) went to the British Schools international at Strathallan.

The spring of 2012 produced the latest stage of the battle for the women's club marathon record. Alison Wilson, with 3:27:08, had earlier taken the record from Lesley Clarkson (3:34:30) and further improved it to 3:25:24 in her native Lochaber in April 2012. A week later Clarkson regained the record with 3:18:44 in London. There was a lighter side to the distance programme too with, on consecutive days in May 2012, Man v Horse and Race the Steam Train contests in Inverness and Boat of Garten.

The summer season got off to a dreadful start for Kirsty Law following a head-on car crash which put her out of the District Championships. She only just made it back for the Loughborough international later in May and, still fragile, posted 49.72 before retaining her Scottish title with 52.02 two weeks later. This meant that the District haul of 34 gold, 18 silver and 14 bronze was one gold medal down. The top performers were Anna Nelson with an under 20 400H/100H/HJ treble while Chalmers slipped under 2 minutes for 800 (1:59.98) and also won the under 17 1500.

These two were the backbone of the under 17 section of the Young Athletes' League Team which edged Aberdeen for the North East title on their way to another final as Team North, the former Team Hippo, missed out. Chalmers and Nelson were to the fore again at the Scottish Schools where Sean's 1:59.10 800 and Anna's 45.50 for 300 hurdles both gained international selections. George Evans also began to make a mark with an under 15 discus win (36.25).

Off-track endurance athletes were not idle that summer and a new race, the 5.5 mile Dochfour Dash on the canal banks with Lee and Ian Ross as principal organisers, filled an important gap in the club's rather sparse promotion of open events. Paul Raistrick was the inaugural winner in 31:19 from Craig Campbell (32:15) and Ross Nixon (33:20). Campbell's earlier performance at Ben Lomond gained him a Scottish under 19 hill running international. Meanwhile an impromptu appearance at the Gairloch 10K saw Jenny Bannerman improve her 10K to 37:35 - one second faster than her father's lifetime best!

Over the years four women, Audrey Munro, Dianne MacKenzie, Kathryn Nicholson and Dorothy Bannerman, had all been prolific veteran title winners. By 2012 Bannerman was the only one still competing and won the Scottish W45 80 hurdles and 100 at Pitreavie. By now Ian Johnstone, his 1973 chilly canal dip a distant memory, was back with the club and took the over 60 1500 and 5000 gold medals.

Sean was third in 1:56.71 in the Schools international before going on to set a new club under 17 record of 1:54.79 for fourth in the AAA under 17 championships.

By this time the entire Hippo organisation, in which Inverness Harriers were generally reluctant participants after an enthusiastic courtship, was beginning to struggle. They had to cancel their August open graded meeting due to lack of officials and this was taken up instead by the club. Soon after, the club took back under its own umbrella the whole series of meetings which it had founded in 1976.

One element of the London 2012 Olympic celebrations which did not go down well at all in Inverness was the omission of Colin Baillie from the list of local torchbearers. It is difficult to assess the impact of the overall Olympic "legacy" on recruitment because the club was already several years into a steady phase of expansion which, in 2014, still continues. Certainly the strong suggestion with the young athletes is that the higher the activity levels required on training nights, the more of them started attending. In the summer of 2012 membership went back above 300 again before reaching a new record of 351 the following year and hitting 416 in at the end of August 2014.

Kirsty Law produced the performance of her life to win the Inter Counties discus at Bedford that August, setting one pb of 56.61 in qualifying and then a massive 57.79 in the final. This created great early optimism about possible Commonwealth Games selection in two years' time. There were further international honours for George Evans and Alison Horne (throws) and Chris Brown (sprints) in the Celtic International. This was followed by a

A group of young athletes

temporary curtailment of the momentum when, after eight out of ten Petrofac titles in the previous two years, 2012 produced only the senior and under 18 women's and the under 10 girls'.

However it was still with considerable optimism that the club assembled in the Lochardil Hotel early that September for a 65th anniversary dinner attended, among others, by two former Scottish National record holders in the 110 hurdles. Neil Fraser made the trip North while 2006 Commonwealth silver medallist Chris Baillie was also present along with Brian Donaldson and high jump coach Ken Allan with whom he was sharing a coaching weekend. At the end of the month the AGM saw Keith Geddes take over as President from Charlie Forbes. Inevitably Jamie Bowie retained the MacKenzie Cup and there was a family double when Jenny Bannerman received the Hunter Cup while her mother Dorothy won the George Bannerman Memorial Trophy for the best veteran.

That late summer saw a purple patch on the road for Roma Shepherd who won the North District half marathon at Nairn in 97:37 and six weeks later the 10K title at Dyke in 41:04. Meanwhile Liz Gray and husband, Highland Council Convener and ex-Inverness Provost

Jimmy, celebrated their ruby wedding by completing the Great Scottish Run.

As expansion continued, the Millburn Academy gym, after over 20 years as the club's home on winter Thursday nights, became too small. In order to accommodate the increasing demand, half the Sports Centre Games Hall had to be hired instead, along with the track. A welcome need to hold separate boys' and girls' club handicaps also arose at a time when an official Inverness Challengers' Wednesday night group of disabled athletes became part of the club.

Into the cross country season, Mhairi MacLennan made her senior debut as a member of the winning trio at the District Relays in Nairn. Raigmore Hospital doctor Joe Symonds began a brief second claim spell with the club and won the District Championship but was ineligible for the team. Missing that day in Evanton were Sean Chalmers, Mhairi MacLennan and Stephen MacKay at a UK event in Liverpool. Chalmers' third place gained him a Scottish under 20 selection for the Celtic Nations international in Cardiff where he again finished an excellent third a fortnight after successfully defending his under 17 Scottish Inter District title in January 2013.

By now the seeds of resurgence were being sown in men's cross country. On January 12th, headed by individual winner Donnie MacDonald, the club posted its first men's North League team win since February 1995. They failed to follow that up in the remaining two matches but on the road won the team contest at the Nairn 10K. This did give an insight into what was possible - and became reality the following season.

The women extended their run of league titles to 10 in a row. Although existing leading runners for various reasons were not available, Mhairi's arrival in the senior team made a big difference, with Alison Wilson, Julie Wilson and Roma Shepherd among the other contributors. The only other team victory was for the under 15 boys as East Sutherland gained the upper hand in the young athletes' contests, edging Inverness into second place in several of them.

In 2012 George Mitchell had officially become Scotland's fastest Old Age Pensioner when he won the V65 cross country title. In 2013 George was runner up in Forres in what was his last championship run. Sadly this club stalwart died, aged 68, in September 2014. There was further national championship glory for the under 15 boys' team of Scott Lisle (9th) Luke Shaw (10th), James Geddes (22nd) and Andrew Johnstone (31st) who took silver medals at Falkirk.

Earlier safety concerns about the club cross country championship course were heightened by the death of a cyclist on the A82 close to the route. Ross Nixon undertook a major revamp which kept the race in the same area but avoided the road completely. He also won the title over this course of his own devising after a tough battle with Finlay MacLennan while Jenny Bannerman made it five women's championships in a row.

The throwers did especially well indoors and George Evans threw the 4kg shot a huge 16.20 to break the Scottish schools under 16 record and win the Jack Sutherland Trophy for the best shot performance. Jamie Bowie had a fast indoor 200 of 21.88 while trips to Austria and Belgium helped his 400 drop further down the 47 second bracket. By now Duncan Flockhart's specialist throws group, which also included athletes like Daniel Wilby, Katie Stark, Alex Geddes and Duncan's own daughter Mary, was well into its stride and well placed to become the club's major source of national medals. His success gained him the Inverness Area Sports Council Coach of the Year award in December 2012.

Two very valuable recruits to the club's team of officials had been Roy and Mary Payne who lived in Aviemore. Sadly Roy died in 2012 and Mary donated a trophy in his memory, matched by an award from the club to go to the best under 15 cross country runners. She presented the inaugural awards to Scott Lisle and Lauren Fraser on a night when Sean Chalmers and Mhairi MacLennan won the Banks trophies at the end of a fine season.

In 2010 Roy and Lorraine MacDonald stepped down as highly successful organisers of the Inverness Half Marathon and the club was given the opportunity to take this on, but rapidly expanding core activities made that impossible. Consequently the organisers of last resort became the company which promoted the Loch Ness Marathon, Caledonian Concepts. This was not over-popular with a number of club runners in the North who for some time had been unhappy with what they saw as the company's over-commercial attitude.

Sure enough, it did not take long for a rise in entry fees for the half marathon and especially the 5K which had for long been the club's road race championships. The 5K fun run entry fee had previously been £3, of which £1 went to charity, but very quickly tripled to £9.

Indignation at these huge price increases was accentuated when fun run competitors crossed the line in 2013 and looked at their GPS devices, only for their delight at apparently huge PBs to evaporate when they realised that the course was only 4.62K. There had been a course marking error but this did nothing to reduce the annoyance and Keith Geddes commented: *"This is completely unacceptable because runners are paying a lot of money nowadays for an event* advertised as a 5K and the organisers can't even get the distance right. We've run our own club championships here for years and what we find here is that our members are quite simply being overcharged and short changed."

The narrative has now reached April 1st 2013, the beginning of the qualification period for the 2014 Commonwealth Games in Glasgow, so we now need to step aside and take a look at the fortunes of the club's contenders for team places during these 14 months. The standards were set at an average 8th place across the previous three Games, to be achieved twice by June 8th 2014.

The most obvious candidate was Kirsty Law whose massive 57.79 in August 2012 was well above the necessary 55 metres in the discus although too early to count. Bowie's target in the 400 was a phenomenally difficult 45.65, only ever achieved by the three Scotsmen ahead of him on the all-time list. The 4 x 400 was also a highly challenging 3:05.50 although eventually relaxed to a more realistic 3:07.00.

On April 1st 2013 these appeared to be Inverness Harriers only Commonwealth Games prospects, but that summer produced two exciting developments. The women's high jump standard was a slightly more athlete friendly 1.80 but Rachael, whose PB of 1.76 dated from back in 2009, had had her quietest season ever in 2012 with just 1.65. That would soon change. There was also a new club member, 17 year old Jason MacLean, from Nairn, a cerebral palsy athlete who had been recommended as a sprinter to Charlie Forbes whose day job by now was High Life Highland's Disability Sports Manager. The T37 100 standard of 13.40 would soon be very much in their sights.

A dislocated rib meant that Kirsty's season did not start until June and just four weeks later she came frustratingly close with

Jason MacLean

54.71 in Loughborough. She missed out again with 53.41 whilst retaining her Scottish title but on 8th September threw a fairytale 55.66 at her home track at Queens Park for her first standard performance. A week later she almost reached her target with 53.42 in

Liverpool but after a good winter, confirmation was not long coming. As early as 23rd March 2014 a 55.25 effort in Birmingham completed the job. This opened the floodgates because by the end of the qualification period she had breached 55 metres on six further occasions.

Rachael bounced back from her barren 2012, upped her training into 2013 and popped over 1.77 at the Queens Park the same September day as Kirsty threw 55.66. It wasn't a qualifying height but it was a crucial turning point which suddenly made it clear to her that an attempt was very much on. The indoor season, which is very high jump friendly, was critical and on 2nd February 2014 she won the Scottish indoor championships. Far more importantly she did it with a height of 1.80. A further 1.80 indoors in Aberdeen was of no further value since the second one had to be done outdoors and that very soon came to pass with 1.80 at the very first event of the season. Better still, this was Inverness Harriers' own open meeting on 13th April and a 1.81 followed in Aberdeen a week later.

With Kirsty and Rachael both achieving qualifying performances at Queens Park open meetings, it was clearly vital to have these properly ratified to the satisfaction of possibly sceptical central belt authorities. Here highly qualified North District officials, and in particular Elspeth Allan who would ultimately preside over the women's high jump among other field events in Glasgow, played a hugely proactive role in producing the necessarily high levels of verification.

Jason meanwhile made steady progress and achieved his target with four runs between 12.95 and 13.03, including the first two by September 2013. On a visit to Dubai to confirm his T37 classification he also had a wind assisted 12.90.

By mid-April 2014, three Inverness Harriers were therefore set for Glasgow but ironically the man who had achieved most was not yet among them due to the demands of his personal situation and very tough qualifying standards.

During the summer of 2013 Jamie Bowie was on fire. Before a 400 PB of 46.06 in Belgium in July, his progress to fifth place in the British championships and World Championship trials included a 46.31 and a 46.11. At this point the increasingly familiar theme of having to meet sometimes conflicting Scottish Commonwealth requirements and those of British Athletics began to assert itself. However there were hugely gratifying moments as well, including his selection for the 4 x 400 at the World Championships in Moscow.

Here a blistering 44.64 flying split by the first Inverness Harrier to contest a global senior championship made a decisive contribution to

Team GB reaching the final. But, after what seemed like an eternity, it emerged that he would be left out of the final, a decision which created considerable controversy within the British athletics community. However there was compensation when he was given a place on the British Athletics Podium Support programme, which did have its considerable obligations as well. Although Jamie didn't get a run in that final, the gathering of club members, hastily assembled to watch it on a large screen in the bar at Fairways, went ahead all the same!

The facility to do one qualifying time indoors was of no real help to Jamie since indoor competition on tight bends does not normally produce fast 400 times. However a fifth place in the British indoor championships did get him into the team for the World Indoor championships in Poland where this time he did also get a run in the relay final. He did not disappoint. His 45.92 second leg split made a huge contribution to a silver medal for Great Britain. Jamie Bowie - and with him his first claim club for 13 years - had truly arrived on the world stage.

Then it was off for the first of two trips to the United States. This began a 10 week period up to the qualification deadline where there was incessant pressure to meet the twin demands of Scotland and Great Britain. It goes without saying that this scenario, which saw him visit the USA, the Bahamas, the UK, Belgium, Italy, Switzerland and Germany all during the two weeks before June 8th, was far from conducive to producing his best and the unrealistic individual standard for Glasgow remained unachieved. However on May 28th he did get together with Grant Plenderleith, Kriss Robertson and Greg Louden to post 3:06.58 in the last chance saloon of a 4 x 400 in Namur, Belgium and achieve the single relay time which was required. The team celebration on the finishing line said it all.

With these celebrations, Inverness Harriers history had been made because on June 12th Kirsty Law, Jason MacLean, Rachael MacKenzie

Stirling Castle Group

and Jamie Bowie were duly named at Stirling Castle as members of Team Scotland. Moreover, Rachael and Jason had achieved this whilst entirely based in the Highlands and coached locally by Dianne and Charlie. Jamie lodged an appeal to run the individual 400 at the Games as well since he was already there for the relay but that was rejected. So with four Inverness Harriers now poised to compete at Hampden Park we must now return to the spring of 2013 and the club's other activities which continued to expand and develop up to the start of these Games.

Life continued apace, including a steady increase in marathon competition, especially among the women runners and three of them got together to contest the team title at Lochaber in April 2013. Jodie Lynch was doing her first marathon since the disappointment of arriving in New York the previous November to find the race cancelled due to the ravages of Hurricane Sandy. In Lochaber she just missed breaking 3:20 by half a minute but the women did win the team title with further contributions from Alison Wilson and from Paula Ross who went on to complete the London marathon in 3:33:42 just seven days later.

One of the highlights of the North District track and field championships was Donnie MacDonald coming from away back to take the 5000. Anna Nelson took a remarkable four over 17 Scottish schools gold medals in a week. She posted five PBs in the pentathlon and at the main championships won the individual 100 hurdles (16.58), high jump (1.63) and 400 hurdles (64.24). In the pentathlon 100 hurdles her 15.38 broke the 34 year old club under 20 record of 15.4, originally set by Dorothy Bannerman in 1979 and matched by Jayne Barnetson in 1985.

Donnie McDonald

Silver medals for George Evans in the shot and discus gave him schools international selections in both events and he was one of the athletes to benefit from a midsummer coaching clinic held by Kirsty Law at the Queens Park. George, along with long jumper Alexander Nicholson, was also in the Celtic Games and it was at this stage that Jason MacLean made his entry to the club and was selected for the UK School Games.

There were two fresh undertakings in the summer of 2013, one at home and the other abroad. A team of over 40 athletes visited the Gothenburg Youth Games in the famous Ullevi Stadium at the end of June. After major fundraising efforts and with the help of some Highland Council funding, this was hugely successful yielding four medals. In the age 16 category there was silver for Andrew Smith in the 400 (52.91) and Alexander Nicholson in the long jump (6.27) and bronze for George Evans in the shot (15.60) while Anna Nelson got an age 18 silver in the 300 hurdles (44.04).

On the home front the club re-entered the Men's League after the best part of two decades' absence. There had been mixed feelings about this, but the athletes themselves volunteered to do the administration and duly went in at the bottom of what had been a five division league but was now down to two. They won Division 2 and with it entry to the top flight for 2014. Meanwhile the Petrofac League produced three female titles, including the senior, and two male.

However the Young Athletes' League suffered a serious downgrading when it lost its under 17 age group and became the Youth Development League. Once again the club team reached the final where it won 12 medals including three gold, but the new set up did not have the same presence or value.

Sam Freck and Eoghan MacNamara with the Scottish League Division Two Trophy.

The 100th Inverness parkrun took place in July 2013. A publicity campaign helped the record turnout to shoot up from 86 to 207 and Sarah Liebnitz won the women's race in 18:52. Also on the up was Dean Cunningham who broke the Peterhead 5K record with 17:19 before progressing to 16:13 the following year.

One departure that summer was of Sean Chalmers who began a degree course at Lamar University in Texas. He was greatly missed during the winter but in the States he began to post personal best performances on the track, including 3:56.49 for 1500 in Houston in March 2014. Unfortunately an Achilles injury blighted his 2014 summer season back home.

Caithness again proved an unpopular venue for the North District cross country relays and in the end the only club women's team to compete was an all veteran one. The trio won that title but, despite crossing the line first, were ineligible for the main award. The men finished a close second to Forres while sisters Connie and Heather Campbell took the girls' title with Josie Steele.

There was a major breakthrough for the men in the Elgin league match in November where the counting quartet of 2nd – Donnie MacDonald (34:09), 3rd – Craig Campbell (34:38), 6th – Andrew MacRae (34:59) and 8th – Dean Cunningham (35:42) pulled off a great victory over Forres. This was the next stage of a rise in the men's fortunes while the women experienced a decline in their cross country successes, largely because of a diversification of interests, especially towards road racing.

In November, Jodie Lynch returned to New York and this time took the club marathon

Sean Chalmers

record, which had previously been held by Alison Wilson and then Lesley Clarkson, with a time of 3:05:39. The same month Jenny Bannerman (37:38) and Sarah Liebnitz (63:18) did the women's double in the Glenmoray 10K and 10 miles in Elgin. There was good news in track and field too when Duncan Flockhart was named as a member of Scottish Athletics' coach mentoring scheme in the throws.

Back on the country, it was a slightly disappointing North District championships at Nairn where East Sutherland made significant inroads in the youngsters' events and Highland Hillrunners took the women's title on countback from the Inverness trio. Apart from in 2010-11 where no team travelled to Stornoway, this was a rare failure to win that particular award. This was followed by a deepening decline in the women's team's fortunes in the league where the titlet had to be conceded to Forres Harriers. This was therefore the first season in something like three decades when the women won none of the three North trophies.

However the men continued their surge at Edderton and Forres and completed the season as North league champions for the first time since Bowman *et al* 23 years previously in 1991. Absolutely crucial to this victory was the arrival of Graham Bee to practice medicine in Inverness whereupon he joined the club first claim at the end of 2013. His contribution to the second half of that league campaign was considerable and this famous victory led to the Walter Banks Rosebowl being awarded for the first time to the entire men's team rather than to a specific individual. Mhairi MacLennan had made impressive progress in her first year as a student at Edinburgh University. She was greatly missed by the women's team but received the Salver for a number of high placings in national and regional cross country events.

In the spring of 2014, Jenny Bannerman broke new ground at 10K with 36:39 at Nairn before improving in three further stages to 35:37 at the Scottish championships in Stirling in September. In May she missed a Scottish 5K championship medal by a yard with another best of 17:16.

Mhairi's track season started brightly with club under 20 records of 4:42.54 in the 1500 and 10:02.69 in the 3000. Meanwhile Stephen MacKay's trips to BMC meetings in England paid off handsomely but it was in the Gothenburg Youth Games that he became the club's second fastest 800m runner of all time behind Donald MacMillan. Here he

Mhairi MacLennan

recorded 1:52.17 and also reduced his 1500m time to 3:58.08.

The 25 strong party which visited Gothenburg in 2014 won six medals, two more than 12 months previously. Evans produced a massive 53.42m for bronze in the age 16 discus as well as 15.63 for third in the shot. Andrew McFarlane won the age 14 pole vault with 3.32m and was third in the 80m hurdles in 11.97 sec. Joe Arnaud had a personal best of 2:06.33 for a silver medal in the age 14 800m in the same age group and there was further silver for Andrew Smith with 22.45 sec in the 17 category 200m.

For Evans, Gothenburg filled the gap between his double Scottish schools success in June (52.65/15.78) and his victory the following month in the shot at the British Schools International in Cardiff with a huge personal best of 16.71. This made him only the third Inverness athlete after Vicky O'Brien and Kirsty Law to win the event when all four home countries were competing. Later in the season at the Celtic Games he eclipsed Devine's admirable 53.80 club record with 53.85 and at the Scottish under 17 championships improved further to 17.24 and 55.32. A UK School Games shot win completed a British treble.

For a number of years representation in the Schools international, a key club performance indicator, had been sparse in the extreme but in 2014 no fewer than six athletes, the biggest presence

Six Harriers at the 2014 British Schools International in Cardiff –
Daniel McFarlane, George Evans, Gillian Gordon, Mary Flockhart,
Daniel Wilby, Andrew Smith.

for 25 years, were selected for the Scottish schools team. The others were Mary Flockhart (javelin), Daniel Wilby (discus), Daniel McFarlane (javelin), Gillian Gordon(300 hurdles and 4 x 300) and Andrew Smith (4 x 400). These selections represented a significant return to earlier standards in age group track and field.

Just before the Commonwealth Games there was an unfortunate but unavoidable illustration of the club having become a victim of its own success. As membership raced through the 400 mark it became apparent that the rush into the under 11 and under 13 age groups had become so intense that the existing coaches were having great difficulty delivering credible coaching to groups which at times exceeded 50. As a result the committee made the difficult decision to suspend new under 11 and under 13 intake until October 1st in the hope of recruiting further coaches in the interim.

By now the club was staffed with coaches, officials, committee and helpers on a more or less unprecedented scale, but still more were urgently needed. As of the end of July 2014 the committee comprised: President – Keith Geddes, Vice President – Duncan Flockhart, Secretary – Dianne Chisholm, Treasurer – Donnie Fraser, Membership Secretary – Charles Bannerman, Coaching coordinator – Charlie Forbes. Committee members- Wendy Flockhart, Laurie MacIver, Ross Cairns, Dougie and Averil Lamont, Ross Nixon, Joan Mack, Wendy Macintosh.

Committee, officials and helpers 2013 – 2014.

Photo – Andy Shepherd

In terms of coaching, at specialist level, Dianne ran sprints and jumps, Duncan Flockhart throws and Charlie Forbes endurance. Wendy Macintosh operated one young athletes' group and Laurie MacIver another while a third, focusing more on endurance, was looked after by Keith Geddes and Tom McWilliam. Grant Nairn and Joan Mack looked after the under 11 group. In addition, a number of parents including Janis Wilby, Karin Smith, Evon Watts and Alan Brown were recruited to assist in coaching and veteran throws coaches Harry Lakeland and Brian Ross continued to have an input. Mary and for some time Roy Payne made big contributions as officials, while Alister Cameron was a willing minibus driver to Men's League meetings.

Meanwhile July 2014 also saw the Commonwealth quartet, their selections now confirmed, make their final preparations for the now imminent Games. Jamie overcame his travel weariness to post 10.75 and a club record 21.52 when he turned out in the short sprints in maroon and gold at the Men's League at Grangemouth. A week later he converted that into 46.18 over the full lap at Loughborough – his third fastest ever. Kirsty signed off with efforts over 55 metres in Loughborough and Italy while Rachael posted 1.76 at Loughborough and 1.77 in Birmingham on a weekend when both women had competitions abandoned amid monsoon conditions. Jason decided not to compete at this stage but rounded off with a series of encouraging time trials.

And it was Jason, on the morning on Monday July 28th, who was first into action at these Games which by that stage had already captured the public imagination in a major way. Glasgow was vibrant by the time he stepped out on to the track at Hampden to finish second in his heat in 12.96, just 0.01 outside his legal best and the fifth fastest qualifying time. And that was also where he finished in that evening's final when he recovered from a slightly uncertain start to record a legal 12.93, a personal best by 0.02. The Commonwealth campaign was under way with a fifth place.

Next into the fray was Rachael in the preliminaries of the high jump which took place ion the morning of July 30th. She produced fine first time clearances, to the massive applause of the Hampden crowd, at 1.66, 1.71 and 1.76. The bar then went to 1.81, which happened to equal her personal best, but she was unable to reach that on this occasion. A first time clearance would have sent her through to the latter stages of a competition which was of a much higher standard than in Delhi where two jumpers in the final cleared just 1.68. On the way back round the track perimeter after the competition, enthusiastic spectators were to be seen high-fiving her and asking for autographs.

On the evening of Thursday July 31st it was the turn of Kirsty to step into the Commonwealth limelight. One of the pitfalls of the horizontal field events at major championships is that there are just three opportunities at the qualifying stage to stake your claim for a place in the final. The field eventer's nightmare is a foul in the opening round or, in the case of the Indian defending champion, in the first two rounds.

This was a nightmare which Kirsty was spared when, in cold and wet conditions, she spun the implement out to 54.33m for her opener. It was immediately clear that this was comfortably going to be enough to reach the following evening's final 12. She improved slightly in round two before fouling her third attempt by which time she was home and dry with around four metres to spare.

Having watched two previous Commonwealth Games and a couple of other major championships from the terraces, I had decided this time to remain in Inverness and follow events via computer and television since, despite the atmosphere in the stadium, the view you get watching there tends at best to be remote. Consequently, across that Thursday and Friday, with two Harriers having completed their Commonwealth debuts and two more still with business to do, I had a couple of personal experiences in Inverness which brought home vividly the progress that all of this represented for the club.

With the coaches all either spectating at Hampden or away on holiday, all organised training had been cancelled for that Thursday evening. So in stark contrast with the invasions of recent weeks and months, the only athletes who turned up at the track were a few self sufficient seniors. When I arrived that Thursday night to find such a temporarily sparse turnout I was overwhelmed by a vivid flashback to the club's many years of struggle for mere existence, in complete contrast with more recent and more prosperous days.

Then on the Friday afternoon, before heading home to watch Jamie and Kirsty, I went to Fraser Park to do my own session on the grass. The significance of the venue didn't actually dawn on me until I arrived to receive a second stark reminder of the very basic origins of a reconstituted club struggling back into existence on a cricket ground with a 300 metre grass track and no field event facilities.

I could almost hear the strident exhortations of Colin Baillie as Ian Tasker ran up and down, Ted Roodhouse put his girl sprinters through their paces and Brian Milne was quietly sick in the far corner. As I write, apart from myself there is only one other active club member who experienced these formative days of 1969 and 1970 and now she was in Glasgow watching the Inverness contingent, including her own daughter, competing in the Commonwealth Games.

I was soon back home in front of my computer watching the dedicated live feed of the women's discus final. The results of the preliminaries had suggested that, outwith the top two or three, it was going to be tight, but unfortunately Kirsty didn't quite make the small breakthrough that might have made all the difference. The best of her three throws was 52.33 so it was a gallant 11th place.

Before the Games began, Jamie said that, to reach the final, the 4 x 400 team might have to break the national record of 3:04.68 which had won Scotland silver in Auckland in 1990. As it turned out he was only partly correct because although they did break the national record, they didn't have to. The team recorded 3:03.94 in the third and final heat as Kriss Robertson passed to Jamie who unleashed a superb 45.00 flying split to set up Grant Plenderleith and Greg Louden to take Scotland home in third place. Although that meant going through as fastest losers, they also posted the fourth fastest heat time since a string of three disqualifications in the first two heats in the end made qualification very comfortable indeed.

Conditions were very different 24 hours later when lashing rain created puddles right across the Hampden track. The atmosphere was building for Usain Bolt's appearance for Jamaica in the last event, the 4 x 100 final, when the 4 x 400 teams emerged with a not very favourable inside lane draw for Scotland. There was also a tactical switch which saw Bowie change places with Plenderleith and run third.

When the gun went, at the second time of asking after a faulty start, the big three bend stagger seemed slow to unwind as Robertson made his contribution. That was a 47.0 first leg split which took the team into sixth place where they stayed when Plenderleith ran a flying split of 45.8 before passing to Bowie. A storming 45.21 leg from the Inverness Harrier, topped off by a strong finish whilst overtaking an Australian, put Team Scotland into fifth place. And it was there that Louden kept them with his 45.97 for an overall 3:04.07 behind a gold medal winning England quartet which included Jamie's colleagues from Team GB.

Given the dreadful weather which had caused poles to slip clean through vaulters' hands in a soaking wet arena, running as close to the previous night's time and inside a 24 year old national record on a second occasion with the loss of just 0.13 seconds was a miraculous achievement. So also was the Inverness man's 45.21 split which compared very well with rivals who had also contested the individual 400 for which Scotland had refused to select him.

After what Jamie described as the longest lap of honour of his life in front of a crowd which had roared Scottish athletes on all week, the quartet then disappeared back into the inner recesses of Hampden Park, and Inverness Harriers' fourfold contribution to the 2014 Commonwealth Games was over.

However for two of them the season was not quite finished since Rachael (1.75) and Kirsty (50.29) later overcame even worse weather than at Hampden to become Scottish champions at Kilmarnock respectively for the first and seventh time respectively.

This is a story which has come a long, long way in the 67 years since three men took the bold step of founding an athletics club in Inverness in 1947. It has been a frequently difficult but also triumphant journey from the Bught to Hampden via the Queens Park. It is also a journey which is by no means complete and remains ongoing, possibly to even greater heights in the future.

APPENDIX - SENIOR CLUB RECORDS AS AT 7th SEPTEMBER 2014.

100 - Scott Fraser 10.70 1994 - Alison Edmonds 11.9 1988
200 - Jamie Bowie 21.52 2014 - Lesley Clarkson 24.87 1999
400 - Jamie Bowie 46.06 2013 - Lesley Clarkson 54.44 2001
800 - Donald MacMillan 1:50.08 1983 - Lesley Clarkson 2:06.74 2004
1500 - Donald MacMillan 3:48.10 1983 - Sheila Gollan 4:34.33 1991
5000/3000 - Paul Kenney 14:13.0 1983 - Sheila Gollan 9:46.1 1990
10000 - Paul Kenney 29:33.5 1983 - no women's performance. Melissa Whyte 35.05 on road 2010
Marathon - Paul Kenney 2:19.04 1983 - Jodie Lynch 3:05.39 2013
Sprint Hurdles - Neil Fraser 14.11 1987 - Jayne Barnetson 14.50 1989
400 hurdles - Alastair Taylor 54.7 1988 - Jayne Barnetson 60.70 1988
Steeplechase - Iain Johnstone 9:27.0 1977 - No women's performance
LJ - Mel Fowler 7.23 1989 - Jayne Barnetson 6.07 1988
HJ - David Barnetson 2.20 1998 - Jayne Barnetson 1.91 1989
TJ - Mel Fowler 14.59 1992 - Women's record under research.
PV - Ian MacKenzie 4.20 2000 - Anna Watson 3.02 1999
SP - George Patience 15.58 1987 - Kirsty Law 11.99 2013
DT - George Patience 53.48 1987 - Kirsty Law 57.79 2012
JT - Alan Kemlo 50.44 1992 – Paula Gass 42.36 2014
HT - Russell Devine 61.90 1990 - Women's record under research.
4 x 100 - Senior Men SAL 43.82 1990 - 48.2 Senior Women Scottish Champions 1981
4 x 400 - 3:28.0 Senior Men SAL 1990 - 3:54.25 Senior Women Halliburton League 2010.